ANTHROPOLOGICAL PAPERS OF
THE UNIVERSITY OF ARIZONA
NUMBER 70

T0136018

The Safford Valley Grids

Prehistoric Cultivation in the Southern Arizona Desert

William E. Doolittle and James A. Neely
Editors

CONTRIBUTORS

Karen R. Adams
Paul R. Fish
Suzanne K. Fish
Jeffrey A. Homburg
Brenda B. Houser
Betty Graham Lee
Dale R. Lightfoot
Arthur MacWilliams
Guadalupe Sánchez de Carpenter
Jonathan A. Sandor
Marilyn Shoberg

THE UNIVERSITY OF ARIZONA PRESS
TUCSON
2004

About the Editors

WILLIAM E. DOOLITTLE is the Erich W. Zimmermann Regents Professor in Geography and the Chairman of the Department of Geography and the Environment at The University of Texas at Austin. He holds a B.A. degree from Texas Christian University (1974), an M.A. degree from the University of Missouri (1976) and a Ph.D. degree from the University of Oklahoma (1979). His research specialty is agriculture, particularly the technology used in the transformation of so-called "natural" landscapes to cultural landscapes in arid environments. He has conducted both archaeological and ethnographic research, with a decidedly geographical orientation, in the American Southwest, Mexico, and Spain. He has worked extensively on issues of irrigation, terracing, runoff agriculture, and gardening. Doolittle is the recipient of the Carl O. Sauer Award from the Conference of Latin Americanist Geographers and the Robert McC. Netting Award from the Cultural and Political Ecology Specialty Group of the Association of American Geographers.

JAMES A. NEELY is Professor Emeritus of Anthropology at The University of Texas at Austin. He holds a B.A. degree, Magnum Cum Laude, from Mexico City College (1958), now the Universidad de las Americas in Puebla, and M.A. (1968) and Ph.D. (1974) degrees from The University of Arizona. His research specialties include archaeology, cultural ecology, village life and the development of urbanism, irrigation-water control systems, and ceramic technology. He has worked extensively in the American Southwest, Mexico, and Iran.

Cover: An aerial view of rock-bordered grids and terraces in the Safford Valley (photograph by Adriel Heisey).

Contributors

Karen R. Adams
  Crow Canyon Archaeological Center
  Cortez, Colorado
Paul R. Fish
  Arizona State Museum
  University of Arizona, Tucson
Suzanne K. Fish
  Arizona State Museum
  University of Arizona, Tucson
Jeffrey A. Homburg
  Statistical Research, Inc.
  Tucson, Arizona
Brenda B. Houser
  U.S. Geological Survey (Emeritus)
  Tucson, Arizona
Betty Graham Lee
  Department of Anthropology (Emeritus)
  Eastern Arizona College, Thatcher
Dale R. Lightfoot
  Department of Geography
  Oklahoma State University, Stillwater
Arthur MacWilliams
  Arizona State Museum
  University of Arizona, Tucson
Guadalupe Sánchez de Carpenter
  Departamento de Antropología, Universidad de las Americas, Puebla, México
Jonathan A. Sandor
  Department of Agronomy
  Iowa State University, Ames
Marilyn Shoberg
  Texas Archeological Research Laboratory
  University of Texas, Austin

THE UNIVERSITY OF ARIZONA PRESS

Copyright © 2004
The Arizona Board of Regents
All Rights Reserved

This book was set in 11/12 CG Times

∞ This book is printed on acid-free, archival-quality paper.
Manufactured in the United States of America.

Library of Congress Cataloging-in-Publication Data

The Safford Valley grids : prehistoric cultivation in the southern Arizona desert / William E. Doolittle and James A. Neely, editors ; contributors, Karen R. Adams ... [et al.].
   p. cm. -- (Anthropological papers of the University of Arizona ; no. 70)
   Includes bibliographical references and index.
   ISBN 0-8165-2428-9 (pbk. : alk. paper)
   1. Indians of North America--Agriculture--Arizona--Safford Valley. 2. Terracing--Arizona--Safford Valley--History. 3. Rock gardens--Arizona--Safford Valley--History. 4. Plant remains (Archaeology)--Arizona--Safford Valley. 5. Excavations (Archaeology)--Arizona--Safford Valley. 6. Safford Valley (Ariz.)--Antiquities.
   I. Doolittle, William Emery. II. Neely, James A. III. Adams, Karen R., 1946- IV. Title. V. Series.

E78.A7S23 2004
979.1'5401--dc22   2004016105

FRONTISPIECE: *front*, the Safford Valley, with extensive ancient grids in the foreground (photograph by Adriel Heisey); *back*, near-vertical view of ancient grids in the Safford Valley (photograph by Adriel Heisey).   →

Dedicated to

Richard B. Woodbury

Visionary

Who first traversed these ancient grids

some 45 years ago

In appreciation of his contributions to the study of
prehistoric agriculture and water management in
the American Southwest and Mesoamerica

Contents

FIGURES

TABLES

Preface

William E. Doolittle and James A. Neely

In 1959 Jim Neely visited the Safford Valley in southeastern Arizona as part of an archaeological field trip from the University of Arizona. Fascinated by the landscape and the archaeological resources, his impression at the time was: "Someday I have to come back and work here." In 1980 Bill Doolittle, upon seeing an aerial photograph of the rock-bordered grids published in the journal *Kiva* (Woosley 1980: 323, Fig. 1), said: "Someday I have to see those things." Our wishes were fulfilled, finally, in May 1994, 35 and 14 years later, respectively.

In no small way our initial visit to the rock-bordered grids in the Safford Valley was as much accidental as intentional. Having similar topical and regional interests, and having the good fortune of being at the same institution, we have worked together on numerous projects focusing on prehistoric agriculture in the American Southwest. Somehow, however, we seemed never to get to the Safford Valley, except for an occasional drive-through. It was a student, Kyle Woodson, who drew us there to inspect the excavations he was conducting at the Goat Hill Site for his master's thesis (Woodson 1995). While there, we accepted an invitation to visit the grids extended by Gay M. Kinkade, archaeologist then with the Gila Resource Area (Bureau of Land Management, Safford Office), now with the Bureau of Indian Affairs, Phoenix Office.

We spent several hours each day for several days walking about the grids, kicking them, probing them, photographing them, sketching them, pondering them, and discussing them. We probably envisaged every possible scenario for their construction and function. At the time, we were not fully aware of the literature concerning them, but we were reasonably confident that not much research had been done on them and that few publications contained more than mention of them. We were also certain that questions concerning them far outnumbered answers. In other words, they were sitting there waiting to be investigated in depth. And, who better to study them but us, with, as it turned out, a team of others.

From the beginning we realized that this job was larger than the two of us alone could handle, not so much in the amount of work as in the nature of the work that might provide those elusive answers. The project begged to be done by a multidisciplinary team of experienced scholars, each with specialized expertise.

Assessing the local topography and hydrology posed no problem; Doolittle handles that in Chapter 5. Similarly, Neely oversaw the archaeological work and placed the grids in their cultural context: Chapter 2 presents a prehistoric and paleoclimatic overview and Chapter 8 discusses field house excavations and ceramics.

The grid interiors are dirt, and we turned to Jonathan A. Sandor and Jeffrey A. Homburg as soils experts. At the time we began to assemble the team, Jon had approximately 15 years experience studying the soils on prehistoric terraces in various parts of the Southwest. Jeff had been working with him for a few years, specifically in the Tonto Basin and Verde Valley. No two people know more about soils cultivated prehistorically in the Southwest than these two. Chapter 6 and Appendix A are the results of their detailed edaphic studies.

The grid borders are rock, and piles of rocks appear both within grids and outside of them. Rock piles are not uncommon features on the landscape of southern Arizona. Archaeologists have walked over them for a century, stopping to ponder them, only to shrug their shoulders and walk on. During the mid-1980s, Suzanne K. Fish (palynologist) and Paul R. Fish (archaeologist) discovered that rock piles north of Tucson comprised mulch that facilitated the prehistoric cultivation of agave. Could the rock piles associated with the rock-bordered grids in the Safford Valley have been used for a similar purpose? Indeed, could the grid borders themselves have been planted in agave? Chapter 7 by the Fishes and their colleagues is an assessment of vegetation and crops based on present-day and paleobotanical data collection and analyses.

Dirt, rocks, mulch, grids. Hmmm? Grids somewhat similar, but not identical, to those in the Safford Valley have long been known from northern New Mexico. As was the case with the rock piles, these, too, were long-enigmatic but recently explained. The scholar who solved that problem was Dale R. Lightfoot. Dale not only brought additional soils expertise to the project, but a comparative perspective as well. His skills in the interpretation of aerial photographs and geographical information systems (GIS) lent additional dimensions to the project. He contributed to Chapter 6 and authored Chapter 4, which discusses his remote sensing, mapping, and GIS activities.

Other scholars joined the team as the project progressed. Arthur MacWilliams and Guadalupe Sánchez de Carpenter, while graduate students at the University of Arizona, excavated roasting pits and conducted surficial artifact collections. Art assisted Paul Fish with artifact identifications, and Lupita made preliminary identifications of macrobotanical remains from the roasting pits. Further identifications and interpretations of macrobotanical remains were made by Karen R. Adams. Art, Lupita, and Karen all provided valuable contributions to Chapter 7. Betty Graham Lee, a local archaeologist, analyzed the rock art. Numerous petroglyphs were discovered among the grids, and there is a sizable rock art site nearby. Any connections between the grids and the rock art had to be explored, and who better to do it than someone who spent years studying rock art in the local area; Chapter 9 is a joint effort between Betty and Doolittle. Brenda M. Houser, a geologist who had spent years working in the Safford area, joined the team to place the grids in their geologic context; Chapter 3 is her assessment of the local and regional geology. Finally, Marilyn Shoberg, a lithic specialist, conducted a microscopic analysis of a tabular knife (Appendix B).

Gay M. Kinkade was a *de facto* member of the team. Most of the grids studied are located on land controlled by his office at the time. Accordingly, it was Gay to whom everyone else had to answer. Gay's duties left little time for him to work on the project in anything other than an official capacity. Government archaeologists get to be involved in numerous projects, but only superficially. As any kid will tell you, looking at a sandbox is nowhere near as much fun as playing in one.

Acknowledgments

No project of this scope and magnitude could be conducted without generous financial support. Despite ever-increasing costs of archaeological research, we completed this project for less than $40,000, a real bargain if ever there was one. We express deep gratitude to the National Geographic Society for the major portion of research funds, grant number 5834–96. Preliminary work was supported by the University Research Institute, The University of Texas at Austin. Other support included a University Cooperative Society Subvention Grant awarded by The University of Texas at Austin and by the Erich W. Zimmermann Regents Professorship in Geography, College of Liberal Arts, The University of Texas at Austin.

We especially thank all of the team members mentioned above who joined us in this enigmatic quest, who contributed to the data collection and analyses, and who wrote portions of this monograph. Other people provided invaluable field assistance, comments, suggestions, and support.

In addition to a fine professional archaeologist, the Safford Office of the Bureau of Land Management had three excellent and dedicated site stewards: Everett J. Murphy, Lee DeWester, and the late Roy Connors, all retired from previous careers and all with overwhelming enthusiasm for archaeology. They often went to great lengths to ensure that the many tasks were completed. Numerous members of the Graham County Archaeological Society served energetically as volunteer field assistants.

Jennifer R. Rinker, a graduate student in anthropology from The University of Texas at Austin, took valuable time away from the excavations that resulted in her master's thesis (Rinker 1998) to lend her archaeological and mapping skills to various aspects of this project while field work was being conducted.

Some noted scholars visited us in the field while work was underway to offer their insights and expertise. Laurance C. Herold, professor emeritus of geography, University of Denver, conducted detailed studies of the *trincheras* in the Sierra Madres west of Casas Grandes, the largest and most extensive prehistoric terraces in North America. We always knew that we were dealing with something special in the Safford grids, but even Larry was awe-struck at the vastness of the grids across the landscape. David E. Doyel, an archaeologist with Archaeological Resources Services, came out from Phoenix and held court for a day or two. Dave, in his inimitable way, contributed to our leaving no rocks unturned, at least figuratively speaking, in proffering possible explanations.

Stephen Bingham, professor emeritus of botany, Eastern Arizona College, identified some plants collected by Ruth Adams, a physician and Betty Lee's sister-in-law. Henry C. Wallace assisted in the identification of some ceramics. Several scholars who were unable to visit the grids while work was in progress provided unfailing moral support, including Anne I. Woosley, Allan J. McIntyre, David A. Gregory, Patricia A. Gilman, W. Bruce Masse, Linda S. Cordell, Richard I. Ford, R. Gwinn Vivian, and Sharon Urban.

Every archaeological project can benefit from the participation of an artist, and for this project we had one of the best. Adriel Heisey is renown for the stunningly beautiful photographs he takes from an ultralight aircraft. His work not only graces this volume, but his keen eye and genuine interest contributed to the success of our work.

Others who assisted in various ways include Jay Norton and Louis Moran of the soils laboratories of the University of Montana and Iowa State University, respectively; Russell S. Vose, Office of Climatology, Arizona State University; Tory Lightfoot, Arts and Sciences Extension Service, Oklahoma State University; Bruce Battles and Allen Finchum, Department of Geography, Oklahoma State University. We are grateful to Michael P. Larson, Oklahoma State University Cartography Service, who provided superior service in that mysterious realm of transmitting computer illustration files.

Dirk J. Harris, Senior Support Systems Analyst, and David Thompsen, Support Systems Analyst, both in the Department of Anthropology, University of Arizona, showed extreme patience with balky equipment and finessed numerous computer problems. María Nieves Zedeño, Bureau of Applied Research, University of Arizona, ably translated the Abstract into Spanish. We are especially appreciative of Carol A. Gifford, whose masterful editorial skills brought this project to fruition.

CHAPTER ONE

A Checkered Landscape

William E. Doolittle and James A. Neely

The landscape of North America is replete with vestiges of ancient indigenous agriculture. Literally every corner of the continent contains some type of remains, be they corn hills in the Northeast (Heidenreich 1974), ridged fields in the Southeast (Kelly 1965) and Midwest (Gallagher and Sasso 1987), or even potato beds in the Northwest (Suttles 1951). No place, however, has a greater number and diversity of prehistoric agricultural features visible on the surface today than the Southwest. In this region, canals, checkdams, terraces, and rock piles are commonplace. In no small way the prevalence of such features is a function of environment and demographics. Limited amounts of rainfall, runoff, and vegetation all favor natural preservation. These same factors have attracted relatively few people in historic and recent times, thereby resulting in comparatively little destruction of these features from modern development.

The abundance and conspicuousness of prehistoric agricultural features in the Southwest has fostered numerous scientific investigations of them. Canals, clearly the largest and most important features that once supported substantial populations, have garnered much attention and, as a result, are both well known and well understood (Breternitz 1991; Dart 1989; Turney 1929). Checkdams appear to be the most widespread and numerous and, not surprisingly, their functions and ecologies are similarly common knowledge (Doolittle 1985; Masse 1979). Terraces are fewer and more isolated than either canals or checkdams, but are equally spectacular, and they too harbor no mysteries (Herold 1965; Sandor and others 1986; Schmidt and Gerald 1988). And although rock piles, often occurring in clusters, numbering in the hundreds, and covering several hectares, were enigmatic for decades,

we now know that they were used for the cultivation of agave (S. Fish and others 1985).

Rock-bordered grids stand in contrast to these and other ancient "agricultural landforms" (Golub and Eder 1964). Composed of rocks arranged in rows oriented more or less parallel and perpendicular to each other and placed on nearly level surfaces, these features have long been known but little studied and not properly understood. This volume details new revelations about the ecology, mechanics, and cultural implications of these ancient agricultural features.

GRIDS, GRIDS, AND MORE GRIDS

In the Southwest, at least three types of grids have been identified that derived from prehistoric cultivation techniques: waffle gardens, pebble-mulch gardens, and rock-bordered grids. The first two techniques are reasonably well known and understood, but details concerning their functions are not yet fully comprehended. Not inconsequentially, therefore, they have contributed to the less-than-perfect understanding, even *mis*understanding, of the rock-bordered grids.

Waffle Gardens

The Zuni waffle gardens were made famous largely as the result of a series of stunning photographs taken by Jesse Nusbaum about 1910 (Fig. 1.1). These photographs have been republished numerous times (Cushing 1920, Plates 1, 16, 17; Ferguson and Hart 1985: 46, 84; Ladd 1979: 493, 497), and several writers have discussed various aspects of these gardens, albeit typically only briefly.

Figure 1.1. Waffle gardens at Zuni Pueblo, about 1910. (Photograph by Jesse L. Nusbaum, courtesy of and published by permission of the Museum of New Mexico, Neg. No. 8742.)

At least seven attributes of these gardens are visible in Nusbaum's photographs. First, it is most apparent why they are called "waffle gardens"; they look like waffles (Baxter 1882: 81). Second, the grids are constructed of earth, not rock (Ferguson and Hart 1985: 38; Ford 1985: 61; Ladd 1979: 498). Third, the individual grids are small, 50 cm to 60 cm square (Clark 1928: 242). Fourth, they are located close to the river bank and irrigated with water carried in jars (Holmes 1912: 35; Stevenson 1904: 353). Fifth, they are located adjacent to the pueblo (Ferguson 1985: 123). Sixth, the total area devoted to grids is small (Stewart 1940b: 337, 338), perhaps less than 200 square meters. And seventh, the grids are cultivated by women, who intensively tend a number of different food and nonfood plants, many of which are not domesticated (Bohrer 1960: 182).

The first attribute lends character to these features, and nothing more. The other six, however, are important in understanding function. They clearly place these

particular grids in the category of gardens and not fields. Although the terms "gardens" and "fields" are often used interchangeably or without much thought, they are different concepts. Their commonality is the fact that crops are grown in them. By definition, fields are large, distant from houses and certainly towns, and devoted to one or only a few staple grain crops that require relatively little attention or care. Gardens are just the opposite (Gleason 1994: 2; Turner 1992: 265–267). Because of the gardens' small sizes, proximity to dwellings, and intensive cultivation of a wide variety of plants, the term is often prefaced by one of several adjectives, including "urban" (Page 1986), "house-lot," "residential" (Killion 1990), "home" (González-Jacóme 1985), "household" (Niñez 1984), "kitchen" (Ginsberg 1987), and "dooryard" (Kimber 1973).

The Zuni waffle gardens are intriguing and their age remains unknown. Waffle gardens were clearly cultivated early in the 20th century and, contrary to popular myth perpetuated by misreadings of Vorsila Bohrer's

Figure 1.2. One of only two waffle gardens remaining at Zuni Pueblo in 1988. (Photograph reprinted by the permission of the Association of American Geographers, from Doolittle 1992: 396, Fig. 5.)

(1960) observations, they have not disappeared (Fig. 1.2; Doolittle 1992: 396, Fig. 5). How early in Zuni history they first appeared, however, is not clear.

Pebble-mulch Gardens

Pebble-mulch gardens in northern New Mexico have received much archaeological attention, especially during the past few years. These agricultural grids have been documented in the Galisteo Basin and the Chama Valley, and although similar if not identical in morphology and age, they functioned differently in these two locales. Pebble-mulch gardens occur on nearly level land near habitations. They involve borders and fill. Large rocks were gathered from the surface and arranged into grids. Most of the grids are discrete, rectangular in shape, and measure no more than 10 m by 20 m (Fig. 1.3). Some, however, are subdivided into smaller grids measuring only one or two meters square, appearing reminiscent of waffle

gardens (Fig. 1.4). What makes all of these grids interesting, however, is that smaller rocks were scraped up from the surrounding surfaces without grids or from borrow pits and deposited in a 5-to-10-cm thick layer *within* the grids.

The veneer of pebbles was first recognized as a mulch 30 years ago (Ellis 1970), and subsequent studies have revealed several nuances, two of which are particularly significant. Experimental studies showed that grids in the Galisteo Basin functioned principally as moisture control devices (Lightfoot 1993b: 366). Crops are no longer raised on the grids, but natural grass growth is more prolific within the grids than outside of them (Lightfoot 1993a: 116). This finding precipitated the collection of moisture, temperature, and biomass data from the grids themselves and from control areas without grids, revealing that soils within the grids had a higher moisture content than those outside (Lightfoot and Eddy 1995: 468–469). Analyses of soil temperatures showed mixed results be-

Figure 1.3. A pebble-mulch grid field on a Pleistocene terrace overlooking the Rio Chama, New Mexico. The layer of dark pebbles inside the grid contrasts with the lighter-colored soil outside the grid. (Photograph reprinted by permission of Oxford University Press from Doolittle 2000: 244, Fig. 7.16.)

Figure 1.4. A subdivided pebble-mulch grid field in the Chama Valley, New Mexico. (Photograph by James A. Neely.)

cause of post-use accumulation of eolian sediment and they were inconclusive (Lightfoot and Eddy 1994: 431–432). Findings of the biomass analyses, however, paralleled those for soil moisture. There was twice as much biomass on the grids than off. Not only did grasses grow taller and denser, but the roots were more numerous and penetrated to a greater depth (Lightfoot and Eddy 1994: 433–434, 435). These analyses confirmed the mulching properties of the pebble layer of grids in the Galisteo Basin. The pebble mulch reduced soil moisture evaporation thereby increasing crop production.

Drawing on analogs, studies suggested that pebble-mulch gardens in the Chama Valley were designed more to mitigate temperature variations than to control moisture (Maxwell 1995b). The region is not as dry as the Galisteo Basin, but it has a much shorter growing season. Increasing the speed of crop growth and even extending the growing season were two benefits of pebble mulching here (Cordell and others 1984: 236). Being darker than the surface of the areas without grids (Fig. 1.3), the pebble layer apparently absorbed solar radiation more rapidly and dissipated heat more slowly than lighter-colored and less rocky soils. The coarse texture of the pebble layer is suspected of reducing air movements over the surface and, as a result, contributing to an increase in soil temperatures (Cordell 1984: 206). Higher soil temperatures would have hastened seed germination (Maxwell 1995a: 119) and increased plant growth by affecting the rate at which crops took up water and nutrients from the soil (Maxwell and Anschuetz 1992: 65). In sum, it is likely that in the Chama Valley pebble mulching increased soil temperatures, crop growth, and the growing season.

Although pebble-mulch gardens in one locale ameliorated cold conditions and those in another setting compensated for aridity, they shared a common denominator in age and perhaps origin as well as morphology. There is no evidence that such features were cultivated recently or historically, but there is ample archaeological evidence that they were cultivated prehistorically, between A.D. 1200 (Cordell 1984: 207) and the arrival of the Europeans (Maxwell 1995a: 117). Maximum use took place in the 1400s (Lightfoot 1993a: 116). The features may have originated with migrants from the area around Sunset Crater, who practiced pebble-mulching prior to A.D. 1250 (Doolittle 1998).

Rock-bordered Grids

Unlike waffle gardens that occur in one locale, and pebble-mulch gardens that are known in only two areas, rock-bordered grids have been recorded from nearly every corner of the Southwest. In the archaeological literature of native North American agriculture, there are no fewer than 56 references to such grids in 27 different locales (Doolittle 2000, Table 7.1). During the late 19th century for example, Adolph F. Bandelier (1892: 72, 73) reported seeing "traces of garden plots . . . encased by rows of stones" south of the Puye Cliff Dwellings in the upper Rio Grande Valley.

Some accounts of rock-bordered grids portray features that are nothing short of remarkable. The top of Abiquiu Mesa was once described as containing "squares and rectangles . . . single rows of boulders laid upon the surface . . . cross each other at right angles to form . . . checkerboard pattern . . . there are at least *2,000* of the squares" (Hibben 1937: 16, emphasis added). The grids atop Abiquiu Mesa were not only numerous, but they were not adjacent to any habitation structures or towns, and they extended for approximately 850 m (Hewitt 1906: 36). By definition, then, they represent fields, not gardens, if indeed they were even agricultural.

These features have been referred to variously as "grid gardens," "bordered gardens," "stone-outlined gardens," or simply "garden plots" (Rankin and Katzer 1989). None of these terms is clearly descriptive with regard to composition and morphology: what materials were used in the construction of grid and bordered gardens, and what shape are the bordered and stone-outlined gardens? All four terms mention a function, which is only inferred and not actually known. We selected the purely descriptive term "rock-bordered grid" as it includes mention of both composition and morphology and implies no interpretation of function. There are two separate parts to each feature that merit research attention and consideration: the individual squares or the grid interiors that contain few if any rocks and the alignments or grid borders that are comprised entirely and exclusively of rocks.

THE SAFFORD VALLEY GRIDS

This study focuses on one specific set of rock-bordered grids, those north of the present-day town of

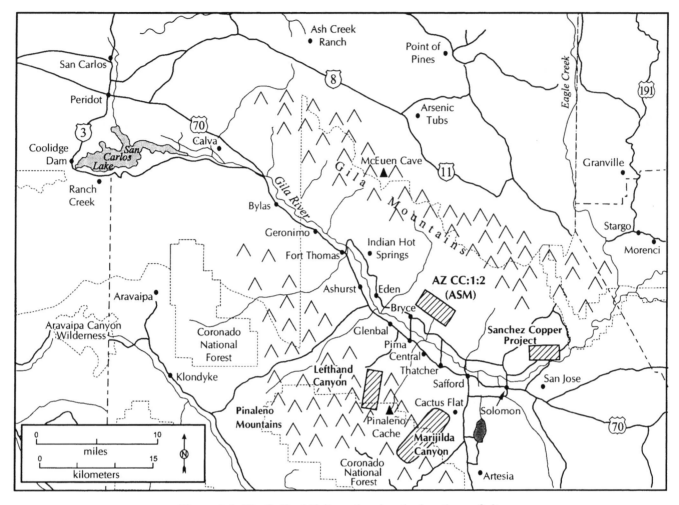

Figure 1.5. The Safford Valley, showing the locations of site
AZ CC:1:2 (ASM) and various physical and cultural features.

Pima in the Safford Valley in southeastern Arizona
(Fig. 1.5). Taking its name from the largest town in the
vicinity today, the Safford Valley is a 70-km-long
basin between the Gila Mountains on the north and the
Pinaleño Mountains on the south. The Gila River flows
more or less southeast-northwest through the center of
the valley. A perennial stream that experiences sizable
seasonal and annual fluctuations in flow, the Gila has
developed an alluvial plain that is nearly 2 km wide in
the Safford Valley. On either side of this plain, and
extending back to the mountains, are broad Pleis-
tocene-aged terraces. Sometimes referred to in the
vernacular by the Spanish term *mesas*, these terraces
are comprised mainly of cobbles and boulders. Their
surfaces are steeper near the mountains than they are

near the river. Toward their downslope ends, surface
gradients are slight and nearly level. The terraces are
also heavily dissected by a number of ephemeral
tributaries. These streambeds ("washes") are typically
dry and vary greatly in size.

Throughout the Safford Valley, rock-bordered grids
are commonly located on the tops of these terraces,
overlooking the alluvial plain of the river. Writing of
the valley's archaeological resources early in the 20th
century, Jesse Fewkes (1904: 177) noted "rows of
stones marking off the surface of the land in rectangles
of great regularity . . . very abundant, especially on the
sides of the mesa bounding Pueblo Viejo." A short
while later, Walter Hough made a similar comment
and was the first to infer both a method of construction

and an interpretation. He noted that on "the gravel terrace . . . are found numerous plots of ground from which the stones have been picked to outline the borders of gardens" (Hough 1907: 33; see also numerous notes in the site files of the Bureau of Land Management, Safford Office).

The rock-bordered grids under investigation here are not the ones reported by either Fewkes or Hough, but they are the largest in areal extent and the most visually striking, especially when seen from the air (Cover, Frontispiece; see also Ahlstrom 1997: 9.10, Fig. 9.5; Woosley 1980: 323, Fig. 1). These grids have two site numbers: most commonly used is AZ CC:1:2 (ASM), rarely used is AZ CC:1:13 (ASM).

The Safford Valley grids are often referred to locally by the misnomer "grid gardens." Features this extensive do not fit the definition of gardens, but rather that of fields.

Previous Research

The earliest mention of the grids at site AZ CC:1:2 (ASM) actually appeared as a footnote in a study of the Pima Indians by Frank Russell (1908: 88–89, n *a*).

At various places in the Southwest the writer has seen extensive areas over which the loose bowlders that were originally thickly scattered on the surface had been gathered in rounded heaps or in rows that divided the ground into rectangles that average about 5 meters to the side. The largest of these "fields" personally inspected is north of the town of Pima, nearly 200 miles east of the Pima reservation. On a lava-strewn mesa that is too high to be irrigated and too far from the hills to be flooded there are a half dozen of these tracts. The largest is a little more than half a mile in length by nearly a quarter in width. There are no signs of human occupation on the surface other than the disposition of the stones.

In this brief note Russell records a surprisingly large number of important points concerning these grids: their (1) location, (2) situation, (3) areal extent, and (4) disjunct nature; and the (5) sizes of individual grids, (6) source of materials, (7) method of construction, (8) water resource problems, and (9) lack of habitation sites nearby.

The Cast of Characters

First among the group of scholars who followed Russell into the Safford Valley and explored these grids was Guy R. Stewart, Senior Soil Conservationist with the Soil Conservation Service, U.S. Department of Agriculture. He examined the grids during the late 1930s and discussed them at some length in two journal articles (Stewart 1939, 1940a). Emil W. Haury of the Department of Anthropology, University of Arizona, also visited the Safford Valley in the 1930s (Stewart 1939: 114; 1940a: 217), but there is no record of his having seen the grids or written about them.

Richard B. Woodbury, an archaeologist then with the Arizona State Museum, surveyed the features twice in 1959 and gave the site its first numerical designation. One of those visits was with Donald R. Tuohy (1960: 29). Woodbury surveyed the grids again in 1960, this time with Don Cassidy, and for reasons not clear gave the site its second number. Woodbury's only published mention of these grids is a brief statement in his famed Point of Pines monograph (Woodbury 1961). His three sets of notes are in the site files of the Arizona State Museum, Tucson.

During the mid-1970s the grids were surveyed by Patricia L. Gilman, Peter Sherman, and Lynne S. Teague, all with the Arizona State Museum. Gilman and Sherman (1975) published a detailed report of their survey and Teague's field notes were appended to Woodbury's. Since the 1970s a number of scholars have visited the grids, mainly on an informal basis. D. Sanders appended his brief notes to Woodbury's and Teague's. Others, like W. Bruce Masse, have not published anything about these grids, but have used their observations in making general statements about prehistoric Southwestern agriculture (Masse 1991). Yet others, working on related topics in the general area, have visited the grids and mentioned them explicitly: Anne I. Woosley (1980), and Gregory R. Seymour, David P. Doak, and Richard V. N. Ahlstrom (1997).

Differing Interpretations

Although Russell appears to have been correct in his assessment of the spatial scale of the Safford grids in his comparison with other grid systems in the Southwest, there has been some dispute as to the exact size of the area they encompass. Stewart (1939: 114,

1940a: 216) claimed that they covered only 10 hectares, but added that they were "probably the most comprehensively laid out of any studied" (Stewart 1939: 131). Woodbury (1961: 41; Woosley 1980: 322; Ahlstrom 1997: 9.3) reported seeing 60 hectares of grids, but his unpublished field notes (on file, ASM) mention 80 hectares. Finally, Gilman and Sherman (1975: 9) did not estimate the hectarage but noted that the grids were observed in an area measuring approximately 1.10 km by 0.75 km (see also Teague, notes on file, ASM). Because of the disjunct nature of the grids, it is difficult to derive a hectarage figure from dimensional measurements.

Russell noted that he saw six sets of grids at AZ CC:1:2 (ASM). Gilman and Sherman (1975: 3, 9) and Teague (notes on file, ASM) reported inspecting 12 fields, and Woodbury (1961: 41; Woosley 1980: 322; Ahlstrom 1997: 9.3, 9.9, Fig. 9.4) claims to have seen "20 separate fields." These differences may reflect the difficulty of distinguishing one set of grids from another at ground level.

More important than the number of tracts with grids on the site are the sizes of the grids themselves, and this, too, is a point on which there are a variety of observations. Russell noted that grids averaged 5 m square, or 25 square meters each. Later scholars reported not only a wide variety in the sizes of the grids, but in their shapes as well. Stewart (1939: 114; 1940a: 216) wrote that the grids were "roughly rectangular in shape," some being as small as 2.4 m by 3.0 m and others being as large as 7.3 m by 9.1 m. In one set of notes (on file, ASM), Woodbury recorded both that grids were "rectangular," and "not always rectangular; very often they are quadrilateral in form." In another set, he describes the grids as being of "Variable size and shape, but on the average each plot is about 3 m. x 4 m."

Teague (notes on file, ASM) observed that "Plot size throughout the system is consistently about 5 x 6 meters. Occasional deviant plots tend to be slightly smaller rather than larger. Patterning of grids is moderately regular." Woosley (1980: 322) said that smaller grids measured "up to 4 m on a side" and larger ones measured "5 to 30 m on a side." Gilman and Sherman (1975: 9) wrote that the grids were "a latticework of various sizes and shapes," and that those in one area "were quite regular" whereas those in another "were less so." The reference to a variety of shapes suggests they observed triangular- and pentagonal-shaped features, as well as rectangular ones.

Nearly everyone who has written about these grids records that the borders are made of rock. Gilman and Sherman (1975: 9) reported further that the individual rocks vary in size, but are generally the larger ones on the surface and that they are unshaped. These same scholars, and Teague (notes on file, ASM), noted though that in at least one place "mounded earth and gravel served" in lieu of rock. Elsewhere, the grid borders vary from one to four rocks wide and are usually only a single course high (Gilman and Sherman 1975: 9).

As for construction, only one researcher since Russell has proffered an explanation. There is a general acceptance of the notion that the borders were made from locally available rocks that were cleared from the centers of the grids. Although he did not mention this clearing-construction in print, Woodbury did include such an inference in his unpublished survey notes (on file, ASM). This idea was not original with Russell, but was actually made a year earlier by Hough (1907: 33), who reported on grids elsewhere in the Safford Valley.

Consensus on Interpretation

Consensus deems that functions of the grids involved agriculture and water management. Interestingly, Russell never claimed that the grids were for crop production or water management, but his use of the term "fields" and his statements about irrigation difficulties certainly allude to these functions. Stewart (1939: 114; 1940a: 213, 216) was the first to suggest that these grids were "water-detention" and "water-retaining" devices. Others have endorsed this interpretation to one degree or another. Woodbury (notes on file, ASM) accepted it with some reservation, noting guardedly that the grids were "Hohokam irrigation pens"(?), an interpretation repeated by Tuohy (1960: 29). In contrast, Gilman and Sherman (1975: 3, 10–11) strongly stated that the "gridded gardens . . . are part of the water control and agricultural system."

If the grids did serve to detain or retain water, how did it get to the grids and then get into them? Tuohy (1960: 29) suggested that they were built "to capture and hold native soil and surface run-off during rainstorms." Presumably, he meant that the grids retained rain water that fell directly into them and prevented it from running off as sheet flow and carrying soil with it. Russell noted that being on the mesa, the grids were too high above the Gila River to be irrigated by canals from the river and that they were too far from the mountains to be irrigated with water originating there. Based on these views, the water must have come from the mesa itself, specifically areas upslope from the grids on the terraces but well below the mountains. There are, in fact, other features that could have diverted surface flow or runoff to some grids.

The Grids Are Not Alone

Russell did not mention any other types of features associated specifically with these grids, but he did mention other rock landforms, specifically rock piles, in his general prefatory comments. Woodbury (notes on file, ASM) was the only scholar to report seeing rock piles among the grids, and Stewart (1939: 112) found two types of rock alignments that did not form grids per se. Other features do exist, however.

The first of these features Stewart dubbed as "dams" and inferred that they were used for "diverting water into rectangular plots." In so doing, they were "forming a complete spreading system." No source of water for this system was evident, but it appeared that subsequent gullying may have changed completely the surface configuration and hence the hydrology (Stewart 1939: 114; 1940a: 216). In addition to both the rock-bordered grids and the rock alignments that he interpreted as water diversion structures, Stewart reported seeing terraces on this site: "a distinct system of terraces had been laid out on a grade of 2½ to 3½ percent. The terraces varied from 14 to 18 feet in width and 180 to 225 feet in length. Soil profile studies showed that the terraces were stabilized by one line of boulders which were either matched together or overlapped." He concluded "that water conservation was clearly the principal purpose of the early cultivators. Soil conservation in many cases was achieved incidentally, since the conservation methods used reduced the run-off and hence slowed down erosion" (Stewart 1939: 114, 131, 1940a: 216–217).

Curiously, none of the researchers who followed Stewart reported seeing any linear rock features other than the grids themselves on this site. There are, however, reports of similar features at other sites in the Safford Valley that have precipitated a number of interesting ideas concerning prehistoric agriculture.

In addition to the rock-bordered grids that he first reported in the east end of the Safford Valley, Fewkes (1904: 178, 179) also found terraces like those mentioned by Stewart and wrote that rock alignments oriented parallel to contours on slopes:

> may be regarded . . . as the walls of terrace gardens, so placed to divide different patches of cultivated soil, or to prevent this soil from being washed down to the plain below. . . . very extensive terraced gardens may be seen not far from San José, and all along the mesa near the Solomonville slaughterhouse. . . . There can hardly be a doubt that water was carried in large earthen vessels to some of the terraced gardens, the altitude of which above the water in the river would make irrigation otherwise impossible.

Russell (1908: 89, n *a*) also found terraces in the Safford Valley "on the north slope of Mount Graham and elsewhere." This brief comment was not lost on two later researchers, whose curiosity prompted them to visit these features. Stewart (1939: 114, 1940a: 217) noted that:

> near Deadman's Gulch, on Graham Mountain . . . terraces had been constructed, apparently by clearing the land and piling the boulders at the outer edge of the terrace. The size of the terraces was very irregular, varying from small areas 20 by 40 feet up to approximately 30 feet wide and over 100 feet in length. Portions . . . were examined by Dr. Haury and have been dated for probable time of occupancy by pottery sherds at A.D. 1200 to 1400.

A short distance west of the grids at site AZ CC:1:2 (ASM), Gilman and Sherman (1975: 7, 11, 23) located site AZ CC:1:17 (ASM), characterized by "10 linear borders," or terraces on a steep slope. These features consisted of unshaped cobbles collected from the surface and piled no more than 30 cm high. Because these alignments retained only limited amounts of sediment, which was not level, they were interpreted as having served a water management function, thereby echoing Stewart's interpretation.

Most recently, all sorts of prehistoric agricultural features have been reported on sites far to the east of these grids, including "rock piles," "checkdams," "terraces," "rock alignments," and even rock-bordered grids (referred to incorrectly as "waffle gardens"; Doak and others 1997). The myriad of ancient agricultural features in the Safford Valley includes remains of prehistoric canal irrigation on the alluvial plain (Bandelier 1892: 406–407, 414; Sauer and Brand 1930: 422; Fewkes 1904: 178; Hough 1907: 33, 34). Many canals occur discretely, others in concert. This diversity has led Woosley (1980: 322) to conclude that the Safford Valley grids "combined systems of ditches and contour terraces, apparently to promote horizontal water control."

Other Evidence of Human Occupation

The nearest known permanent habitation sites of any consequence are located at the mouth of Peck Wash (Fig. 1.6) and 6.4 km (about 4 miles) west of the grids. Little may be said of the Peck Wash Site because of heavy modern disturbance. The Owens-Colvin Site, AZ CC:1:19 (ASM), is a 50-to-100-room pueblo that, on the basis of ceramic evidence, was occupied between about A.D. 900 and 1375. It is situated on the first terrace overlooking the alluvial plain on the north side of the Gila River, which is only 750 m distant (Gilman and Sherman 1975: vi, 8, Fig. 1; see also Ahlstrom 1997: 9.1, 9.2, Fig. 9.1). Although these sites are not far away, they are certainly distant enough that the grids should not be considered gardens. The people who inhabited the settlements at the Peck Wash and Owens-Colvin sites may well have been involved in the building and use of the rock-bordered grids at AZ CC:1:2 (ASM), but that connection remains unproven.

Previous researchers found no habitation sites commensurate in size near the grids comprising site AZ CC:1:2 (ASM). The identification of the Peck Wash Site (Crary 1997) modifies that situation. And it is entirely possible that other habitation sites may lie buried beneath the much disturbed alluvium at the foot of the terraces, awaiting discovery by means of future geoarchaeological research. Other evidence of prehistoric human activity in association with the grids is sparse. Woodbury (notes on file, ASM) saw a "rectan-

gular stone foundation," presumably of a house, and a cluster of fire-cracked rocks approximately 2 m in diameter, both nearby. Teague (notes on file, ASM) reported nine black-and-white Mimbres sherds and some chert and andesite flakes on the site. Sanders (notes on file, ASM) encountered several brown ware sherds inside one of the grids. Gilman and Sherman (1975: 9) listed "four or five hoe blade fragments, scattered lithics, and one small ceramic scatter of Mimbres sherds" on the site. The hoe fragments lend a modicum of credibility to any agricultural interpretation, and the ceramics identify use during the Bylas phase (Ahlstrom 1997: 9.3).

Additional Thoughts

The amount of soil erosion that has taken place on the site since the grids were abandoned is debatable. Gilman and Sherman described the surface as "covered by igneous cobbles, underneath which a heavy gravel or sand is found." They evaluated this grid site as "poor agricultural land" and "marginal land," and the area below, along the Gila, as "prime river bottomland" (Gilman and Sherman 1975: 9, 11). They then went on to postulate about the adaptiveness of using a diversity of lands and agricultural systems and about the sequence of land use. In general, they suggested two things. The first is that prime land was used initially, and as the population grew lands of lesser quality were brought into production. Second, the grids provided an alternative agricultural strategy in years when conditions did not permit the usual harvest of crops on the bottomland (Gilman and Sherman 1975: 11).

At first glance, these ideas make sense. After some deliberation, however, a number of inconsistencies begin to appear. A multiple of nuances and subtleties exist. If Gilman and Sherman are correct, and they may well be, a plethora of factors have to be taken into account. For example, there must be certain positive characteristics about marginal lands that make them acceptable as a back-up to prime lands, that, by extension, must have some negative qualities. Also, exactly how prime are the bottomlands, and how marginal are the mesa tops? Perhaps overlooked is that land that might be classified as poor by 21st-century Americans, could well have been considered prime land by ancient farmers, who had very different tech-

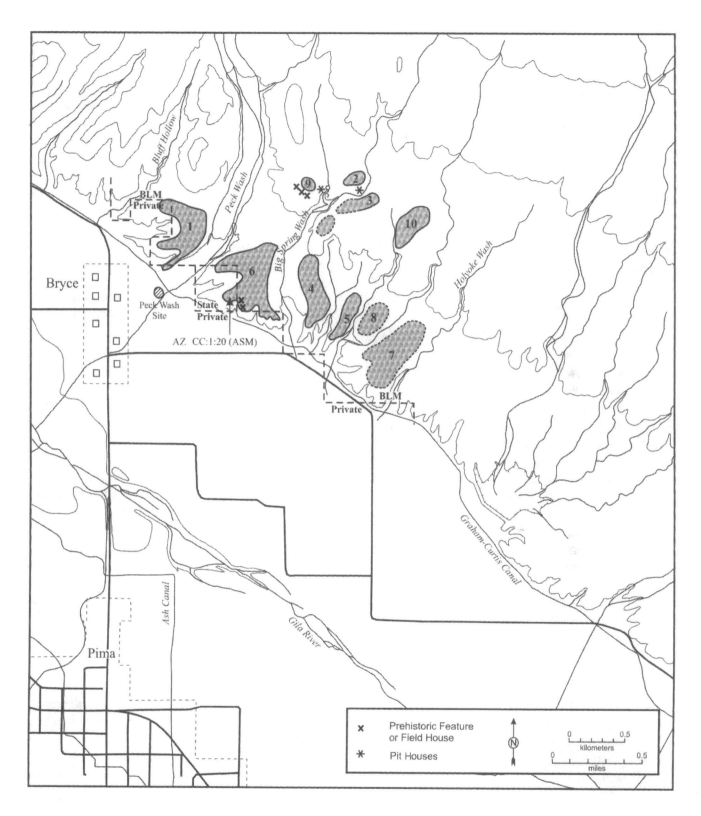

Figure 1.6. Site AZ CC:1:2 ASM (Grid Localities 1–10) and
other cultural and physical features mentioned in the text.

nologies and needs (Doolittle 1980). Gilman and Sherman (1975: 11) raise some interesting points that are of considerable anthropological importance; we address them further in Chapter 10.

The Safford grids remain enigmatic despite being impressive. They are sufficiently impressive to have engendered some support for nomination to the National Register of Historic Places (Doyel 1993: 57; Gilman and Sherman 1975: 12). As impressive as they are, however, they have not been granted registry. The reasons for this denial of official recognition are unknown, but may well rest in these grids not being understood. Correcting this situation is the goal of this project.

1994 RECONNAISSANCE

Our initial visit to site AZ CC:1:2 (ASM) confirmed everything that previous scholars had agreed upon, which is to say that the grids are on the terrace north of the town of Pima. We were unable to resolve certain discrepancies among earlier findings concerning grid size and shape, the extent of the area covered, and the number of groupings, and instead we accepted that variations do exist. For convenience, we categorized the grids spatially into ten localities (Fig. 1.6).

Evidence from the survey confirmed that grid borders in one locality were comprised of large rocks (Fig. 1.7), whereas in another they were comprised of smaller rocks (Fig. 1.8), and yet in another of gravel (Fig. 1.9); that rock piles occurred in the centers of some grids (Fig. 1.10); that there were some relatively long rock alignments (Fig. 1.11) and that there were some short rock alignments, or what most Southwestern archaeologists would consider "checkdams" (Doolittle and others 1993), some even with rock piles in association (Fig. 1.12); and that there were terraces (Fig. 1.13) in association with the grids. Most surprisingly, however, we identified seven things that none of the previous visitors had reported.

1. There are areas adjacent to, but separate from, the rock-bordered grids that are covered with rock piles (Fig. 1.14).

2. There are places where the natural surface gradient changes from relatively slight to relatively steep, and rock-bordered grids on the former merge into terraces on the latter. Viewed dynamically, as the natural surface gradient steepens, rock-bordered grids

become terraces with crosswalls. As the gradients become even steeper, the crosswalls disappear, resulting in simple terraces (Fig. 1.15).

3. Several of the rocks forming the grid borders have different patinas on one side than they do on the other, so rocks were overturned as they were moved (Fig. 1.16). Other rocks appear to be in situ, and differences in patination between the upper and lower parts of rocks are visible a few centimeters above the current ground surface, presumably as a result of post-use deflation or erosion (Fig. 1.17).

4. There are a few circular rock features (Fig. 1.18), whose function is unknown. Gay M. Kinkade proposed in 1997 that they might have been used for storage or ceremonies.

5. There are a few rectilinear rock features similar to structures that Southwestern archaeologists identify as "field houses" (see Chapter 8).

6. There is a thin but substantial scattering of ceramic sherds as well as lithic tools and debitage among the grids.

7. There are a few examples of rock art scattered among the grids (see Chapter 9).

ADDRESSING THE ISSUES

The confirmation of previous findings combined with new discoveries and an incomplete understanding of grid ecology and function raise a number of questions that beg to be answered. Questions concerning the grids at site AZ CC:1:2 (ASM) are classified into four categories: age, construction, purpose, and function. On the basis of other findings in the American Southwest, these questions are reformulated as testable propositions.

Proposition of Age

1. The grids, and associated rock piles, alignments, structures, and rock art were constructed in prehistoric times.

Ranchers, farmers, the federal, state, and local governments all are known to have built rock erosion and water management features that look amazingly prehistoric (Doolittle and others 1993). Those built by the Civilian Conservation Corps (CCC) are frequently confused with their prehistoric counterparts (Wright 1993). The CCC was very active building rock erosion

Figure 1.7. Grids, with large rocks, at Locality 4. (Photograph by William E. Doolittle.)

Figure 1.8. Grids at Locality 5; rocks are smaller than at Locality 4. (Photograph by William E. Doolittle.)

Figure 1.9. Grids at Locality 6, without large rocks. Grid borders are comprised of the largest materials on the surface. (Photograph by William E. Doolittle.)

Figure 1.10. Grids at Locality 2 with a rock pile in the center of one grid. James Neely provides scale. (Photograph by William E. Doolittle.)

Figure 1.11. Long rock alignment ("diversion dam") at Locality 6. (Photograph by William E. Doolittle.)

Fig. 1.12. A short rock alignment ("check-dam") at Locality 1, with rock piles just upslope. (Photograph by William E. Doolittle.)

Figure 1.13. An upslope view of terraces at Locality 1. One member of the research team is standing on each terrace, reminiscent of Woodbury's (1961: 29) Figure 14 in *Prehistoric Agriculture at Point of Pines, Arizona.* (Photograph by William E. Doolittle.)

Figure 1.14. A rock pile field adjacent to, but separate from, rock-bordered grids at Locality 1. (Photograph by William E. Doolittle.)

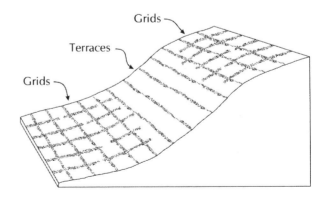

Figure 1.15. Schematic diagram of grid-to-terrace transition at Locality 4.

Figure 1.16. An upturned boulder with distinct variations in patina from one side to the other. (Photograph by William E. Doolittle.)

Figure 1.17. Undisturbed or in situ boulder with distinct variations in patina from top to bottom. (Photograph by William E. Doolittle.)

Figure 1.18. A small rock "ring" at Locality 1. (Photograph by William E. Doolittle.)

control devices in the Safford Valley during the 1930s (Seymour 1998), and its modern counterpart, Ameri-Corps, has been doing the same thing there recently (*Eastern Arizona Courier* 1998). Determining whether or not these grids are prehistoric is, therefore, crucial.

After determining that the grids are prehistoric, it is necessary to identify their ages more precisely, especially for the purpose of establishing their cultural affiliation. Ahlstrom (1997: 9.3), Gilman and Sherman (1975: 9), Sanders (notes on file, ASM), and Teague (notes on file, ASM) all found a few prehistoric ceramic artifacts among the grids, but such fragmentary evidence requires additional support.

Proposition of Construction

2. Grid borders were constructed of rocks from the immediate vicinity, on the terrace surfaces, and not from some remote source.

There is some archaeological evidence that rocks were moved short distances for agricultural purposes elsewhere in the Southwest (for example, Lightfoot and Eddy 1995), and there is no evidence to suggest that ancient people in the region collected rocks from specific source areas and transported them any great distances. Furthermore, it is intuitively logical that prehistoric farmers would not have hauled heavy, bulky, low value materials farther than was necessary, preferring instead to use readily available rocks.

Areas without grids on the tops of the Pleistocene terraces north of the Gila River are littered with loose rocks. In areas with grids, the interiors of the grids are relatively free of rocks, especially large rocks. As was noted by Gilman and Sherman (1975: 9) and Teague (notes on file, ASM), the grid borders tend to be comprised of the largest rocks on the terraces (Figs. 1.7, 1.8). Both Russell (1908: 88, n *a*), and Woodbury (notes on file, ASM) explicitly suggested that the grid borders were formed by the clearing of surface rocks. Their idea merits evaluation.

Proposition of Purpose

3. The grids were used for agricultural production.

As with their assumptions of a prehistoric age, every archaeologist who has seen these grids assumed they were agricultural. But, assuming they were agricultural does not prove it. The few fragments of stone hoes among the grids reported by Gilman and Sherman (1975: 9) resolve little and result in a myriad of questions, not the least of which is: What crops were grown? These questions are framed as a subset of additional propositions.

3a.   *Crops were grown in the interiors of the grids.*

3b.   *Crops were grown among the rocks comprising the grid borders.*

3c.   *Certain crops were grown in the grid interiors and others were grown among the rocks on the borders simultaneously.*

The interiors of the Zuni waffle garden grids are planted in a variety of vegetables (Bohrer 1960: 182; Doolittle 1992: 396). The pebble-covered fields of the Galisteo Basin were planted in staples like maize and beans (Lightfoot 1993a). And, finally, agave was cultivated in rock piles in the Santa Cruz Valley (S. Fish and others 1985). These findings lend validity to propositions of grid purpose.

Propositions of Function

4a.   *The grids collected and retained surface runoff.*

4b.   *The grids captured rainfall and retained runoff.*

4c.   *The grids retarded soil erosion.*

4d.   *Grids are the remains of devices used to anchor brush that retarded wind erosion.*

4e.   *The grids collected sediment, thereby resulting in a deeper growing medium.*

4f.   *Rocks comprising the grid borders provided a mulch, reducing evaporation and soil moisture loss.*

4g.   *Grids served no explicit function. The borders are simply the result of clearing rocks from the surface.*

The first two of these propositions are a direct result of Stewart's (1939: 114, 1940a: 213) interpretations. The second and third propositions (4b, 4c) follow the ideas of Tuohy (1960: 29). The third and fourth propositions (4c, 4d) can also be traced to Stewart, at least in part. They are rooted in his observation of terraces, his interpretation that erosion control was "secondary" (Stewart 1939: 131) and "temporary" (Stewart 1939: 111), and his claim that soil loss has occurred since the grids were abandoned (Stewart 1939: 131). The fourth proposition is also based in part

on the work of one of Stewart's contemporaries. During his investigations of landscape changes, John T. Hack (1942: 72) observed that Hopi farmers often used parallel lines of brush oriented perpendicular to the prevailing breeze in order to reduce wind erosion. This brush was not planted, as in the case of midwestern hedgerows (for example, Hewes 1981), but was cut and anchored with large rocks. Eventually, and certainly after abandonment, the brush deteriorated or decayed, leaving only lines of rock as evidence of fields. Whether or not these grids are remnants of brush anchors warrants consideration.

The fifth of the grid function propositions (4e) is inversely related to the fourth. It assumes that soil loss was a normal condition and that the grids impeded it. Furthermore, it assumes that grid function terminated at abandonment and that subsequent erosion has taken place. This proposition is based on a number of factors. First, many rock alignments in the Southwest are known to have trapped sediment (Sandor and others 1986). Second, many such alignments were eventually breached, resulting in the release of trapped sediment (Doolittle 1985). Third, Gilman and Sherman's (1975: 11) assessment of the grids at AZ CC:1:2 (ASM) presents a less-than-flattering image of present-day land quality. And, fourth, our discovery of top-to-bottom differences in patina on rocks still in situ (Fig. 1.17) would indicate that the darker patina is the result of a long-term exposure to the atmosphere and that the lighter patina is a function of short-term exposure. Accordingly, on rocks that have not been moved, the light patina evident just above the current ground surface might be a function of post-use exposure as soil was removed either through deflation or erosion.

Grid function proposition six (4f) is related to propositions 3b and 3c. Evaluation of pebble-mulch fields in northern New Mexico (Lightfoot 1993b) and rock piles in the Santa Cruz Valley (S. Fish and others 1985) are invoked as supportive correlates.

In a similar manner, the final grid function proposition (4g) is related, at least in part, to proposition 2, dealing with construction and related to purpose like propositions 3a and 3c. If the grids, and specifically their interiors, were farmed, rocks had to be cleared from the planting surface, unless they were needed as mulch. Under this scenario, the grid borders would have been "constructed" inadvertently as the result of rock clearance (Doolittle 1984), something suggested by both Russell (1908: n 88) and Woodbury (notes on file, ASM). If the grids were not agricultural (Proposition 3), then an entirely different tack must be taken.

The Research Team

Testing these propositions required numerous lines of investigation. As outlined in the Preface, this project was multidisciplinary. The team involved several scholars who, within their respective disciplines and subdisciplines, are among the world's foremost authorities with regard to prehistoric agriculture in the American Southwest. Members of the research team were assigned the simple task of applying their respective skills and expertise, however best they saw appropriate, to address the propositions. The specific methods and techniques we used are outlined in the following chapters by the persons responsible for certain aspects of the work.

CHAPTER TWO

Paleoclimatic and Archaeological Contexts

James A. Neely

There is a strong correlation between climatic conditions (the availability and predictability of moisture for agricultural pursuits) and major cultural changes in prehistoric times. Climate played an important, but not the only, role in the processes of cultural change documented by the archaeology of the Safford Valley (Neely 1997b).

HISTORY OF CLIMATE FROM 150 B.C. TO A.D. 1450

Although dendroclimatic information derived specifically from this area is not yet available, Jeffrey S. Dean told me in 1998 that specialists in the Laboratory of Tree-Ring Research at the University of Arizona have started analysis of data assembled from the Pinaleño Mountains (Figs. 1.5, 2.1). Detailed climatic information is available, however, from adjacent regions and, following Dean and Robinson (1982: 50) who have noted the interrelated nature of climatic conditions throughout the Southwest, I use it here to provide a period-by-period overview of climatic conditions in the Safford Valley. Because of proximity and physiographic similarities, precipitation records from the nearby Tonto Basin (Fig. 2.1; Rose 1994), geological and geomorphological studies of the Middle Gila River region (Huckleberry 1995; Waters and Ravesloot 2000), and tree-ring based reconstructions of stream flow in the Gila River (Graybill and others 1999) provide a tentative, but reasonable, reconstruction of moisture conditions in the area, arguably the most important of the climatic conditions for agriculture in the Southwest.

Early Formative Period (150 B.C.–A.D. 800)

The Tonto Basin precipitation record begins at A.D. 740. From that date until the end of the 8th century, the record is characterized by broad fluctuations in moisture (Rose 1994: 356), with the period of 752 to 809 having the highest percentage of extreme variation in the 631–year dendroclimatic record for this region (Van West and Altschul 1994: 402). In general, the dendroclimatic record of the last 60 years within this cultural period is predominantly characterized by dry conditions. These conditions introduced a pattern of aridity and variability that has continued in the Tonto Basin, and in the Safford Valley, to the present day, making these regions challenging for human groups of any size to establish a stable subsistence base.

Beginning somewhat earlier, in A.D. 534, the tree-ring record analyzed by Graybill and his colleagues (1999) documents basically the same pattern of climatic variability in the flow of the Gila River. These findings suggest that the nature of the Gila River would have made the use of the floodplain difficult for agricultural pursuits and occupation, but any canal irrigation ventures undertaken would have been relatively successful.

Late Formative Period (A.D. 800–1150)

During the first 117 years (A.D. 808–925) and the last 28 years (A.D. 1122–1150) of this period, episodes of reduced precipitation and drought were frequent, with the highest ratio of dry-to-wet years recorded for

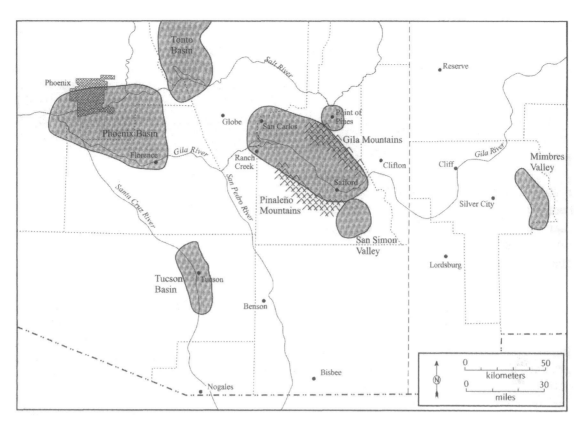

Figure 2.1. The Safford Valley, showing its geographic relationship to neighboring archaeological areas.

the Tonto Basin (Van West and Altschul 1994: 402–403). However, perpetuating the pattern of variability noted for the Early Formative period, most of the latter part of this period apparently was a time in which precipitation was particularly abundant. Altschul and Van West (1992: 180; see also Ciolek-Torrello and others 1994: 445–446), in their study of agricultural productivity for the Tonto Basin during the period of A.D. 740–1370, reported that the prehistoric agricultural potential in the Tonto-Globe area for the 124–year period between A.D. 977 and 1100 represented: "the longest continuously productive years in the entire 631–year sequence." In a subsequent publication, Van West and Altschul (1994: 399) modified the above statement somewhat by saying:

> the most striking feature of the Sedentary period is its relatively salubrious nature. It possesses a uniquely long period between A.D. 1042 and 1083 (42 years) when, with the notable exception of A.D. 1067, there were almost no drought years of any magnitude. These were the longest

continuously productive years in the entire 631–year sequence.... Thus the Sedentary is considered to be the most benign of all periods in the 631–year sequence in the Lower Tonto Basin. The generally favorable conditions of the eleventh century persisted through the first two decades of the twelfth century. Theoretically, these moderate conditions would have been conducive both to the proliferation of agricultural techniques and to population growth in the lower Tonto Basin.

Van West and Altschul noted that this period, when compared with the previous one, was a time of greater predictability in local agricultural productivity and sustainable population size, making it the period of greatest agricultural predictability on record in the Tonto Basin (Van West and Altschul 1994: 396, 403–404). On the other hand, the Gila River flow study (Graybill and others 1999) indicates this period to have been one of very high discharge variability. Such variability would mean that the floodplain of the

Gila River was an area of low agricultural predictability and that canal irrigation from the river was a risky enterprise during this period. Huckleberry (1995) and Waters and Ravesloot (2000) support this view by documenting a contemporary cycle of Gila River flooding and widening-downcutting.

The combined moisture and Gila River data related above may well explain the development, and later expansion, of the dry-farming areas and the foothill irrigation and field systems during this period. Although there is currently little information concerning contemporaneous river-associated canal irrigation and field systems, it seems probable that they would have been frequently in a state of disrepair.

Classic Period
(A.D. 1150–1450)

The climatic good fortunes of the peoples of southeastern Arizona apparently came to an end in the Classic period. The reversal of the Late Formative climatic optimum probably contributed greatly to modifications in the form and complexity of the subsistence and sociopolitical systems of the resident groups, and ultimately to their collapse and apparent disappearance from the area.

The Early Classic Period
(A.D. 1150–1300)

Rose (1994: 357, 358) and Van West and Altschul (1994: 400–401) document the early part of the Classic period as having had a high degree of climatic variability, with volatile conditions in which the clustering of drought years and occurrence of isolated wet years made successful agriculture unpredictable and hazardous. The Early Classic period had droughts of serious intensity and an extreme amount of interannual variation, and it represented the interval of least agricultural predictability in the 631-year dendroclimatic record of the Tonto Basin (Van West and Altschul 1994: 402–403). The latter part of the Early Classic period witnessed the so-called Great Drought of A.D. 1275–1299. In the words of Van West and Altschul (1994: 404), in the Tonto Basin the Early Classic period (A.D. 1150-1300) was, "the worst time to practice agriculture." The climate of the Safford Valley area surely mirrored that condition. Graybill and his colleagues

(1999) interpreted this as a time of relatively low mean flow, with numerous periods of prolonged low flow and low discharge variability for the Gila River. The preceding climatic conditions would not have been conducive to dry farming and foothill canal irrigation agriculture, but, in spite of low flow conditions, would have been generally favorable for the establishment and intensification of canal irrigated fields, both on and above the floodplain, serviced by the Gila River. Tempering the latter benefits, however, the low flow conditions of the Gila River would have limited irrigation agricultural productivity.

Late Classic Period
(A.D. 1300–1450)

In the Tonto Basin, the 71-year climatic documentation representing the first part (A.D. 1300–1370) of the Late Classic period records some relief from the preceding climatically disastrous times, but the intermixed patterning of dry and wet years may well have been more than the by-then agriculturally beleaguered inhabitants could withstand. Van West and Altschul (1994: 401) noted that, climatically, the Late Classic period was one of relatively high potential for agricultural productivity and population growth, but was also a time of only moderate agricultural predictability. Although conditions were conducive to yield abundant harvests from nonirrigated fields, they were probably disastrous to the fields that were irrigated, destroying the canals and related field systems beyond reasonably rapid repair. During this period, the Gila River experienced unusual discharge variability. High magnitude annual discharges would have severely affected canal irrigation by stranding intakes, destroying canal segments closest to the river, and filling canals with sediment (Graybill and others 1999).

These climatic conditions probably facilitated a subsistence strategy markedly different from that of the Early Classic period. The conditions would have been conducive to dry-farming and foothill irrigation agriculture, but would have been generally disastrous for the use and maintenance of Gila River canal systems and fields on the Gila River floodplain.

THE ARCHAEOLOGICAL PERSPECTIVE

Professional archaeological work has been conducted in the Safford Valley for more than a century, but most studies have been relatively restricted and have lacked regional and interregional perspective. As a result, the picture that has emerged is fragmented, but illustrates a surprising complexity. Despite its importance, and the fact that it was evidently one of the last major unstudied prehistoric population centers, the Safford Valley area remains one of the least known and poorly understood regions of the American Southwest. In her publication describing the excavations at the Owens-Colvin site, Pam Rule (1993: 6) has accurately summarized the situation as follows:

> The Safford Valley is one of the least studied and most complex regions of the Southwest, confronting a researcher with a bewildering array of pottery types, no established chronology, and a curious admixture of cultural traits. Local sites have suffered intensively from both agricultural activities and plundering, with most larger manifestations essentially destroyed. . . .
>
> Local culture history is so poorly documented that the descriptive ground-work available to researchers in most of the Southwest is lacking and must be built up by the same painstaking methods used by investigators of decades ago. Only after a firm descriptive and temporal foundation has been established will it be possible to approach the higher order questions already under consideration in better known areas of the Southwest.

Fortunately, this situation has begun to change in the past decade through the coordinated efforts of both professional and avocational researchers. Perhaps the single most important event to make inroads into this problem was the 1997 seminar titled "The Archaeology of a Land Between: Regional Dynamics in the Prehistory and History of Southeastern Arizona," organized by Anne I. Woosley and sponsored by the Amerind Foundation, Dragoon, Arizona. Fourteen scholars were invited to participate in the seminar, two of whom prepared papers that combined their own research with syntheses of disparate studies conducted in the Safford Valley throughout the late 1800s and the 1900s.

This section borrows heavily from the papers of Joseph Crary (1997) and Neely (1997b, 2001a). It is a brief overview of the prehistory of the Safford Valley and sets the cultural scene for the construction and use of the rock-bordered grids. Emphasis is placed on agricultural systems and paleoclimatic conditions.

PREHISTORIC CULTURAL DEVELOPMENTS IN THE SAFFORD VALLEY

The model of cultural development formulated for the Safford Valley (Neely 1997b) is divided into four chronological periods (Fig. 2.2; Crary 1997). Their salient features are: (1) Paleoindian and Archaic periods (about 8,000–150 B.C.), which witnessed the earliest occupants as well as the beginnings of agriculture and irrigation in the region; (2) Early Formative period (150 B.C.–A.D. 800), characterized by tribalism, a dispersed settlement system, a mixed subsistence strategy, the development of agriculture, and the beginnings of population aggregation and regional differentiation; (3) Late Formative–Pre-Classic period (A.D. 800–1150), characterized by an increasing focus on agriculture and the development of complex agricultural systems that incorporated water-management and irrigation technology, the occupation and utilization of marginal areas, population aggregation, regional differentiation, and increasing cultural system complexity; and (4) Classic period (A.D. 1150–1450), characterized by an emphasis on regionalism, the influx of substantial numbers of immigrants from the north, increasing population aggregation, the formation of subregional centers, agricultural intensification, emerging complexity of the religious and social systems, the development of new exchange-alliance networks, and, finally, system collapse.

Paleoindian and Archaic Periods (About 8,000–150 B.C.)

Limited information exists on the Paleoindian and Archaic periods of occupation in the Safford Valley. The best evidence for a Paleoindian occupation, which began around 8,000 B.C., is a single fluted Clovis type projectile point. Roy Conners reported to me in 1997 that he found the point in the northern foothills of the Pinaleño Mountains (Fig. 2.1). Evidence for Archaic occupation, which terminated about 150 B.C., is also scant, but two recent projects have significantly increased knowledge of this period. The relevance of these two projects to the rock-bordered grids is that their findings provide solid evidence for early and con-

DATES	Period Designations used in this monograph	Phase Designations Safford Valley (Crary 1997)	Hohokam Period Designations (Elson 1996)	Phase Designations Tonto Basin (Elson 1996)	Phase Designations Phoenix Basin (Elson 1996)	Phase Designations Tucson Basin (Mabry 1998a)
AD 1500	?	?		?	Pima / Papago	
AD 1400	CLASSIC	Safford-Gila	CLASSIC	Gila	Civano	Tucson
AD 1300		Safford-Gila		Roosevelt	Civano	Tucson
AD 1200		Bylas		Miami	Soho / Santan	Tanque Verde
AD 1100	LATE FORMATIVE/ PRE-CLASSIC	Eden	SEDENTARY	Ash Creek / ?	Sacaton	Rincon
AD 1000		Two Dog		Sacaton	Sacaton	Rincon
AD 900		Talkali	COLONIAL	Santa Cruz	Santa Cruz	Rillito
AD 800		Talkali		Gila Butte / Snaketown / ?	Gila Butte	Cañada del Oro
AD 700	EARLY FORMATIVE	Pinaleño	PIONEER		Snaketown	Snaketown, Sweet-water, Estrella
AD 600		Dos Cabezas		Early Ceramic	Sweetwater	Tortolita
AD 500		Peñasco		Early Ceramic	Estrella	Tortolita
AD 400		Peñasco	ARCHAIC	Early Ceramic	Vahki	Agua Caliente
AD 300		Peñasco		?	Vahki	Agua Caliente
AD 200		Witlock		Late Archaic	Red Mountain	Agua Caliente
AD 100		Witlock		Late Archaic	Archaic	Cienega
AD/BC		Witlock		Late Archaic	Archaic	Cienega

Figure 2.2. Chronology, period, and phase sequences for the later occupations of the Safford Valley and adjacent regions. Double horizontal lines indicate poorly defined temporal boundaries.

tinuous sedentary village life, agriculture, and associated landscape transformations in the Safford Valley.

In 1997 Steven M. Shackley (UCLA) and Bruce Huckell (University of New Mexico) conducted test excavations in McEuen Cave in the Gila Mountains a short distance north of the rock-bordered grids (Fig. 1.5). Radiocarbon dates recovered from the Late Archaic period strata ranged from 2790 to 2200 B.P. A date of about 3690 B.P. came from a maize kernel, and it is one of the oldest dates on maize in North America. Shackley (2000: 9) concluded that McEuen Cave is: "The only site with buried deposits that is known to span this critical transition period from purely hunting-gathering to mixed farming-foraging economies."

The second project, more directly applicable to the rock-bordered grids, was conducted in 1999 and 2000 under the direction of Jeffery J. Clark of Desert Archaeology, Tucson. Excavations on the floodplain and at the edge of the adjacent terrace, south of the Gila River near the present-day town of Thatcher (Fig. 1.5), yielded evidence of occupation in the form of pit houses and agricultural use in the form of irrigation canals. These features date to, or near, the transition from the Late Archaic period to the Early Formative period, and similar features continue through the Late Formative and Classic periods (Clark 2000, 2002; Clark and others 1999).

Materials from the Late Archaic period components suggest an early local development of ceramic technology and irrigation agriculture. This evidence opposes the theory that such developments in the Southwest were a function of Mesoamerican influence during the Early Formative period (for example, LeBlanc 1982), but is congruent with recent findings in the Tucson area (Mabry 1998a, 1998b, 2002; Mabry and others 1997; Muro 1998a, 1998b).

Early Formative Period
(About 150 B.C.–A.D. 800)

As with the Paleoindian and Archaic occupations, information is sparse for the Early Formative period in the Safford Valley. What few data exist, however, suggest that there was a similar uniform cultural expression throughout southeastern and central Arizona, as well as southwestern New Mexico and northwestern Mexico. The period is characterized by what appears to have been a kinship-oriented, egalitarian, "tribally"

organized society (Neely 1997b); a dispersed settlement system with pottery-producing pit house communities; and a mixed subsistence strategy consisting of a hunting and gathering base augmented by horticulture and agriculture.

Agricultural Systems

Various types of evidence (settlement patterns, architecture, plant remains, and tool types) point toward a heavy reliance on wild foodstuffs in the beginning, but the use of cultivated plants increased throughout the period. This "mixed" (Welch 1994) or "broad-spectrum" (Flannery 1965) economy was similar to that documented for the Western Apache (Pool 1985; Welch 1994) and Tohono O'odham (Fontana 1983; Hackenberg 1983).

The location of the sites where maize was found indicates that the occupants were using naturally fertile and well-watered areas for small agricultural plots, in some cases alluvial fans at the mouths of intermittent drainages. Water from seasonal precipitation and run-off was used to provide the necessary moisture for successful germination and maturation. However, the recent findings of Clark (2002) indicate some irrigation agriculture was also practiced. A roasting pit excavated just east of the city of Safford yielded evidence of cultivated crops and a radiocarbon date (with a two-sigma range) of A.D. 430–660 (Seymour, Doak, and Ahlstrom 1997). These findings roughly approximate those made nearby in the Tonto Basin (see Ciolek-Torrello and others 1994: 443).

Agricultural Artifact Assemblage

The chipped stone assemblage, the types of handstones and metates present, and the archaeobotanical remains recovered indicate the practice of a mixed subsistence economy. Much of the artifact assemblage, like small handstones (convex, flat, plano-convex, multifaceted), pestles, mortars (portable and bedrock), milling stones (basin and slab), flaked stone tools, and a few dart and projectile points that characterized the sites of this period, confirms a heavy dependence on wild resources. Some of the flaked stone tools were well designed for cutting and pulping agavelike plants (Sayles 1945, Plates 41, 49*f*). Gilman (1997: 135) noted that short manos seemed to indicate a strong dependence on wild plant foods and that longer manos appeared with the increasing inclusion of corn in the diet. Her findings parallel an earlier study of manos from the Cave Creek Site and San Simon Village by Hard (1990: 138), who discovered that mano length increased from an average of 13.2 cm for Peñasco phase specimens to an average of 16.3 cm in the later Encinas phase.

Late Formative Period
(A.D. 800–1150)

The Late Formative period appears to have been characterized by a "tribally" organized society, but with an increase in cultural system complexity (Neely 1997b), an increasing focus on agriculture and the development of complex agricultural systems that incorporated more sophisticated water-management and irrigation technology, the occupation and utilization of agriculturally marginal areas, population aggregation, changes in ceramic production and exchange, and regional differentiation. Although the beginning of the period saw a continuation of a relatively mobile settlement system still based on the San Simon Valley tradition, significant changes took place throughout the period. This mobility and the San Simon tradition were apparently affected through external ties with the more sedentary systems of the expanding Hohokam and Mimbres traditions to the west and east, respectively.

The relationships remain tenuous, but the establishment of the Hohokam cultural tradition in the Phoenix and Tucson basins (Fig. 2.1) around A.D. 800 (Wallace 2000; Wallace and others 1995) appears to have played a significant role in the cultural development of the Safford Valley beginning at this time. After about A.D. 900 a full-fledged Hohokam affiliated community formed that was centered on the Ranch Creek drainage of the San Carlos district (Fig. 2.1) and the extreme western end of the Safford Valley (Crary 1997). Permanent settlements, fine-line ceramic decoration, house-in-a-pit architecture, the development of small-scale complex irrigation systems, and the construction of at least two ballcourts typify the Hohokam influences. At the eastern end of the Safford Valley, cultural ties appear to have been with the Mimbres Valley tradition of southwestern New Mexico (Fig. 2.1), expressed by sedentary villages, certain architectural characteristics, but most specifically painted broad-line ceramic decoration.

Although the San Simon core tradition survived in a somewhat reorganized form in the San Simon Valley, by the beginning of the 11th century A.D. many communities in the Safford and Duncan valleys had effectively become Hohokam and Mimbres affiliates. Ceramics from the last half of the period are characterized by the distinctive scroll and textile motifs that appear on the Mimbres Classic Black-on-white Style III. In the interval from about A.D. 1000 to 1150, a Safford Valley tradition and lifeway developed that incorporated architectural and artifactual influences, and perhaps immigrants, from the Point of Pines region to the north (Fig. 2.1). The manufacture and exchange of fine-paste brown plain ware, as well as plain and indented corrugated ceramics, indicate interaction and possibly demographic shifts from the east-central Arizona uplands to the Safford Valley. The termination of the Late Formative period coincides with the collapse of the San Simon, Hohokam, and Mimbres regional traditions.

At the transition into the Classic period, the Eden phase (Crary 1997) represents the formation of a discrete Safford Valley tradition and the repeated realignment of exchange networks. Between A.D. 1100 and 1150, interaction with the Phoenix Basin and San Simon Valley declined, whereas exchange with the Cliff and Mimbres valleys in New Mexico increased. However, after A.D. 1150 the focus of exchange had shifted to the Point of Pines area and to the Sulphur Springs Valley, as the Mimbres tradition collapsed.

Agricultural Systems

The emphasis on agriculture continued to increase throughout this period, with canal systems for domestic use and irrigation increasing in number and size (Crary 1997; Neely 1995a, 1997b, 2001a; Neely and Crary 1998; Neely and Doolittle 1996; Neely and Rinker 1997). Archaeological dating is based on diagnostic ceramics found on sites and fields associated with water management infrastructure and canals. Compared with the beginning of the period, by the end of this period, at about A.D. 1150, these canal systems had become more complex, longer and wider, and they were associated with larger field areas. It is also during this period that the inhabitants of the Safford Valley intensified their dry-farming agricultural pursuits by increasing the size of nonirrigated fields and constructing labor-intensive "permanent" infrastructures in the form of various water-management features (like checkdams, linear borders, and terraces). Despite the relatively dramatic, complex, and far-reaching cultural changes that the archaeology documents for this period, we view the communities and their associated agricultural system technologies as the result of efforts by a society little different from the kinship-oriented egalitarian one that existed in the Early Formative period (Neely 1997b).

Although small-scale irrigation systems were used in the Safford Valley during the Early Formative period, Talkali phase (Fig. 2.2; Crary 1997) systems of canals associated with agricultural fields formed the earliest securely dated complex agricultural manifestations yet documented in the region. Their remains appear in the eastern and central portions of the Safford Valley (Neely 1995a, 1997a, 2001a; Neely and Crary 1998; Neely and Doolittle 1996; Neely and Rinker 1997). Later Two Dog phase canals revealed during construction of the current BLM administrative office (Botsford and Kinkade 1993) and at the Methodist Church Site (Crary 1997) in the city of Safford were located on the second terrace above the Gila River and apparently had intakes located several miles upstream (Doolittle 1997). These formed a series of parallel secondary canals, possibly interconnected by a network of smaller tertiary canals.

With the adoption of complex irrigation systems in the riverine setting associated with the Gila River, canals were also constructed in the upper bajada (for example, Lefthand Canyon and Marijilda Canyon; Fig. 1.5) of the Pinaleño Mountains (Doolittle 2000: 318–321; Neely 1995a, 1997a, 2001a; Neely and Crary 1998; Neely and Doolittle 1996; Neely and Rinker 1997; Rinker 1998). In the uplands, there was a proliferation of small rock-bordered canals paralleling the narrow floodplains of the intermittent streams that drained the upper bajada. Evidence suggests that the genesis of the small dry-farming systems, which are located throughout the bajada in both the San Carlos and Safford districts (Figs. 1.5, 2.1), occurred during this Late Formative period. Initially these systems were composed of small and dispersed clusters of rock piles, linear borders, checkdams, and low terraces. The temporal placement of these sites hinges on the presence of small residential and processing localities thinly scattered among the field systems. The

development of the bajada dry-farming and canal irrigated fields may have been a response to the greater quantities of more predictable percipitation as well as the cycle of Gila River flooding and channel widening-downcutting documented by Huckleberry (1995) and Waters and Ravesloot (2000).

The Eden phase and the Late Formative to Classic period transition throughout southern Arizona experienced subtle yet important changes. Although some changes were directly related to agricultural intensification, others clearly were not. Much of the area peripheral to the Phoenix Basin was abandoned at this time, and populations from the Gila River between Riverside and Winkleman may have resettled in the San Carlos district, just west of the Safford Valley (Crary 1997). Interestingly, the San Carlos district is the only area outside of the Phoenix Basin where Classic period buff ware was manufactured (Crary 1997), suggesting continued interaction of some kind.

The one thing that has become increasing clear through recent studies is that by the end of this period the inhabitants of the Safford Valley were heavily exploiting the waters of the Gila River for domestic uses and for agricultural irrigation. Some evidence is based on the discovery of canals that carried Gila River waters, but most of the evidence comes from settlement pattern data. Although it is difficult to discern a pattern because of the extensive and intensive historic use of the Gila River floodplain and adjacent terraces, there was a general decrease through time in the number of small riverine settlements and an increase in the development of relatively large aggregated communities. The distribution of these large aggregated communities may well reflect their construction along major canals carrying water from the Gila River. The communities were roughly 3 km to 6 km (1.8–3.7 miles) apart along the first terrace above the floodplain of the San Carlos River, as well as along both sides of the first terrace above the floodplain of the Gila River between the small modern communities of San Carlos and Geronimo (Fig. 1.5; Crary 1997). This same settlement pattern occurred in the Casa Grande region of the Gila River (Crown 1987).

Farther east, the Late Formative settlements between the small modern communities of Fort Thomas and San José (Fig. 1.5) formed a nearly continuous distribution along the first and second terraces paralleling the Gila River floodplain (Chapter 10). In 1997

Frank Quinn, a local historian and life-long (90+ years) Safford resident, reported to me the locations of some sites within the city of Safford that may well have been positioned along the higher (that is, more southerly) canals (see also Botsford and Kinkade 1993). Although these sites were severely affected by modern constructions, evidence of their locations may still be present below the ground surface. The recent findings of Desert Archaeology in the Thatcher-Safford area (Clark 2002) indicate it is likely that communities were also present on the Gila River floodplain as well.

Agricultural Artifact Assemblage

Although basin metates, grinding slabs, and one-hand manos remained dominant tools early in this period, the adoption of shallow trough metates and rectangular two-hand manos indicate changes in the subsistence patterns. By the end of the period, the trough metate and two-hand mano had become the dominant milling tools. Following the research and reasoning of Hard (1990) and Mauldin (1993), the modification of milling tool shape and its larger size reflect the increasing importance of and dependence on maize agriculture in the subsistence system. The need to produce increasing quantities of processed corn probably resulted from an increasing population and greater interregional trade (Crary 1997).

Stone hoes and knives associated with subsistence activities formed a major portion of the lithic assemblage associated with the Late Formative sites of the Safford Valley. The hand-held flaked stone hoes or digging tools were of various shapes and materials, but laminated schistose-rich gneiss and other schistlike stones predominated (Haury 1945: 134–137, Plates 50–56; Neely 1993a, 1993b, 1995b, 2002; Sayles 1945, Plate 40*a*; Towner 1994: 479–480, Fig. 9.8). The most likely uses of the stone hoe were digging and turning the earth for cultivation. Its size, shape, and weight indicate that it would also have functioned well for digging canal channels. These tools appear in association with habitation sites, in dry-farming and irrigated field contexts, and adjacent to canals (Neely 2002). The tabular agave or mescal knives were of fine-grained to aphanitic gray rhyolite and basalt (S. Fish and others 1985; S. Fish and others 1992: 83–84; Johnson and Wasley 1966: 246). The use of the agave or mescal knife for cutting the large leaves from agave

hearts prior to their roasting is ethnographically documented from the American Southwest (Castetter and others 1938). These knives occur mostly on the surface of dry-farmed fields, but are also found in relatively large numbers at habitation sites, in the vicinity of roasting pits, and, in small numbers, on the surface of irrigated fields.

Both stone hoes and tabular knives came from Tonto Basin excavations (Towner 1994), but the number of specimens recovered shows that these tools were more prevalent in the Safford Valley. Only two hoes came from the Tonto Basin (Towner 1994: 479 480, Fig. 9.8) and they were dated to the Pre-Classic (Crary's Late Formative) period. The Tonto Basin stone hoes came from limited activity and dry-farming field contexts (Towner 1994: 489, 502), which correspond with only two of the four proveniences in which they were recorded in the Safford Valley.

Classic Period
(A.D. 1150–1450)

Population increases through internal growth and immigration, perhaps intra- and interregional conflict, and decreasing agricultural productivity resulting from a major climatic shift contributed to the formation of large aggregated communities in the Classic period. Some of these communities have been tentatively labeled as "regional or subregional centers" (Crary 1997). They are characterized by large "public" or "communal" architecture and were positioned so as to be near, and possibly control, water sources, prime agricultural lands, and infrastructure (like irrigation canals). This period also was a time for the development of new exchange and alliance networks, as indicated by changes in ceramic production and exchange, and increasing regionalism. Early influences appear to have come from northern Mexico and later influences from east-central Arizona and west-central New Mexico. The continuing modifications in the settlement pattern, the construction of Compact Room Groups or "CRGs" (Crary and others 1992; Germick and Crary 1992) and platform mounds, the aggregation of population, as well as the growth of agriculture and intensification of water-management systems reveals a concomitant change in some aspects of the religious and sociopolitical systems at this time. Any changes that occurred may well have been a matter of an expansion of already existing aspects of the religious and sociopolitical systems, rather than major reformulations of those systems (Neely 1997b). Finally, this period culminates with the collapse of all cultural systems and the general abandonment of the Safford Valley between about A.D. 1400 and 1450.

Early Classic Period
(A.D. 1150–1300)

Changes in the Safford Valley Classic period archaeological remains reflect transformations in the social and ceremonial organization that apparently occurred in response to alterations in the subsistence and sociopolitical systems. These modifications were required primarily by negative changes in broad regional climatic conditions, unusual population growth, and perhaps an increase of intergroup conflict (Neely 1997b). These events began early in the period and were exacerbated near the end of the period by severe drought conditions and the influx of large numbers of immigrants.

The Early Classic period affiliations of the Safford Valley were to the south during the first portion of the period, and then to the north at the end of the period. Marking these affiliations, the interval from about A.D. 1150 to 1275 witnessed the formation of local traditions within the major drainage areas. Here, populations resided in large formal communities. Collectively, these drainage groupings appear to have been integrated as a regional corporate body that indirectly had affiliations with the northern Chihuahua regional system (Crary 1997).

From about A.D. 1275 to 1300, the Safford Valley experienced an intrusion of Anasazi communities from the Tusayan and Kayenta regions of northeastern Arizona. In addition, the Safford Valley shared affinities with the Maverick Mountain complex, an enclave of late 13th-century western Anasazi immigrants into the Point of Pines region (Haury 1958; Lindsay 1987) just north of the Safford Valley. Crary (1997) has named this intrusion the Goat Hill complex, as the phenomenon was first disclosed in the Safford Valley through the excavation of the Goat Hill Site (Woodson 1995, 1999). Subsequently, several other sites containing architectural and ceramic evidence associated with the Tsegi phase of the Tusayan and Kayenta Anasazi (Lindsay 1987; Lindsay and Jennings 1968) have been discovered in the Safford Valley.

Late Classic Period
(A.D. 1300–1450)

The infusion of immigrants, probably combined with major climatic change, played a key role in the demise of the Safford Valley's Early Classic period communities and the acceptance or formation of the Salado regional system early in the 14th century. Population growth and drought may have created sociopolitical stresses, and perhaps even armed conflict, over a finite supply of land and water. Developing directly from an existing system that could expand through the coalescence of relatively small groups, a change occurred that amounted to an expansion of already present aspects of the sociopolitical system. This change is modeled as the development of horizontal sociopolitical stratification in a format that did not cause a major reformulation of the existing system (Neely 1997b). This expansion apparently involved the intensification of agriculture, growth of aggregated communities, the construction and use of platform mounds for ceremonial purposes, and a new multiregional art style and ceremonialism that has been named Salado (Neely 1997b).

The cultural merging of the Point of Pines Mogollon and the Tusayan, Kayenta, White Mountain, and Little Colorado proto-Hopi people with local populations and traditions resulted in an initial resurgence of population and further reformulation of the sociopolitical and religious systems. Thus, the Safford Valley tradition was incorporated within the Salado interaction sphere and it adopted characteristics of the Salado phenomenon. In fact, the Late Classic period may be defined by realignments of exchange networks, the relocation of ceramic manufacturing centers, and economic competition with the White Mountain and Chihuahuan interaction spheres (Crary 1997). The increasing population continued to live in aggregated communities and subregional centers that may have initially increased in size. The last few decades of the Classic period were apparently characterized by a decline in the population, and the final aggregated communities and subregional centers were abandoned sometime between 1400 and 1450 (Crary 1997).

The trend away from a diversified subsistence base in several environmental settings and toward increasing population, movement into aggregated large communities, and dependence on Gila River irrigated agriculture may have resulted in a momentum in settlement and subsistence system change. This momentum may not have been slowed and modified quickly enough to offset environmental changes. Furthermore, social problems may well have been emerging with a burgeoning population of peoples with diverse cultural and linguistic backgrounds living in large aggregated communities (following Johnson 1982, 1989; Levy 1992; Schlegel 1992). Having adapted to large, aggregated communities that were heavily committed to the Gila River based irrigation agriculture of the floodplain and lower terraces, people found it impossible to revert back quickly enough to successfully pursue a more appropriate scattered ranchería style of habitation with small dry-farming and irrigation agricultural activities in diverse environmental contexts. Also perhaps hindering the dissolution of the large communities and reversion back to the ranchería pattern was the threat of raiding or warfare; the large, unified communities could better withstand the onslaughts of attacking groups. The abandonment of the Tonto Basin and Safford Valley and the local collapse of the Salado system appear linked to the shifting environmental and subsistence patterns of the late 13th and 14th centuries, the contemporaneous threat of warfare, and the inability of the sociopolitical system to sustain the complex level of organization that had been attained.

Dry Farming Systems

Marking the initiation of the Early Classic period in the Safford Valley was greater variability in the occurrence of, and a decrease in the amount of, effective moisture for agricultural production (Van West and Altschul 1994). Partially offsetting this negative turn in precipitation for the valley during this part of the period was the limited availability and dependability of water from the Gila River and its use in the development of canal irrigation agriculture (Graybill and others 1999).

The Early Classic period is represented by the expansion of large upland dry-farming and irrigation systems such as those occurring in Lefthand Canyon and Marijilda Canyon (Fig. 1.5; Neely 1995a, 1997a, 2001a; Neely and Crary 1998; Neely and Doolittle 1996; Neely and Rinker 1997; Rinker and Neely 1998). The use of nonirrigated, dry-farmed fields in the Classic period represents the continuation of a

tradition that began in the Early Formative period. Because of the large numbers of these fields, and their extensive acreage, this type of agriculture formed an integral part of the overall subsistence system utilized by the resident farmers. The presence of water and soil management features constructed of stone at these sites facilitates their detection and should permit measurement and mapping of field areas. These fields are in several different topographic and geographic locations within the Safford Valley, all of which would have been difficult or impossible to reach with canal irrigation.

Early Classic period communities of the Safford Valley area were often surrounded by extensive dry-farming systems (Crary 1997; Neely 1997b) that consisted of rock piles, rock-bordered grids, linear borders, chevrons, checkdams, and terraces. These systems were probably used in a symbiotic relationship with the expanding irrigated agricultural systems in marginal nonriverine settings. This pattern of communities surrounded by dry-farming systems contrasts with the linear pattern recorded in the Casa Grande region down river (Crown 1987).

Although dry-farmed areas increased in size during this period, small plots were still common. They occurred in close association with habitations and were probably gardens for the cultivation of herbs and other plants. They may have served as seedbeds from which seedlings could be transplanted to larger fields.

Dry-farmed fields dating to the Early Classic period represent a continued use and augmentation of agricultural infrastructure constructed during the Late Formative period and new fields developed during the first half of the Bylas phase. Many of these fields may have become unusable due to the severe lack of precipitation during the Great Drought years between A.D. 1275 and 1299 (Dean and Robinson 1982, Figs. 8.3, 8.6).

The Late Classic period represents the culmination of large upland dry-farming systems (Neely 1995a, 1997b; Neely and Crary 1998; Neely and Doolittle 1996; Neely and Rinker 1997; Rinker 1998). The few remaining upland settlements in the Safford Valley were abandoned by about A.D. 1385, as indicated by the absence of key diagnostic ceramics at any of the sites studied to date. By A.D. 1450, the Safford Valley appears to have been effectively abandoned.

The Sanchez Copper Project (Fig. 1.5) just east of Safford investigated dry-farmed fields characterized primarily by rock piles and rock-bordered grids (Seymour, Doak, and Ahlstrom 1997). Ceramics recovered indicated that these fields, too, were used during the Late Classic period. Pollen revealed that maize and cotton were grown on the rock piles and among the rock-bordered grids (Cummings and Puseman 1997). A roasting pit adjacent to cultivated fields at site AZ CC:1:54 (ASM) in Lefthand Canyon (Rinker and Neely 1998) produced burned agave(?) remains that have been radiocarbon dated (TX–9259) to the Late Classic period.

Canal Irrigation Systems

As the Classic period seems to be the time when the maximum prehistoric intensification of canal irrigation took place in the Safford Valley, and probably in adjoining areas as well, it is appropriate to make the following observations. First, the Safford Valley evidently contained the largest expanse of arable alluvium in the Circum-Sonoran uplands of central and southern Arizona. Second, referring to the canal irrigated land area in the Safford Valley between the head of the San José canal to the east and the town of Fort Thomas to the west (Fig. 1.5), Doolittle (1997) stated that "perhaps no more than 7,400 hectares (18,278 acres) could have been irrigated in the Safford Valley prehistorically." This makes the Safford Valley second in size only to the Phoenix Basin in the amount of potentially irrigable land available in what is now the state of Arizona.

The nature of the foothill agricultural irrigation systems of the Safford Valley changed in the Early Classic period with a perceptible increase in number and length of such systems and in their extension northward farther from the Pinaleño Mountains and closer to the floodplain of the Gila River. Archaeologists have not discerned any modifications in the features characterizing the systems or in the size range of the associated fields. However, many of these systems and fields were probably abandoned by the beginning of the Late Classic period.

Considering the adverse climatic conditions at the end of the Early Classic period, it is likely that reservoirs were used in conjunction with foothill canal irrigation agriculture. Based on diagnostic ceramics recovered on survey, reservoirs evidently date to the Early Classic period, although some may date earlier.

Reservoirs are traditionally thought of as domestic water resources, but they may have served for irrigation as well. Survey (Neely 1995a; Neely and Crary 1998) also indicated the possibility that these reservoirs were originally natural marsh or *ciénega* areas (Doolittle 1997) that were modified in ancient times to become larger water impoundment areas. These reservoirs were associated with the ancient foothill systems along the north face of the Pinaleño Mountains. They may have served functions similar to those recorded for the Tohono O'odham (Papago) in southern Arizona and northwestern Sonora by Castetter and Bell (1942). In such systems, water is impounded and collected and in times of need drained from the reservoirs by canals that carry water to the fields. Reservoirs 1 and 2 of the Lebanon irrigation system in Marijilda Canyon (Fig. 1.5), at the southern edge of the city of Safford, are two examples of such features functioning today.

Beginning about A.D. 1250, the onset of drought conditions, increasing populations, a change in the discharge of the Gila River, and probably environmental degradation caused by agricultural intensification appear to have overtaken the technologies that supported the development of Early Classic period communities. The Great Drought (Dean and Robinson 1982, Figs. 8.3, 8.6) and the low annual flow of the Gila River (Graybill and others 1999) characterizing the Late Bylas phase would have had lasting effects on all irrigation systems. These climatic conditions would not have been favorable for foothill canal irrigation agriculture, and many such systems were probably abandoned. In spite of the low flow conditions, however, these same climatic conditions would have been favorable for the establishment and intensification of canal irrigated fields, both on and above the floodplain, serviced by the Gila River.

The first few years of the Late Classic period witnessed the final use of the few remaining large upland irrigation systems, such as those in Lefthand and Marijilda canyons. Reservoirs may also have been briefly revitalized, but because of climatic reversals, the occupation of the upland settlements (with their associated irrigation systems) apparently ended by approximately A.D. 1385. This termination date is based on the failure of surveys to recover post–A.D. 1385 diagnostic ceramics from the foothill sites studied thus far.

The end of the Early Classic period and the entire Late Classic period were times characterized by large settlements situated adjacent to the floodplain of the Gila River. In addition, this period probably witnessed the expansion in area coverage and an increase in the sizes of canals carrying water from the Gila River for irrigation and domestic use. Several of the major historic canal systems functioning in the mid–1870s were actually prehistoric canals that had been renovated (Colvin 1997; Neely 2001a; Ramenofsky 1984). Their size and association with major sites, such as Buena Vista-Curtis, suggest that the prehistoric versions of these canals probably dated at least as early as the Late Classic period. These canals span a distance of about 47 km (29 miles) along the course of the Gila River, from just northeast of San José to Fort Thomas. Renovation of the Safford Valley canals should not be considered an isolated event. A growing body of evidence shows that the reuse of prehistoric canals was commonplace, not only with the Hohokam canals of the Phoenix Basin (Masse 1981) but around the world, including Peru (Gelles 1996); Sri Lanka (Stanbury 1996); Sonora, Mexico (Doolittle 1988); and Puebla, Mexico (Neely 1995c, 2001b, 2001c).

Agricultural Artifact Assemblage

In addition to the hand-held flaked stone hoes or digging tools and the tabular knives noted for the Late Formative period, three other kinds of stone tools appeared in association with Classic period sites in the Safford Valley (Neely 2002): (1) a large prismatic blade cutting tool made of chert, aphanitic basalt, or a fine grained to aphanitic gray rhyolite; (2) a moderately large pointed digging tool, generally shaped like an Acheulean hand-ax and made of a material that appears to be aphanitic basalt; and (3) a large, heavy, pestle-shaped "mattock" digging tool with an adzlike bit, made of various materials but most often of a schisty gneiss. Haury (1945: 124, Plate 32*e–f*) reported a similar mattock tool from the Salt River Valley, and Johnson and Wasley (1966: 246) described another from a Bylas phase site (AZ V:16:8 ASM) just west of the Safford Valley. Except for the fact that they were made of stone and thicker, the mattocks found in the Safford Valley are similar to the wooden "hoes" of the Pima described and illustrated by Castetter and Bell (1942: 136–137, Fig. 1*b*) and by Russell (1908: 88, Fig. 10*c*).

Future excavations may determine a more precise beginning date for these types of tools. All three types appear to be associated with multicomponent sites, and it is possible that these tools actually first appeared in the Late Formative period.

FINDINGS AND MEANINGS

Although the Safford Valley has attracted few scholars interested in collecting and assessing paleoclimatic data, some studies have been undertaken in adjacent areas that provide enough insight to at least suggest some trends that should be substantiated and accepted with minimal modification by future research. The archaeological record from the Safford Valley is meager compared with records elsewhere in the American Southwest. Regardless of how few projects have been undertaken and how few data have been reported to date, a sufficient amount of evidence does exist to place the rock-bordered grids in a prehistoric cultural context.

CHAPTER THREE

Geologic Setting

Brenda B. Houser

Understanding certain archaeological features and sites often requires detailed knowledge of the geological context in which they are situated (Butzer 1982: 35–156). This requirement is particularly important when it comes to understanding how ancient agricultural systems functioned (Schmidt and Gerald 1988). Fortunately, a great deal of detailed reconnaissance and geologic mapping of the Safford Valley was accomplished in the 1980s (Drewes and others 1985; Houser 1991; Houser and others 1985; Richter and others 1983), including the vicinity of the rock-bordered grids and related features comprising site AZ CC:1:2 (ASM). In this chapter I describe the regional geologic setting and then discuss the local stratigraphy, the geological deposits of the Gila Mountains from which all basin-fill and piedmont rocks are derived, and the geology of the southwest piedmont slope on which the site is located. After recording surficial materials, I discuss erosional, depositional, and tectonic processes, especially with regard to how they have controlled the distribution of materials and hence the location of rock-bordered grids.

REGIONAL GEOLOGIC SETTING

The Safford Valley is in the southern Basin and Range geologic province near the middle of a large structural basin that extends more than 300 km (186 miles) from the present-day town of Globe, Arizona southeastward to beyond the U.S.–Mexico border. The southern Basin and Range Province of the southwestern United States is a region of northwest-southeast-trending sediment-filled basins separated by fault-bounded mountain ranges. In southeastern Arizona this topography began to form during the Miocene, approximately 17 million years ago (Ma), as a result of northeast-southwest-directed crustal extension (Houser and others 2004; Stewart 1998). As the basins subsided and earlier stream systems were disrupted, the basins developed interior drainage and were filled with sediments derived from the adjacent mountain ranges. Aprons of coalescing alluvial fans consisting of poorly sorted bouldery to pebbly gravel were deposited near the ranges at the edges of the basins. Finer-grained sand, silt, and clay were carried beyond to the center of the basins, where this sediment was deposited as overbank, playa, and lacustrine facies.

In much of the southern Basin and Range Province, tectonic activity and subsidence of the basins began to wane between approximately 2.0 and 1.6 Ma (about the end of the Pliocene and beginning of the Pleistocene). Through-flowing streams were established in many basins accompanied by erosion of older basin-fill sediments deposited during the Miocene and Pliocene. In the Safford Valley, a thickness of 300 m or more of basin-fill sediments have been eroded by the Gila River (Houser and others 1985).

As basin-fill rocks were eroded, large thick aggrading alluvial fans at the margins of the basin were replaced by smaller, thinner alluvial fans with short residence time. That is, coarse-grained alluvium was deposited on piedmont slopes by streams and then, within a few thousand to tens-of-thousands of years, was moved farther downslope again by the same stream systems. Ultimately, alluvium being transported down the piedmont slopes reached the Gila River. In the meantime, as the river cut down through the older basin-fill rocks, it migrated back and forth across the basin and left deposits of axial valley alluvium on terraces adjacent to the floodplain. During these on-going

Figure 3.1. Simplified geologic map of the Safford Valley and Gila Mountains, showing locations of rock-bordered grids. See text, *Local Stratigraphy*, for descriptions of symbols and map units. (Modified from Houser and others 1985. Base is a Landsat thematic mapper image.)

processes of erosion and sedimentation, the interaction between streams on the piedmont slopes and the Gila River in the axial valley resulted in the complex mosaic of various alluvial deposits (Fig. 3.1; Houser and others 1985). In some places, including the area around the site, the pattern is further complicated by the presence of Pleistocene faults that caused minor uplift, exposing older alluvium and basin-fill deposits lying beneath younger alluvium (Figs. 3.2, 3.3).

LOCAL STRATIGRAPHY

Site AZ CC:1:2 (ASM) is located at the toe of the southwest-sloping piedmont of the Gila Mountains adjacent to and overlooking the Gila River floodplain (Figs. 3.1, 3.2). The map units situated between the middle Tertiary volcanic rocks (Tv) of the Gila Mountains (30 to 19 Ma) and the river are: (1) upper basin-fill sedimentary rocks (Unit Tbf, Pliocene); (2) Gila River alluvium on terraces (Unit Qgra, Pleistocene);

(3) loess (Pleistocene); (4) piedmont alluvium (Unit Qpa, Pleistocene and Holocene); and (5) Gila River alluvium of the floodplain and channel (Holocene).

Upper Basin Fill (Tbf)

The oldest map unit underlying the piedmont surface is upper basin fill consisting of coarse-grained alluvial-fan facies near the Gila Mountains grading to finer-grained fluvial facies near the Gila River. The alluvial-fan facies consists of gravel and sandy gravel containing volcanic clasts (rock fragments, in this case chiefly basaltic andesite through dacite composition) derived from the Gila Mountains. The fluvial facies consists of pale brown, cross-bedded to thick bedded to laminated, calcareous sandy mudstone with zones of discontinuous 1–cm-thick limestone lenses (Fig. 3.3). Age dates obtained from interbedded tephra (volcanic ash) in the fluvial facies indicate that the age of the upper basin fill ranges from at least as old as 5.02 Ma (Wrucke and

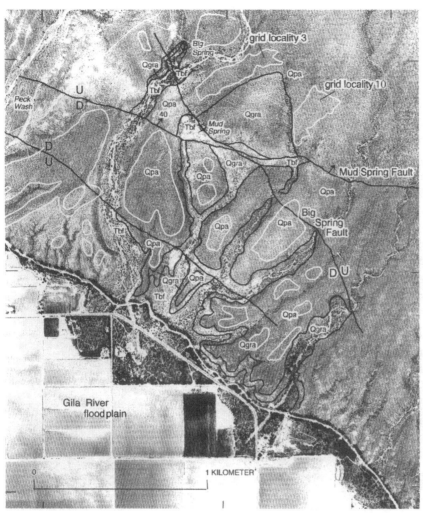

Figure 3.2. Partial map of geologic contacts in part of the area of rock-bordered grids (outlined in white), showing there are no grids in the area underlain by Gila River alluvium north of the Mud Spring Fault. See text, *Local Stratigraphy* for description of symbols and map units. Recent alluvium in washes not shown. Location of faults and sense of movement inferred from map patterns, aerial photographic lineaments, and a few exposures. Base is a U.S. Geological Survey orthophoto quadrangle.

others 2004) to younger than 2.17 Ma (Dickson and Izett 1981). Upper basin-fill sedimentary rocks are overlain unconformably by Gila River terrace alluvium (Qgra) and by piedmont alluvium (Qpa) where terrace alluvium was not deposited. Exposures of upper basin-fill sedimentary rocks are confined to the sides of washes and canyons and to the bluffs overlooking the Gila River floodplain. The maximum thickness of the unit may be more than 750 m.

Gila River Alluvium on Terraces (Qgra)

Pleistocene Gila River alluvium on terraces ranges from silt to boulder size clasts with the most abundant size range being sand through small cobbles. Sorting and bedding are good; sandy silt is commonly restricted to beds 0.3 m to 0.5 m thick rather than being distributed throughout the sandy matrix. Pebbles and larger clasts are conspicuously well rounded and cemented locally by sparry calcite.

Typical exposures of Gila River terrace alluvium are shown in Figures 3.4 and 3.5. Clast composition reflects both distant and local sources, and includes volcanic rocks, pink and red granite, orthoquartzite, chalcedony, and rare limestone. Glen Izett (U.S.G.S., retired) told me in 1981 that tephra interbedded with Gila River alluvium on a terrace across the river from Safford correlates with the 0.6 Ma Lava Creek B ash. Gila River terrace alluvium is overlain by the loess unit or by piedmont alluvium and is exposed in the upper part of the bluffs bordering the Gila River floodplain, along the sides of tributary washes and canyons, and in the upthrown fault block northeast of the Mud Spring Fault. Its maximum thickness is approximately 20 m.

Loess

A lenticular layer of pale-yellow and yellowish brown sandy silt, 2 m to 3 m thick, commonly overlies Gila River terrace alluvium (Fig. 3.4). The sandy silt probably was deposited initially as loess on abandoned parts of the Gila River floodplain and later was re-worked and carried into ponds in a swampy overbank environment. Some zones are massive appearing and poorly bedded (typical of loess), others show discontinuous laminae; vertical calcareous root casts are abundant in some zones, and paleosol horizons are common (Fig. 3.6). The base of the sandy silt is conformable with the underlying Gila River terrace alluvium. The upper surfaces show channels and potholes that were eroded by the streams that carried the overlying piedmont alluvium (Fig. 3.7). Both the paleosol horizons and the eroded upper surfaces suggest that these deposits formed throughout a considerable period of time and were semi-indurated when they were covered by the piedmont alluvium. The loess layer (not visible in Fig. 3.2) is discontinuously exposed above Gila River terrace alluvium in the bluffs bordering the Gila River and along the sides of washes and canyons.

Piedmont Alluvium (Qpa)

Piedmont alluvium consists of silt-size to boulder-size sediment, comprised mainly of angular to subrounded volcanic clasts derived from the Gila Mountains. Cobbles and boulders are abundant and piedmont alluvium is overall coarser grained than Gila River terrace alluvium. Silt is common in the matrix and in thin discontinuous beds. The silt beds are semi-indurated with calcite cement, which makes the beds stand out in relief in outcrop, emphasizing the low-angle cross bedding of the piedmont alluvium (Fig. 3.7). Well-rounded clasts of granite and orthoquartzite reworked from the underlying Gila River terrace alluvium are common to uncommon. From near the site northeastward to the coarse-grained basin fill bordering the Gila Mountains (Fig. 3.1), piedmont alluvium is the principal rock unit present on the surface of the piedmont slope where it is as much as 10 m thick. The volcanic clasts are composed of basaltic andesite, andesite, and dacite, the dominant lithologies present in the Gila Mountains. These are the rocks that were used to construct the rock-bordered grids and rock alignments.

Figure 3.3. Fine-grained fluvial facies of upper basin fill. Mud Spring reverse fault cuts both basin fill (Tbf) and Gila River terrace alluvium (Qgra), which has been incorporated along the fault plane. Hammer shows scale; view is to the east. (Photograph by Brenda B. Houser.)

Gila River Alluvium of the Floodplain and Channel (Qgra)

Holocene Gila River alluvium comprises the floodplain and river channel. It is virtually identical to Pleistocene Gila River alluvium except that it is not cemented. Only the surface of the unit is exposed, but well-drilling data indicate that it is as much as 15 km thick. This unit dates to the last ten thousand years.

GEOLOGY OF THE GILA MOUNTAINS

The Gila Mountains are composed chiefly of middle Tertiary volcanic rock (Tv). However, at the southeast

Figure 3.4. Gila River terrace alluvium (Qgra) capped by a lenticular loess deposit. (Photograph by Brenda B. Houser.)

Figure 3.5. Pebbly Gila River terrace alluvium (Qgra) overlain by loess that is overlain by piedmont alluvium (Qpa). (Photograph by Brenda B. Houser.)

end of the range, southwest of the drainage divide between Bonita Creek and the Gila River, Late Cretaceous and early Tertiary (70 to 50 Ma) volcanic and shallow intrusive rocks (TKv) are present in addition to middle Tertiary volcanic rocks (Fig. 3.1; Houser and others 1985). The presence of these older rocks is important because of their weathering properties. The older volcanic rocks have been propylitically altered by the shallow intrusions to lithologies that contain clay and chlorite minerals and that weather rapidly. These minerals weaken the rocks and cause them to break up rapidly, particularly when they are transported. Thus, the sediment derived from weathering of the older

volcanic rocks tends to be composed of smaller clasts on average than those derived from the unaltered middle Tertiary volcanic rocks.

The Gila Mountains are topographically asymmetrical as is evident by the drainage divide being located closer to the southwest side of the range than to the northeast side (Fig. 3.1). The range has been tilted to the northeast approximately 5 to 25 degrees by late Tertiary crustal expansion (Stewart 1998). The effect of this tilting on the composition of the piedmont alluvium at the southeast end of the range is two-fold. First, the tilting has led to exposure of the band of older altered volcanic rocks adjacent to the southwest

Figure 3.6. Loess deposit, showing root casts and paleosol horizons. (Photograph by Brenda B. Houser.)

piedmont slope. Second, most of the detritus derived from the younger overlying Tertiary volcanic rocks is carried northeast to Bonita Creek rather than to the southwest piedmont slope. Thus, the piedmont alluvium at the southeast end of the Gila Mountains is composed chiefly of relatively small clasts derived from the altered Late Cretaceous and early Tertiary volcanic rocks.

GEOLOGY OF THE SOUTHWEST PIEDMONT SLOPE

The southwest piedmont slope of the Gila Mountains (Fig. 3.1) consists of upper basin-fill sedimentary rocks (Tbf), Gila River terrace alluvium (Qgra), and piedmont alluvium (Qpa). Figure 3.1 depicts only coarse-grained basin-fill alluvial-fan facies adjacent to the range; the finer-grained fluvial facies at the toe of the

piedmont is shown in Figure 3.2. Exposures of Gila River terrace alluvium (Unit Qgra) make up a large part of the southeast end of the piedmont surface. The terrace alluvium actually continues on to the northwest past Black Rock and to the northeast approximately half way up the piedmont slope, but in both directions it is covered with piedmont alluvium (Figs. 3.2, 3.5, 3.7). The northwest extent of the terrace alluvium exposures correlates well with the northwest extent of the Late Cretaceous and early Tertiary volcanic rock outcrop in the Gila Mountains. This correlation suggests that the small clast size and altered, weathered condition of detritus derived from the older volcanic terrain does not provide a very thick or complete cover of piedmont alluvium. The clasts readily weather in place chemically, break up into smaller and smaller fragments, and are easily removed by erosion. In contrast, piedmont alluvium derived from middle Tertiary volcanic rock provides a thick, very coarse erosion-resistant covering layer.

One of the few places where any Gila River terrace alluvium is exposed on the piedmont (other than at the southeast end) is within the area of the rock-bordered grids. There, a triangular area of terrace alluvium, approximately 0.5 km on each side, is exposed on a low hill on the north side of the Mud Spring reverse fault (Figs. 3.2, 3.3). Figure 3.2 shows that two areas of grids, constructed on piedmont alluvium, stop at the contact of the piedmont alluvium with terrace alluvium. The importance of this exposure is that it indicates that Gila River terrace alluvium was avoided for the purpose of constructing rock-bordered grids.

Field observations suggest two possible reasons for avoidance of the Gila River terrace alluvium in grid construction: (1) clast size, and (2) soil properties. On average, clasts of terrace alluvium are smaller and rounder than those of piedmont alluvium, meaning that building rock-bordered grids with terrace gravel would have required more time and effort than if larger materials were used. Also, the mechanical, and probably chemical, properties of soils developed on the two kinds of alluvium are quite different. Based on qualitative observations only, the terrace alluvium is sandier and contains less silt than the piedmont surface. Finally, and anecdotally, vegetation provides a hint that soils on the two kinds of alluvium may be different. In November 2000, following an especially wet October, there was a significant difference in the species of low

Figure 3.7. Pebbly Gila River terrace alluvium (Qgra), overlain by loess that is overlain by piedmont alluvium (Qpa). Visible are channels and potholes on the surface of the loess and low-angle cross-bedding in the piedmont alluvium. (Photograph by Brenda B. Houser.)

annual plants growing on Gila River terrace alluvium versus piedmont alluvium. Terrace alluvium had abundant heron's bill (*Erodium* sp.), whereas piedmont alluvium had virtually no heron's bill.

FINDINGS AND MEANINGS

Evidence indicates an association between geology and the location of the rock-bordered grids and related features of site AZ CC:1:2 (ASM) in the Safford Valley. The composition and exposure of surficial materials were influenced both by the geology and structure of the Gila Mountains and by local faulting. The composition of the surficial materials in turn apparently affected directly the location of the rock-bordered grids, both on a local scale and, by inference, on a valley-wide scale. Detailed mapping shows that the grids were constructed only on gently sloping terraces where bouldery piedmont alluvium derived from the Tertiary volcanic rocks of the Gila Mountains

is the underlying surficial material. The grid borders are composed of rocks comprising this alluvium and Proposition 2, as outlined in Chapter 1, is thereby confirmed. The grid borders were constructed with materials that were available in the immediate vicinity, on the respective site localities, and materials were not transported in from even a short distance away.

Areas underlain by Gila River terrace alluvium were avoided for the construction of grids, perhaps because of the smaller boulder size compared to piedmont alluvium or perhaps because of differences in the soils. Whatever the reason, it may explain the absence of grids on river terraces upstream from site AZ CC:1:2 (ASM), all of which are underlain by Gila River terrace alluvium. Thus, it appears that the piedmont alluvium next to the floodplain was the preferred substrate for construction of rock-bordered grids. The underlying reason for this preference was most likely a function of differences in either rock types or soil or some combination of the two.

CHAPTER FOUR

Landscape Context: GIS Analysis and Mapping

Dale R. Lightfoot

Despite the numerous times site AZ CC:1:2 (ASM) has been visited by archaeologists, no clear picture of the areal extent of the rock-bordered grids and related features has previously emerged. Estimates of the area they encompass range from 10 to 80 hectares, and various scholars have reported seeing as few as six and as many as twenty separate clusters of grids during surface surveys of the site (Gilman and Sherman 1975; Stewart 1939, 1940a; Woodbury 1961). Comments about the vastness of these enigmatic features helped to generate interest within the academic community, but amounted to little more than speculation by scholars who were clearly impressed but unwilling or unable to provide additional information. Furthermore, even a systematic accounting of the collective area covered by all of the grids would still reveal nothing of their spatial configuration. For example, were they comprised of like-sized clusters designed to use land within a given area most efficiently, or were they arranged haphazardly, perhaps through incremental construction as the grid area developed? Were they contiguous or fragmented? Were they distributed uniformly within a given area, or was there a distinct core and periphery to the distribution? Were they associated consistently with certain combinations of topography, soils, and geologic materials, or did outliers exist off of the Pleistocene terraces, unrelated to either edaphic or geologic controls? Until these details were mapped in their entirety and accurately overlaid (transformed in GIS) with a detailed map of the site, it was impossible to see any relationships between the grids and the regional landscape. Using aerial photography produced specifically for this project, and the spatial analytical capabilities of a geographic information system (GIS),

a comprehensive regional view of the rock-bordered grids has been created and mapped at the level of individual grids (Fig. 4.1).

AERIAL PHOTOGRAPHY AND MAPPING

Aerial photographs provide nonbiased, nondescriptive, quantifiable, and retrievable data for prehistoric landscape survey (Lyons and Scovill 1978). Aerial photo-derived data offer much finer resolution than satellite-borne imagery or aerial digital scanner imagery, in this case permitting individual rock alignments or grid borders to be mapped with precision, while still providing the advantages of broad-coverage analysis available with digital imaging systems. Such large-scale surveys are the principal source of regional archaeological data, especially where such studies are conducted in advance of land modification projects (Schiffer and others 1978).

Photographic analysis can be effective in reducing time, labor, and costs during a project by decreasing the amount of ground survey required (Lyons and Scovill 1978). This is especially true when working in areas as large as the 6–square-kilometer (2.3–square-mile) study area encompassed by site AZ CC:1:2 (ASM). Because aerial survey is geometrically more accurate than most ground surveys conducted across a large area, this procedure facilitates more precise and rapid location positioning. One experienced air-photo interpreter with a stereoscope and a pair of large-scale aerial photographs can scrutinize, in a short time, an area that would take a ground survey team days to cover adequately. Furthermore, without the aerial images a ground team might miss some of the smaller grid clusters, and a regional map of the grids would not be available for subsequent comparison to soils or geologic maps.

The scale of the photographs, the time of day and season, and the time elapsed since rainfall last moistened the ground can all affect the appearance of landscape features on aerial photographs. The extreme subtlety of the rock alignments in the photographs can result in slightly different depictions of grid details by different researchers using the same aerial photographs. Still, the spatial extent and orientation of grids should be similar, especially if followed by an extensive ground verification exercise (called ground-truthing), as was done here.

Individual rock-bordered grids and surrounding landscape features were mapped from a series of stereo pair aerial photographs (scale = 1:6350) with the aid of a stereoscope and zoom transfer scope. Most of the rock alignments appear very subtle on the aerial photographs. Considerable care, therefore, was taken to map only those features that were clearly grid borders. Lines about which there was some doubt were not mapped. With a first draft of the map in hand, every grid locality was then subjected to ground-truth verification.

It is essential for serious archaeological study that any transcription of data from aerial photographs should not only be meticulous in its rendering of detail, but should be metrically accurate as well. This affects both the representation of individual features and their location in relation to each other (Wilson 1982). To this end, some researchers encourage the use of more geometrically accurate (albeit more expensive) ortho-photo maps created from rectified (nondistorted) aerial photographs (Prewitt and Holz 1976). However, the direct overlay tracing of landscape features from nonrectified aerial photographs (using a zoom transfer scope or tracing directly onto an overlay sheet of mylar) can still result in a measurement or positional accuracy of 90 to 95 percent (Ebert and others 1979). Therefore, the accuracy of the photo-derived map was further enhanced by digitally overlaying it ("rubber sheeting" it) to a topographic map to more accurately portray the landscape configuration of the rock-bordered grids and to tie geocoordinates to the map for overlays with other maps within a geographic information system (GIS).

GIS ANALYSIS

Other studies of known or suspected prehistoric agricultural sites have demonstrated relationships between fields and features and microenvironments. In a study of a prehistoric agricultural site in western New Mexico, Sandor and his colleagues (1986) reported that ancient terraces "occur primarily within a narrow range of possible locations, implying deliberate placement with respect to climatic, topographic, and soil factors." In the Galisteo Basin of northern New Mexico, Lightfoot (1993b) demonstrated that prehistoric farmers constructed pebble-mulch fields only where a certain topography and soil type combined to provide an ideal agricultural microenvironment. Prehistoric agricultural-environmental relationships have been established elsewhere, and the findings presented in Chapter 3 demonstrated that, if agricultural, the rock-bordered grids were sited intentionally to take advantage of specific topographic, edaphic, and geologic niches on the landscape.

With the computer generated map of the study area, overlaid with maps of physical landscape attributes and manipulated by a geographic information system, it is possible to examine the spatial units and areal relationships and to summarize and present complex spatial information. ArcInfo, ArcView, and ArcGIS systems were each employed during this research. Each software system has its special strengths, and they were exploited in accordance with the computational requirements of each analytical problem. The spatial analytic abilities of these geographic information systems were used to: (1) calculate the total area and combined lengths of the rock borders constituting the grids, (2) spatially and statistically analyze the correspondence of grids with particular soil and geologic units, and (3) conduct a buffer analysis to compute a distance decay function to examine the pattern of clustering of grids around Big Spring Wash, a place of special environmental (Chapter 3) and cultural (Chapters 7, 8, 10) importance.

Measures of Area and Length

Each cluster of rock-bordered grids depicted on the digitized map of the study area was outlined on-screen to convert contiguous grid lines to a single polygon. Any gap in the grid lines, visible at the scale of the

Prehistoric Features

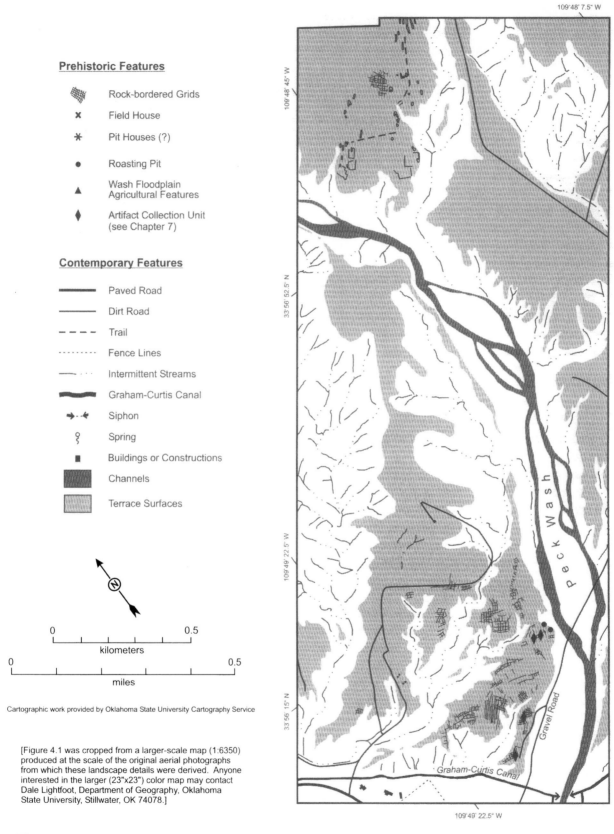

Rock-bordered Grids

✘ Field House

✱ Pit Houses (?)

● Roasting Pit

▲ Wash Floodplain
   Agricultural Features

◆ Artifact Collection Unit
   (see Chapter 7)

Contemporary Features

━━━━ Paved Road

──── Dirt Road

─ ─ ─ Trail

········· Fence Lines

──·── Intermittent Streams

〜〜〜 Graham-Curtis Canal

➤·◄ Siphon

⚲ Spring

▪ Buildings or Constructions

███ Channels

▒▒▒ Terrace Surfaces

0   0.5
      kilometers

0   0.5
         miles

Cartographic work provided by Oklahoma State University Cartography Service

[Figure 4.1 was cropped from a larger-scale map (1:6350)
produced at the scale of the original aerial photographs
from which these landscape details were derived. Anyone
interested in the larger (23"x23") color map may contact
Dale Lightfoot, Department of Geography, Oklahoma
State University, Stillwater, OK 74078.]

Figure 4.1 (*a, b*). Map of the rock-bordered grids and associated ancient and present-day landscape features.

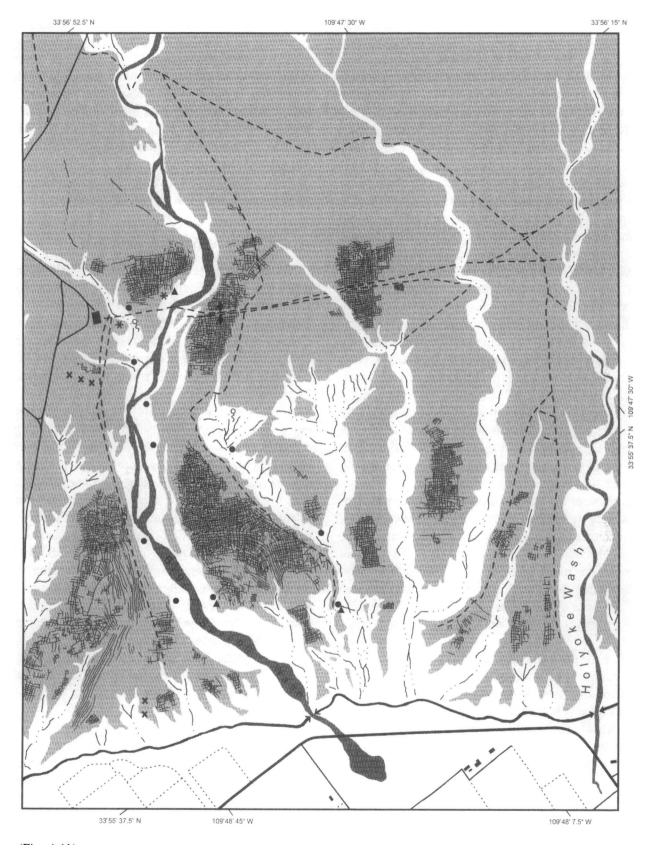

33°55' 37.5" N   109°47' 30" W

Holyoke Wash

33°55' 37.5" N   109°48' 45" W   109°48' 7.5" W

(Fig. 4.1*b*)

aerial photos, constituted a break in contiguity and therefore led to the creation of separate polygon areas. Thirty-six separate grid clusters (36 polygons) were mapped. With the map scaled to the earth's surface, the area covered by each polygon unit was computed and the sum of all grid polygons calculated. Collectively, grids covered 822,000 square meters or 82.2 hectares (203 acres) within the 6–square-kilometer area. Assuming that all available surface area was used and crops were planted both on the grid borders and grid interiors (that is, if Proposition 3c, as outlined in Chapter 1, is correct), this figure provides the maximum total area on which crops could have been grown.

It is also possible that crops were planted principally or exclusively on the rock borders, with crop production less important or absent in the grid interiors (Proposition 3b). If so, it is not the area encompassed by the rock-bordered grids that is important for calculating the amount of growing surface, but rather the total length of the rock alignments themselves. This value, the total plantable linear meters of rock alignment, was calculated by converting each rock alignment (originally traced from aerial photos and digitally retraced before GIS analysis) into a GIS arc line defined by nodes at both ends of each discrete arc. Each of these arc segments was summed to produce a total arc line length.

Because of the internal nature of ArcInfo and Arc-View node (intersection) counting, overlapping lines are counted each time they touch a node. For a crossing intersection this results in the end of the four line segments that touch the node being counted four times. In theoretical GIS space this presents no problem since the lines have no width, but in the real world of rock-bordered grids, the rock alignments have an average width of 1.4 meters. Geometry was therefore introduced to the geometry-less GIS line segments to avoid double, triple, or quadruple counting the meter-wide grid line overlaps. With so many intersecting rock alignments across this vast area of grids, such overlap error would significantly inflate the total length measurement. Where two alignment segments shared a common node, one overlapped line (1.4 m) was subtracted. Where three alignment segments shared a common node, the two overlapped grid lines (2.8 m) were subtracted. For each four-way intersection (the most common intersection on the site), the three overlapped lines (4.2 m) were subtracted from the

original total alignment length. This procedure, extracted from a total of 10,643 nodes (most of which were intersecting nodes) yielded 24,899 m of overlap error that were omitted from the final tallied length.

A total of 13,527 rock alignment segments was tallied with a mean segment length (average distance between rock-borders or alignment intersections) of 8.4 m. The maximum rock alignment length is 361.2 m (a terrace line) and the shortest is 2.1 m. The length of the rock alignments comprising the grid borders totaled 89,089 linear meters or 89 km (55 miles).

Association with Soils

To test for any relationship between rock-bordered grids and soil type, the transformed (geographically rectified) grid map was digitally overlaid with a Soil Conservation Service (SCS), now the Natural Resource Conservation Service (NRCS), soils map (Gelderman 1970). The overlap between areas covered with rock-bordered grids and specific soil types is highlighted in Figure 4.2. Although a strong relationship was detected between the placement of features and topography on a microscale (flatter slopes nearer the margins of the Pleistocene terraces; see Chapter 5), this overlay exercise showed no clear relationship between soil type and the siting of rock-bordered grids at the macroscale. This finding appears to contradict other studies where relationships between ancient agricultural features and soils have been identified (Homburg and others 1999; Lightfoot 1993b; Sandor and others 1986). This apparent lack of relationship is largely a function of the relatively uniform soils associated with the terrace surfaces when viewed at the regional scale of the soils map. More than 98 percent of the rock-bordered grids are situated on surfaces containing Pinaleño soils (soil types CkD, PuB, PnB, and BpB), but these gravelly or cobbly soils exist in various soil complexes on terraces throughout the Safford Valley.

Association with Geology

Unlike the nonexistent relationship between soil type and features, there is a strong relationship between the rock-bordered grids and geology. Analysis resulting in the initial discovery of the association of grids with piedmont alluvium (rock unit Qpa) was articulated in Chapter 3. It involved manually overlaying a map of

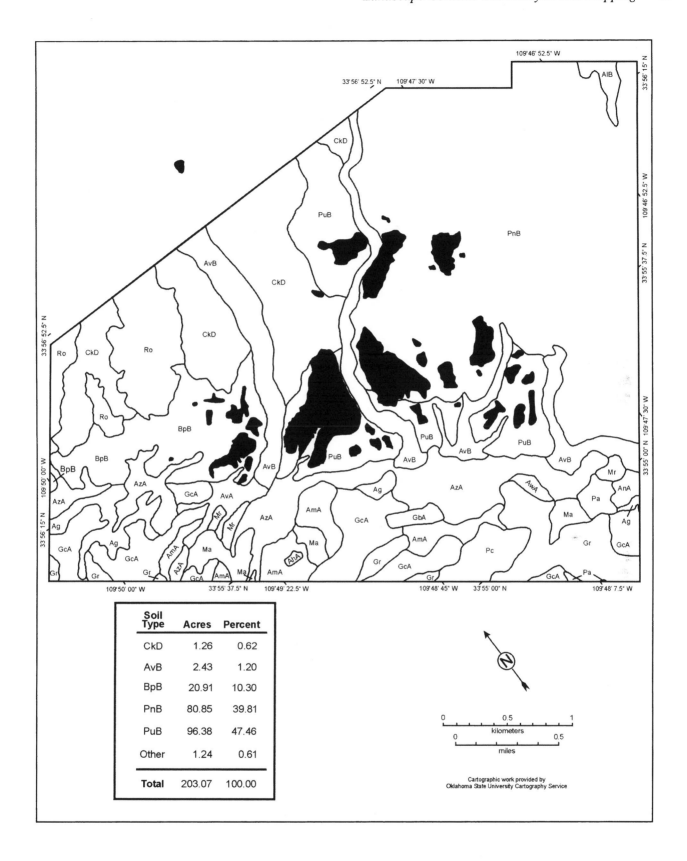

Soil Type	Acres	Percent
CkD	1.26	0.62
AvB	2.43	1.20
BpB	20.91	10.30
PnB	80.85	39.81
PuB	96.38	47.46
Other	1.24	0.61
Total	203.07	100.00

Cartographic work provided by
Oklahoma State University Cartography Service

Figure 4.2. Map showing the association between rock-bordered grids and soils.

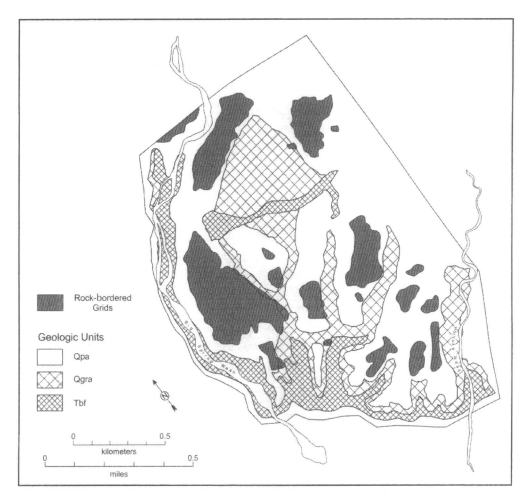

Figure 4.3. Map showing the association between rock-bordered grids and geology.

two of the grid groups on a geology map of the region. The relationship between grids and geology was further tested through GIS analysis by digitally overlaying a transformed (digitally rectified) version of the geology map used in the analysis in Chapter 3 with the portion of the digital grid map covering the area between Big Spring Wash and Holyoke Wash (see Fig. 3.2). The union of grid polygons with geologic units confirms the finding made in Chapter 3: 95.2 percent of the rock-bordered grids in this area are situated on piedmont alluvium (Qpa; Fig. 4.3). Although not every grid is associated with this specific geologic unit, a convincing relationship between grids and geology nevertheless extends across the entirety of the area mapped. The alluvial geology of this region may be controlled tectonically, but the consistent exploitation of cobbly alluvium by the builders of the rock-bordered grids appears to be a methodical cultural construct.

Those small areas of rock-bordered grids that are in association with Gila River alluvium on terraces (Qgra: 4.1%) and upper basin fill (Tbf: 0.7%) may be more apparent than real, the result of registration errors (for example, the arbitrary placement of a "fuzzy" geologic unit boundary, or slight skewing of grid polygon boundaries as the digital grid map was rubber-sheeted to the geographic coordinates of the transformed-rectified geology map). Regardless, these lesser associations are minor and do not explain the siting of rock-bordered grids.

A Symmetry of Pattern: Big Spring Wash as Central Place

Visual inspection of Figure 4.1 reveals a symmetrical pattern in the distribution of rock-bordered grids on either side (roughly east and west) of Big Spring Wash.

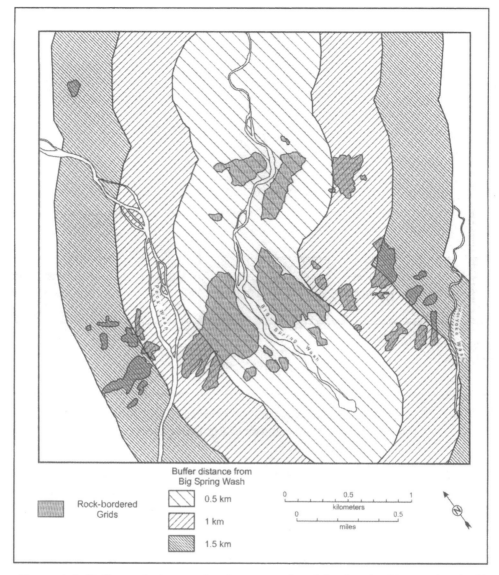

Figure 4.4. Buffer analysis map showing areas of rock-bordered grids associated with corridors set at 0.5 km, 0.5-1.0 km, and 1.0-1.5 km on either side of Big Spring Wash.

The greatest concentration and best-preserved examples of roasting pits occur in or near this drainage (see Chapter 7). This wash appears to be the functional and cultural center of site AZ CC:1:2 (ASM; Chapters 8, 10). A large cluster of grids is located close to the wash, with important clusters seemingly mirrored on either side. As distance from the wash channel increases, there is a gradual diminishing of rock-bordered grids. Buffer (corridor) analysis (at 0.5 km intervals, centered on Big Spring Wash) was used through GIS to statistically examine this distance decay phenomenon (Fig. 4.4). Results show a remarkable

balance on either side of the wash with regard to the diminution of grid area across space (Fig. 4.5). Whether Big Spring Wash was actually a convenient path of ingress and served as an access route to the central part of the grids, or whether this symmetry is an artifact of the distribution of Qpa geology, is discussed in Chapter 10.

If the siting of rock-bordered grids was a function of distance from the principal dwellings, then the dwellings must be those located in the vicinity of Big Spring Wash. Alternatively, Big Spring Wash could have been at the terminus of a path or trunk road connecting more

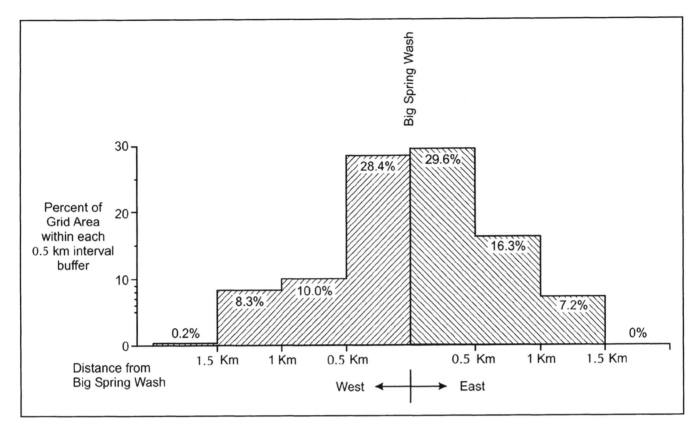

Figure 4.5. Graph of symmetrical diminution of rock-bordered grids with distance east and west of Big Spring Wash.

distant dwellings to the grids. Both scenarios offer transportation access as an impetus to grid placement or, at least, the clustering of rock-bordered grids about this wash. This cultural explanation for clustering cannot be borne out because the ancient paths or roads, if they ever did exist, are no longer visible, and no principal habitation area has been observed among the grids or near the floodplain of the wash (Chapter 8). The nearest large habitations, the Peck Wash site and AZ CC 1:19 (ASM), are located on the first terrace, overlooking the floodplain of the Gila River, approximately 1.4 km (0.9 mile) and 8 km (5 miles) respectively downstream from the mouth of Big Spring Wash (Chapters 8, 10; Gilman and Sherman 1975: 8–9).

It is possible that the noted symmetry of rock-bordered grids is autocorrelated with a symmetry of Qpa geology on either side of Big Spring Wash. If this particular alluvial deposit was in such proximity to Big Spring Wash, with progressively less of this unit extending to the east and west and eventually none of it farther than 2 km (1 mile) from Big Spring Wash, then the grids, already demonstrated to have a pre-

ferred siting in this particular geologic unit, would reflect a similar spatial distribution. It is not likely, however, that the Qpa geologic unit is confined in such proximity to, and symmetry around, Big Spring Wash. Furthermore, this geological coincidence cannot be demonstrated at this time because a complete geologic map of the area, produced at a scale useful for this type of analysis, remains to be made (Fig. 3.2 extends only a short distance to the east of Big Spring Wash).

FINDINGS AND MEANINGS

The acquisition of large-scale aerial photographs provided a valuable tool for analyzing the landscape context of the rock-bordered grids comprising site AZ CC:1:2 (ASM) and allowed mapping of the full extent of all grid and terrace alignments across this expansive site. Indeed, inconsistencies concerning areal extent, disagreements over grid size, and propositions related to geology and soils could only be corrected or confirmed through the broad-scale aerial perspective afforded by these images. Additionally, with the aerial photo-derived map, geographically rectified to a topographic map and overlaid with maps of geology and soils, it is possible to calculate spatial statistics that contribute to the understanding of some of the environmental decision-making that may have determined the siting of grids.

Using aerial photographs, we produced a large-scale map (1:6350) depicting grid and terrace alignments, other prehistoric cultural features associated with the grids, contemporary cultural features (roads, canals, buildings), and natural landscape features such as terraces, washes, and springs. This map offers the first comprehensive view ever produced of this set of rock-bordered grids and provides a source of data that, once digitized, geographically rectified, and overlaid with other features of the landscape, supports a detailed analysis of the grids and landscape milieu using the spatial statistical functions of geographic information systems (GIS). Perhaps most importantly, the computational abilities of GIS provided an accurate measure of both total area and collective length of the rock grids, thereby ending speculation on these attributes and allowing calculations of crop production and carrying capacity heretofore not possible.

Specifically, GIS analyses were performed to examine the relationships of grids to soil type and geology and to examine the visually distinctive pattern of grid clustering on either side of Big Spring Wash. Within the 6–square-kilometer area, rock-bordered

grids collectively cover an area of 822,000 square meters (82.2 hectares or 203 acres). The combined length of all grid and terrace lineaments equals 89,089 m (89 km or 55 miles). There appears to be no particular soil type preferred by the builders of the rock-bordered grids, though this apparent lack of relationship is probably a function of the lack of variation of soil types in this area when aggregated to the broad-area scale of this analysis.

A more distinct relationship is visible in the overlay of grids with geology. More than 95 percent of the rock-bordered grids (within the area covered by a detailed geology map) are sited on coarser-grained piedmont alluvium surfaces containing abundant cobbles and volcanic clasts that were used in the construction of the grid and terrace rock lines. The clustering (and subtle mirroring pattern) of grid areas on either side of Big Spring Wash was examined through buffer analysis to highlight the reduction of grid area with distance away from this channel, with a roughly equal rate of diminution east and west of the channel. It appears that this pattern is the result of both the cultural centrality of Big Spring Wash to habitations and naturally occurring waters from the spring (Chapters 8, 10). Whether or not the pattern was also a result of the natural distribution of the piedmont alluvium geology (Chapter 3) cannot be determined unless a more complete map of the geology of the area is completed.

CHAPTER FIVE

Site Topography and Hydrology

William E. Doolittle

Understanding the exact function of rock-bordered grids requires, among other things, detailed description and analyses of the features themselves. With the large number and widespread spatial extent of the grids, describing and analyzing the entire complex would be a monumental task, and probably one that would eventually become redundant and counterproductive. To obtain a representative amount of data in a reasonable period of time, we decided to conduct detailed microscale assessments of topography and hydrology on one discrete set of rock-bordered grids and on one set of rock alignments or terraces, both of which are parts of Locality 1, AZ CC:1:2 (ASM; Fig. 1.6). The equipment used was a Nikon A20LG Total Station with a single prism.

TERRACES

In terms of understanding function, the rock alignments are certainly less problematic than the rock-bordered grids. Alignments tend to occur on the relatively steep slopes and are assumed to be terraces (see Chapter 1). Terraces can serve a number of functions, often simultaneously (Donkin 1979: 34; Spencer and Hale 1961: 4–5). The possible functions of these terraces include: (1) to create nearly level, or at least less-steeply sloping, planting surfaces; (2) to increase soil depth; (3) to control erosion; (4) to manage water; and (5) to clear the land of rocks (Fig. 5.1).

The slope chosen for in-depth study has a southeastern aspect. A transect from the base to the top (near where the slope levels-off and not at its crest) measured 88.3 m. We did not record actual elevations because the nearest U.S.G.S. benchmark with vertical control

Figure 5.1. An uncleared and unterraced portion of a slope, with a roughly uniform distribution of cobbles and boulders on the surface. (Photograph by William E. Doolittle.)

was more than 6 km (3.7 miles) away and beyond the range of the surveying equipment. Instead, we established an arbitrary datum and from it determined that the top of the slope was 9.651 m higher than the base (Figs. 5.2, 5.3).

The overall gradient of this slope is 10.930 percent. However, the slope is not uniform; it is convex and steeper at the bottom than at the top (Fig. 5.3). In fact, the slope can be viewed as made up of two segments of approximately equal length. The lower part of the slope is 43.8 m long with a gradient of 12.418 percent. The upper part is 44.5 m long with a gradient of 9.465 percent. The steepness of the lower slope is largely a function of a gully with its head less than 50 m from the point where the profile was drawn; the gully parallels the toe of the slope. The comparatively slighter gradient of the upper slope reflects the overall gentleness of the Pleistocene terrace surface.

Figure 5.2. View from the base toward the top of the terraced slope. The rock alignments forming the terraces are clearly visible among the creosote vegetation. (Photograph by William E. Doolittle.)

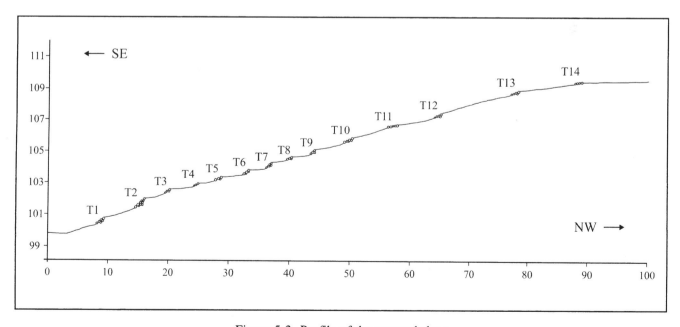

Figure 5.3. Profile of the terraced slope.

Table 5.1. Cross-Section Dimensions of Terrace Alignments

Terrace	Width (m)	Height (m)
1	1.441	.416
2	1.853	.620
3	1.235	.243
4	1.081	.223
5	1.441	.263
6	1.235	.284
7	1.544	.366
8	1.184	.276
9	1.133	.241
10	1.665	.354
11	2.170	.179
12	1.413	.315
13	1.363	.207
14	1.360	.114
Terraces 1–14 (N, 14)		
mean	1.437	.293
sd	.298	.123
var	.089	.015
Terraces 1–8 (N, 8)		
mean	1.377	.370
sd	.247	.169
var	.061	.028
Terraces 9–14, with cross walls (N, 6)		
mean	1.506	.235
sd	.337	.169
var	.114	.008

Figure 5.4. Close-up view, upslope, of intact terrace alignments. (Photograph by William E. Doolittle.)

Fourteen terraces parallel the topographic contours of the slope. They vary somewhat in width, but average 1.437 m, with those on the lower slope being slightly narrower than those on the upper slope (Table 5.1). In terms of height there is marked variability. The overall average terrace height is 29.3 cm. The eight terraces on the lower slope average 37.0 cm in height, and the six on the upper slope average 23.5 cm in height. Paralleling this trend, the tallest terrace (Terrace 2) is near the bottom of the slope (the second one up from the toe of slope), and measures 62.0 cm high, and the lowest terrace (Terrace 14) is the one at the top of the slope, measuring only 11.4 cm high.

Gravity and time have taken their toll on the integrity of portions of these features. On the whole, however, they appear remarkably intact (Figs. 1.13, 5.4), sufficiently so that details of morphology and hence construction can be inferred, especially from excavated cross-sections. At first glance, one gets the impression that these terraces are comprised of unshaped rocks, ranging from tennis ball size to basketball size, piled on the ground surface with minimal or no care, one to three courses high. If terraces were constructed in such a manner, their overall cross-section, regardless of slope, would be more or less parabolic, although it might not appear that way from the surface because of partial burial from subsequent sedimentation on the upslope side. On closer inspection, and from excavations, a different picture emerges.

The downslope faces of these features, or risers to use appropriate terrace terminology (Wilken 1987: 114), are not semiparabolic but sloping planes (Fig. 5.5). To be sure, they are not vertical or even close to it, but they are planes and they do have a pronounced slope. The slopes of the risers are greater than the slope of the natural surface. To construct these sloping risers, the builders first laid down small rocks and then placed larger rocks in front (downslope) and on top of them to form the risers (Figs. 5.6, 5.7). The upslope

Figure 5.5. Close-up view along a terrace alignment. (Photograph by William B. Doolittle.)

Figure 5.6. Close-up view of Terrace 6 after excavation. (Photograph by William E. Doolittle.)

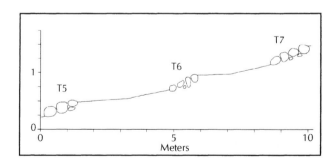

Figure 5.7. Profile of Terraces 5, 6, and 7.

Figure 5.8. View down the terraced slope, showing both risers (oriented from lower left to upper right) and cross walls (oriented from upper left to lower right). (Photograph by William E. Doolittle.)

Figure 5.9. View up the terraced slope. The exceptionally large rocks standing on end are part of the terrace risers but are aligned with each other up and down the slope; they may be boundary markers. (Photograph by William E. Doolittle.)

faces of the alignments, although concealed by sediment, are neither sloping nor parabolic, but instead are nearly vertical. Their uppermost edges are clearly visible on the surface.

This verticality cannot be deemed accidental or inadvertent, a situation that would normally indicate incremental change (Doolittle 1984). It sets these terraces apart from the rock-bordered grids, which slope on both sides. Instead, this verticality was intentional, implying that the builders knew that the upslope face would be buried by sediment. In terms of cross-sectional morphology, these terraces are almost identical to the "stone alignments," and "piled rubble" known from the Sierra Madres farther south in Mexico (Herold 1965: 111–112, 114-115, Fig. 12), features identified and long-accepted as terraces. On the basis of locale, morphology, and parallels from elsewhere, the interpretation of these alignments as terraces cannot be in doubt. But the precise terrace function was not the same from one part of the slope to another.

The six terraces on the upper slope are slightly different from their eight counterparts on the lower slope. The upper terraces are not different in morphology, but rather in an association of features not present lower down. Upper terraces have low cross walls spaced 5 m to 8 m apart and oriented perpendicular to the topographic contours and terraces proper (Fig. 5.8). These cross walls are morphologically similar to, and hence were probably constructed in a manner like, the alignments that comprise the rock-bordered grids

and not to the terraces. Their exact function remains unknown, but they may have served as boundary markers. Dispersed along this entire slope larger than average and elongated rocks have been positioned on end (Fig. 5.9), and they appear much like boundary markers found in fields elsewhere (see Chapters 8, 10; Doak and others 1997: 4.3; Woodbury 1961: 13–14).

The presence of cross walls on a terraced slope renders the appearance of grids when viewed from the air. The hill on which these terraces are located does not have a pronounced crest or peak. Instead, it levels off or, more accurately, is characterized by a gentle, almost imperceptible, convex curve. Not inconsequentially, the top of this hill is covered with rock-bordered grids. Visually, then, rock alignments on this slope change as one proceeds from bottom to top: from terraces to terraces with cross walls to grids.

Terraces on this slope have characteristics that can be correlated to variations in terrain and that compensate for natural impediments to cultivation. The terraces are higher and more numerous on the steeper lower slope than on the more gradual upper slope. Differences in number mean that distances between alignments vary. Combined with differences in height and elevation, differences in horizontal distance result in different gradients, which are critical in terms of understanding the details of terrace functions. It is every bit as important to look at each feature in relation to its nearest counterpart as it is to look at each individually. Accordingly, the focus now shifts

Table 5.2. Terrace Surface Gradients

Terrace	Gradient (%)
1	11.360
2	11.751
3	4.126
4	4.814
5	4.584
6	6.160
7	4.848
8	6.798
9	9.030
10	11.042
11	7.654
12	10.340
13	5.761
14	0.317
Terraces 1–14 (N, 14)	
mean	7.042
sd	3.329
var	11.081
Terraces 1–8, lower slope* (N, 8)	
mean	6.805
sd	3.060
var	9.362
Terraces 10–14, upper slope* (N, 5)	
mean	7.023
sd	4.305
var	18.529

*Terrace 9 is excluded from both slope segments as the dividing line between upper and lower slopes falls in the middle of that terrace surface.

Table 5.3. Detailed Terrace Surface Gradients

Terrace	Front to Middle Gradient (%)	Middle to Back Gradient (%)
1	11.483	11.209
2	9.096	15.022
3	2.063	5.777
4	1.617	8.016
5	2.964	6.662
6	1.791	9.715
7	3.591	6.545
8	4.002	10.247
9	6.760	12.711
10	7.523	13.320
11	7.853	7.481
12	11.828	7.392
13	6.607	4.817
14	0.317	0.000
Terraces 2–14* (N, 13)		
mean	5.535	8.285
sd	3.732	3.983
var	13.925	15.863
Terraces 2–10* (N, 9)		
mean	4.379	9.779
sd	2.745	3.319
var	7.532	11.018
Terraces 11–14 (N, 4)		
mean	6.651	4.923
sd	4.774	3.506
var	22.789	12.295

*Terrace 1 is excluded because of its anomalously steep gradients and convex surface.

from the rock alignments or terrace walls themselves to the terrace surfaces behind (or upslope) and in front (or downslope) of each wall.

The 7.042 percent overall gradient of the terrace surfaces is, not surprisingly, less than that of the natural slope (Table 5.2). What is surprising, however, is that at 6.805 percent the terrace gradient mean for the lower slope is less than the gradient mean on the upper slope. To complicate matters further, individual terrace surfaces do not have uniform gradients, and there is a difference in terrace surface configurations between the lower and upper slopes.

There exists a change of gradient at approximately the center of each terrace, or close to the mid-point between respective terrace walls (Fig. 5.7). Although this change of gradient is nearly imperceptible on some terraces, on others it is sufficiently marked to be visible to the naked eye. On average, the gradients of the front portions of terrace surfaces (those areas immediately upslope of terrace walls and extending to approximately one-half the distance to the next riser) are less than the gradients of the rear portions of terraces (those areas extending from the mid-points of terrace surfaces upslope to the next riser), 5.535 percent as compared to 8.285 percent (Table 5.3; Fig. 5.5).

The gradient and the surface area of the first terrace are anomalous, and the terrace itself may be anomalous. It has a convex surface area, with the front of the surface being steeper than the back and both surfaces being not much more gradual than the natural slope gradient. With its extreme downslope location and position near the gully defining the bottom of the slope, this terrace may have served principally as an erosion control device rather than as an agricultural feature (Doolittle 1985).

The surface areas of Terraces 2 through 10 are concave in configuration. Their back portions have an average gradient of 9.779 percent and the front portions have an average gradient of 4.379 percent (Table 5.3). In contrast, surface areas of Terraces 11 through 14 are convex, with a 4.923 percent average gradient for the back portion and a 6.651 average gradient for the front portion. Something interesting happens at Terrace 11 (actually beginning on Terrace 10 and ending on Terrace 12), a transition from concave to convex at around the 7.5 percent gradient.

The front area of Terrace 10 has a gradient of approximately 7.5 percent and a back area gradient of more than 13 percent. In contrast, Terrace 12 has a front area gradient of nearly 12 percent and a back area gradient of almost 7.4 percent. Terrace 11 is truly the fulcrum of this front to back gradient transition, with an overall gradient (Table 5.2) and front and back gradients of approximately 7.5 percent.

What can be inferred from this situation? It is possible that areas with slopes of 7.5 percent or less were preferred for cultivation. If such areas did not exist, they were created. If this interpretation is correct, then only one-half of most terraced surface areas were actually farmed. In some cases, such as Terrace 12, the cultivated area was not immediately upslope of the terrace wall, but some distance yet farther upslope.

Accepting the 7.5 percent maximum slope gradient means that nine terraces on this particular slope (Terraces 3-11) served at least in part to create less-steeply sloping surfaces. Terrace 2 has front, back, and overall gradients greater than 7.5 percent and, as with its immediate neighbor downslope (Terrace 1), might not have been cultivated. Erosion control seems to be the most likely function. The entire surface areas, from front to back, of the two terraces farthest upslope were probably cultivated, as was the back half of Terrace 12. In these three cases, terrace construction served a function other than decreasing the surface gradient, and increasing the depth of soil or controlling water are possibilities.

In sum, two (14.3 percent) of the 14 terraces on this slope seem to have functioned principally for erosion control; these were the farthest downslope where the natural gradient was the steepest. Three (21.4 percent) of the terraces probably served to increase the depth of soil and perhaps control water; these were the terraces farthest upslope where the natural gradient was slight.

Nine (64.3 percent) of the terraces in all likelihood served primarily to create less-steeply sloping planting surfaces. Looked at another way, in terms of gradient, alignments on extremely steep surfaces apparently functioned mainly to control erosion, those on moderate slopes served primarily to level surfaces and secondarily to deepen soils and control water, and, finally, those on slight slopes were built to increase the depth of soil and control water. Assessment of soil depth and soil moisture functions is presented in Chapter 6. For now, attention turns to water runoff and surface hydrology, topics that can best be addressed by a detailed focus on a set of nonterrace alignments.

GRIDS

Rock-bordered grids tend to be located on nearly flat or gently rolling surfaces with slight slopes. This type of setting makes grids enigmatic in that they seem to serve no obvious function, unlike terraces that may serve as many as four functions, sometimes simultaneously. It makes no sense that grids were intended to create nearly level planting surfaces when the natural surface was already nearly flat. It is also improbable that they were used to increase soil depth, unless the soil was hand-carried and deposited inside the grids. Nor could grids have trapped eroding sediment, as there was no source on such low relief surfaces and being bordered by rocks there would have been no way for the sediment to wash into the enclosures. Similarly, there is no readily apparent way the grids could have functioned to control erosion. That leaves water control as the most likely function, but how?

As in the case of erosion and sedimentation, there are no large catchment areas to generate surface runoff. Even if there had been such areas, the runoff velocity would have been slow because of the absence of relief. And again, the rock borders fully enclosed the grids and there would have been no way for runoff to flow into a grid area, much less from one grid to another. One is left to wonder, then, if the grids are not related to direct rainfall.

The notion that rock-bordered grids are linked to precipitation is not an easy one to accept. The area in which the grids are located is characterized by scant rainfall. The city of Safford, for example, receives only 224 mm annually, 88.4 mm (39.5 percent) of which falls in the months of July and August (Sellers

Figure 5.10. Rock-bordered grids on an apparently flat surface. (Photograph by William E. Doolittle.)

Figure 5.11. Rock-bordered grids on a surface that slopes more than is first perceptible. The base of the fence post in the rear center of the image is much lower than the feet of the person, James Neely. (Photograph by William E. Doolittle.)

and others 1985). The region does receive some snowfall each winter, but it is highly unlikely that what little snow is received would produce sufficient amounts of meltwater to be retained in the soil until the spring planting. The key, then, may well lie in conserving the scant amount of rain that does fall.

Conserving moisture has long been recognized as an ancient alternative to capturing it (usually by diversion) in agricultural practices of the Southwest (Vivian 1974). Water can generally be conserved in one of two ways, by mulching and by retention. Mulching involves making additions to the surface to prevent evaporation (Lightfoot 1993b). Retaining water typically involves some type of barrier that slows surface velocity, thereby inhibiting runoff. The issue of mulching as a possibility is discussed in Chapter 6. The issue of retention is problematic because the local relief is nearly flat, but it seems to be the only option with even a hint of merit.

The grid area chosen for an in-depth microscale study of topography and hydrology is 100 m southeast of the terraced slope discussed above. It is near the southern edge of the Pleistocene terrace at the rear of a northeast-southwest oriented lobe that overlooks the Gila River (Fig. 1.6). The southeast edge of this lobe overlooks Peck Wash. The northwest edge of the lobe is defined by a narrow, deep, and steep-gradient gully that has its head immediately north of the study site. At first glance, the area appears to be flat (Fig. 5.10), but on further inspection relief is detectable and substantiated by Total Station mapping (Fig. 5.11).

The exact number of rock-bordered grids that covered this area remains unknown, almost entirely because of postutilization destruction through erosion (Fig. 5.12). The rock alignments forming this grid complex are visually distinctive, but deceivingly so. The rocks provide conspicuousness, but they are neither closely fitted nor tightly stacked. As a result, the grids are broad, low, and discontinuous.

A sample of 10 points along these borders revealed that widths varied between 1.08 m and 1.81 m, and averaged 1.42 m. In contrast, the average height was only 14.5 cm, with the tallest point measuring an unimpressive 21.7 cm and the lowest measuring a mere 7.8 cm (Table 5.4, Fig. 5.12 points A-H, J, K). In other words, with a height-to-width ratio of nearly 10 to 1, these rock borders are not as definitive as they might seem. When their relatively great widths and low heights are combined with the discontinuous nature of rock placement, these borders become gossamery, and their fragility is highlighted.

The impact of erosion on these borders is evident in several ways. In at least two places, between Grids 1 and 2, and Grids 13 and 14 (Fig. 5.12), the rock borders separating grids have distinct openings or breaks; portions of these borders jut-out from adjacent walls leaving the distinct impression that portions have eroded away. Similarly, borders defining Grids 11, 12, 13, 20, 21, and two unnumbered grids west of Grids 29 and 30 are oriented perpendicular to, and terminate

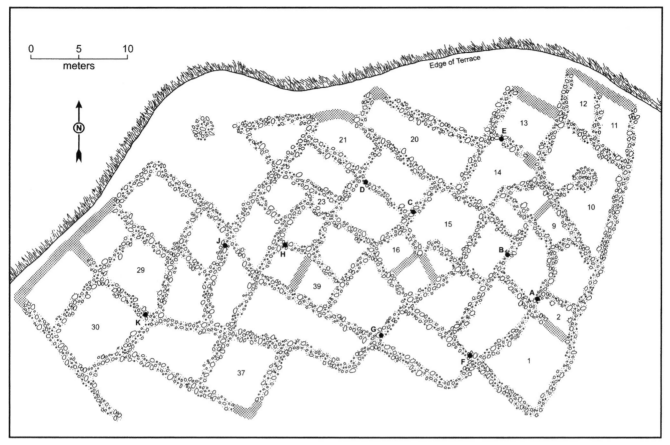

Figure 5.12. Plan of the rock-bordered grids at the eastern edge of Locality 1, with certain details added. Letters A-H, J, and K indicate the places at which cross-section dimensions of the borders were sampled (Table 5.4). Shaded lines indicate places where borders are absent today but may have existed in times past.

Table 5.4. Cross-section Dimensions of Rock Borders

Sample Point	Width (m)	Height (m)
A	1.54	.153
B	1.28	.103
C	1.40	.078
D	1.08	.214
E	1.81	.190
F	1.50	.166
G	1.34	.100
H	1.28	.097
J	1.43	.217
K	1.52	.129
Total (N, 10)		
mean	1.418	.145
sd	.196	.059
var	.038	.026

at, the terrace edge (Fig. 5.12). The lack of connecting alignments here strongly suggests that rock borders once paralleled the escarpment but have long since tumbled in pieces to the bottom of the gully.

In addition to the few presumed alignments that are missing, there are an even greater number of rock borders that may have been destroyed. At least three factors support this idea. One is the extreme diversity of grid sizes. Average grid size is nearly 22 square meters (Table 5.5). Some grids, such as Grid 10 at 50 square meters, are large and others, such as Grid 23 at 2.5 square meters, are small (Fig. 5.12). Accepting that a complete border existed between Grid 2 and Grid 1, it is possible that the larger grids could have been divided into more numerous smaller ones (Fig. 1.4), the borders of which are no longer present. Another factor is that some grids, such as Grids 9 and

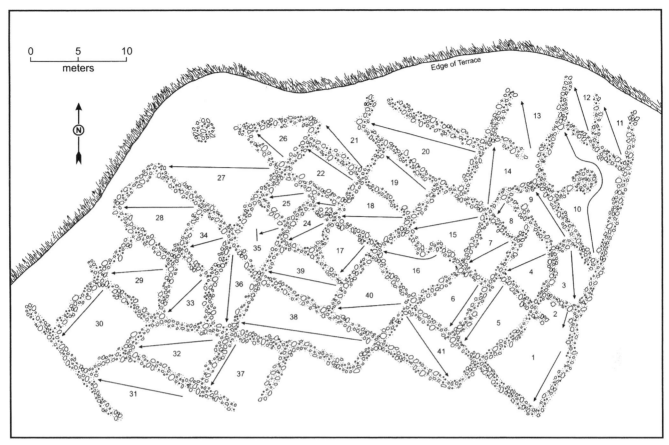

Figure 5.13. Plan of rock-bordered grids at the eastern edge of Locality 1 with
arrows showing the directions of surface gradients and hence runoff (Table 5.6).

39, have no internal signs of dividing borders, but the
midpoints of their longest sides are intersected by
borders of adjacent grids. It is possible, therefore, that
these "T" intersections are the remains of truncated "+"
intersections. Finally, the irregular configuration of
certain rock borders hints at possible grid division.
This is no more evident than in the case of the border
between Grids 15 and 16 (Fig. 5.12). Characterized by
two 90–degree bends, this border may indicate that its
adjacent grids were subdivided into several smaller
grids.

Two observations mitigate the idea that grids were
divided into greater numbers of smaller units than
appear today. First, if these grids did contain more
rock borders in the past than can be seen today, where
did the rocks constituting them go? Certainly they
could not have eroded out of the grids without the
borders themselves being more heavily eroded. There
simply are not enough rocks on any grid surface to be

collected into additional borders (Figs. 5.10, 5.11).
Second, even if there were more rock borders, their
presence would have greatly reduced the areas within
the grids. The grids are not all that large (extensive),
and the borders are not all that small (narrow). An
areal analysis based on the sum of individual grid areas
subtracted from the total area of the rock-bordered
complex revealed that grid interiors comprised 61.6
percent of the area and rock borders covered 38.4
percent (Table 5.5). The ratio of borders to grids was
remarkably high. If the grids were cultivated areas, it
would have been counterproductive to reduce them in
size.

Accepting that what can be seen today reflects what
was there in times past, 41 grids were studied in detail
regarding surface configuration and runoff. Four
hypotheses were tested: (1) individual grids had flat
surfaces; (2) individual grids were lower in the centers
than at the borders; (3) individual grids were higher in

Table 5.5. Rock-bordered Grid Sizes

Grid	Area (sq. m)	Grid	Area (sq. m)
1	37.5	22	15.0
2	5.0	23	2.5
3	15.0	24	10.0
4	17.5	25	10.0
5	27.5	26	12.5
6	20.0	27	NA
7	15.0	28	30.0
8	5.0	29	25.0
9	15.0	30	40.0
10	50.0	31	NA
11	12.5	32	30.0
12	12.5	33	20.0
13	20.0	34	15.0
14	22.5	35	17.5
15	30.0	36	17.5
16	25.0	37	30.0
17	17.5	38	45.0
18	22.5	39	22.5
19	22.5	40	30.0
20	40.0	41	27.5
21	17.5		

Total Area with Grids (100%)	1380.0
Area of 39 Individual Grids (61.6% of total)	850.0
mean	21.795
sd	10.851
var	117.746
Border Area (38.4%) (total area with grids minus total of individual grids)	530.0

the centers than at the borders; (4) individual grids had gradients that conformed to some general direction.

Considering that the natural relief of the grid area is slight, the first hypothesis of creating nearly level planting surfaces seems counterintuitive, unless the leveling was for the purpose of retaining runoff. In such light, it is only logical that the modified surface would be flat. The second hypothesis follows the reasoning of the first, but goes one step further, concentrating in addition to retaining runoff. With a central depression, each grid would serve as a microcatchment area, presumably for a single specialized crop plant in the center of the grid. This concept is supported by abundant references from the arid lands agricultural literature (for example, National Academy of Sciences 1974: 29–31).

In one sense, the third hypothesis turns the second hypothesis around 180 degrees, but in another sense it is exactly the same. That is, perhaps it was not the grid areas that were cultivated, but the borders. It has been demonstrated that specialty crops were cultivated in rock piles in ancient times, with water captured off of bare surfaces and retained under the rocks, which acted as mulch. Grapes in the Negev Desert have been put forth as one example (Mayerson 1961: 41–47). More importantly, agave was cultivated in rock piles across the southern Southwest (S. Fish and others 1985), and this possibility cannot be ruled out for the borders (see Chapters 6 and 7).

Least enchanting of the hypotheses is merely that the gradients of the grids parallel the gradients of the natural ground surface. If supported, this hypothesis means that rock borders did indeed serve principally to retain rainfall on the grids by inhibiting runoff, however slight it might have been. The area receives very little rain, however, so there would have been an inverse correlation between the amount of runoff and its value; every little bit helped.

We established a datum and determined elevations at the center and the corners of each of 41 identifiable grids with surface areas that seemed reasonably well intact, that is, with few or no signs of erosion. We calculated gradients on the basis of the highest and lowest elevations within each grid (Table 5.6), and plotted the directions of flows (Fig. 5.13), with some surprising results.

The surfaces were nowhere near as flat as seemed during initial and even prolonged visual inspection (Fig. 5.11). Gradients ranged from a low of 0.925 percent (Grid 25) to a high of 5.473 percent (Grid 13), and they averaged 2.346 percent (N = 40). The first hypothesis, that grids were intended to produce level planting surfaces can clearly be rejected. The second and third hypotheses can be rejected as well. In only one case, Grid 35, was the low point of the grid in the center of the grid. In no case was the high point in the center. The grids, therefore, did not function as either microcatchment areas or as a means to concentrate moisture along the grid borders.

It could be argued on the basis that 40 of the 41 grids have low points at their margins that the borders adjacent to these downslope points benefitted from concentrated runoff. It should be borne in mind that at best, this is replacement and not concentration. Local-

Table 5.6. Topography and Hydrology of Rock-bordered Grids

Grid	Direction of Slope	Drop (m)	Gradient (%)	Grid	Direction of Slope	Drop (m)	Gradient (%)
1	Normal	.228	4.100	22	Terrace Edge, interior	.146	2.655
2	Normal/Terrace Edge, interior	.038	1.900	23	Terrace Edge, interior	.053	2.650
3	Terrace Edge, interior	.096	1.920	24	Normal	.076	1.900
4	Normal	.101	2.244	25	Terrace Edge, interior	.037	0.925
5	Normal	.207	3.090	26	Terrace Edge, interior	.119	3.132
6	Normal	.194	3.880	27	Terrace Edge, open	.222	2.114
7	Normal	.098	2.177	28	Terrace Edge, interior	.163	2.233
8	Normal	.038	2.533	29	Normal/Terrace Edge, interior	.107	1.877
9	Terrace Edge, interior	.106	2.000	30	Normal	.140	2.154
10	Terrace Edge, interior	.197	1.407	31	Normal/Terrace Edge, interior	.162	1.800
11	Terrace Edge, open	.076	1.382	32	Normal/Terrace Edge, interior	.130	1.625
12	Terrace Edge, open	.193	3.712	33	Normal	.143	2.860
13	Terrace Edge, open	.301	5.473	34	Normal/Terrace Edge, interior	.056	1.474
14	Terrace Edge, interior	.106	2.000	35	Center	.073	2.920
15	Normal	.120	1.791	36	Normal	.109	1.557
16	Normal/Terrace Edge, interior	.159	2.446	37	Normal	.128	2.560
17	Normal	.092	2.421	38	Terrace Edge, interior	.163	1.283
18	Normal/Terrace Edge, interior	.122	1.968	39	Terrace Edge, interior	.101	1.443
19	Terrace Edge, interior	.172	3.127	40	Terrace Edge, interior	.151	2.188
20	Terrace Edge, open	.335	3.102	41	Terrace Edge, interior	.176	2.286
21	Terrace Edge, open	NA	NA				

Total (N, 40)	Drop (m)	Gradient (%)		Normal/Terrace Edge, interior (N, 7)	Drop (m)	Gradient (%)
mean	.135	2.346		mean	.111	1.870
sd	.066	0.884		sd	.048	0.307
var	.004	0.782		var	.023	0.940
Normal (N, 13)				Terrace Edge, including interior (N, 20)		
mean	.129	2.559		mean	.153	2.345
sd	.054	0.761		sd	.077	1.067
var	.003	0.579		var	.059	1.138
Terrace Edge, open (N, 5)				Normal and Terrace Edge, interior (N, 34)		
mean	.225	3.157		mean	.124	2.210
sd	.101	1.574		sd	.049	0.704
var	.010	2.478		var	.024	0.495
Terrace Edge, interior (N, 14)						
mean	.127	2.055				
sd	.048	0.685				
var	.023	0.470				

ized moisture increases created by runoff flowing toward certain borders was the result of water flowing away from opposite, upslope borders where moisture deficits would then exist. Such deficits could, arguably, have been compensated for by increased moisture from adjacent grids upslope, as is best exemplified in the cases of Grids 24, 18, 15, and 8, in that order. Such replacement, however, would not have resulted in net increases of soil moisture in particular places, and may even have resulted in net decreases due to the greater distances that surface runoff had to travel. The only

borders that would have experienced net increases are those at the extreme downslope edges of grid complexes, such as the western corners of Grids 28, 29, and 30. Furthermore, the borders separating certain interior grids would have experienced extreme net decreases, as in the case of the borders between Grids 3, 4, and 9. In sum, the grids did not serve to concentrate moisture along the rock borders.

Only the fourth hypothesis appears to have explanatory value; the individual grids do have gradients that conform to a single general direction (Fig. 5.13). On further examination, however, one detects distinct anomalies in the trend first perceived.

Two general trends exist in the gradients of the grid surfaces: one is along the normal gradient of the Pleistocene terrace, more or less toward the southwest; the other is toward the nearest edge of the terrace. To be considered "normal," a grid surface gradient can be any direction ranging from due south to due west. Complicating matters, however, is the fact that this grid complex is on a relatively narrow lobe of the terrace and in proximity to its edges, especially on the north and west sides. It stands to reason, therefore, that grids near these edges and even on the east side of the complex would slope toward the washes. But, there is more.

Some grids on the edges of both the terrace and the complex, such as Grids 13 and 27, lack rock borders on their downslope sides, undoubtedly due to erosion as discussed earlier. Others, such as Grids 26 and 28, are on the edges of the terrace and the complex but remain fully enclosed by borders. And yet others, such as Grids 9 and 39, are located neither on the edges of the grid complex nor the terrace, but have gradients that are not normal; they slope toward the terrace edge. Were these variations not confusing enough, some grids, such as 29 and 32, could be classified as having gradients that are normal or slope toward the terrace edge, or both. A quantitative assessment of gradients by direction is clearly needed.

The average gradient for grids comprising this complex is 2.346 percent (Table 5.6), steeper than might be expected, but far less than the average of the frontal areas of terrace surfaces on the lower slope and the back areas of terraces on the upper slope (Table 5.3). Not surprisingly, the five grids that are on terrace edges but lack downslope borders have relatively steep gradients. At 3.157 percent, the gradients of these grids are steeper than for any other category of grid (Table 5.6), thereby confirming the effects of erosion.

Thirteen grids follow the normal slope of the terrace and have gradients averaging 2.559 percent, slightly greater than the complex as a whole. In contrast, those 14 grids located either at the edge of the terrace (but fully enclosed by borders) or on the interior of the complex (and sloping toward either of the lateral washes) have gradients of 2.055 percent, slightly less than that of the complex average. The seven grids with slopes that can be envisaged as normal, toward the

terrace edge, or both have the slightest gradients of all grid categories, 1.870 percent (Table 5.6).

Exactly what all these variations mean, if anything, is difficult to say. Regardless of how one views them, reasonably undisturbed or non-eroded grids have gradients that are remarkably uniform, within a range of approximately 0.6 percent. Second, there is no substantial difference between grids with gradients normal to the terrace and those that slope toward the edges. Third, and most importantly, gradients of all of the grids are slight.

Although the surfaces of these grids are not flat, they are remarkably close to it. Without rock borders, some water from precipitation would run off and a certain amount of this precious resource would be lost for agriculture. With the borders, the hydrologic picture changes markedly. As low as they are and as porous as they may seem, the rock borders are sufficiently high and have enough integrity to prevent water from running off. As a result, they retained all of the rain that fell on the grids, thereby facilitating agriculture in an area that otherwise would be impossible to farm.

FINDINGS AND MEANINGS

The two types of rock alignments, terraces and bordered grids, functioned differently according to microscale topographic and hydrologic analyses. The terraces may have served more than one function, and a few appear to have been used for erosion control exclusively. Most terraces aided the creation of slopes less steep than normal. The reasons for creating slopes with gradients of less than 7.5 percent may well rest with a need to increase the depth of soil and control runoff. Some terraces were built on slopes with naturally slight gradients and almost assuredly served either or both of these purposes. In sum, assuming that the propositions outlined in Chapter 1 for the rock-bordered grids apply to terrace functions, Propositions 4b, 4c, and 4e are accepted, at least tentatively. Propositions 4a, 4d, and 4g are rejected. These features did not collect diverted runoff, they did not anchor brush that retarded wind erosion, and although they did result from land clearing, such was not their sole function. The verdict on Proposition 4f is still undecided. Terrace risers may have provided mulch that reduced evaporation and soil moisture loss, but confirmation requires detailed soil analyses (Chapter 6).

One of the truly remarkable findings to come out of this analysis is that only approximately one-half of the land area on steep slopes, those parcels immediately behind or upslope of risers, benefitted from surface leveling and increased soil depth by terracing. Presumably, the back areas of terrace surfaces, those areas immediately in front of or downslope from risers, were either uncultivated or planted in crops with shallower roots than crops grown on the terrace fronts. There is a possibility that yet other crops were grown on the risers themselves. In other words, the terraced slopes are much more complicated than they first appear.

The rock-bordered grids seem to be much less complicated than the terraces. Their principal function was probably to capture rainfall and retain surface runoff, thereby substantiating earlier speculation (Stewart 1939: 114, 1940a: 213, 216; Tuohy 1960: 29) and confirming Proposition 4b, and refuting Propositions 4a, 4c, 4d, 4e, and 4g (Chapter 1), at least tentatively. As straightforward as this may seem, however, the cultivated landscape was not necessarily a simple one. The grids themselves are small and the rock borders take up a large percentage of the land area. It is possible, therefore, that different crops were produced on different components of the system, as per Propositions 3c and 4f (Chapter 1). Confirming these notions, and those concerning terraces, requires additional analyses, first in the way of soils and then in the way of crops.

CHAPTER SIX

Soil Investigations

Jeffrey A. Homburg, Jonathan A. Sandor,
and Dale R. Lightfoot

I f the rock-bordered grids comprising site AZ CC:1:2 (ASM) served an agricultural purpose, as suggested by previous researchers (Gilman and Sherman 1975; Stewart 1939, 1940a) and as proposed in Chapter 1, then it is imperative that related features (terraces and rock piles) and the areas where they are located be subjected to rigorous soil analyses. Successful agriculture is dependent in large part on the medium in which the crops are grown, and, as demonstrated in Chapter 5, the rock features at the site did have an effect on soil properties. The grids retained runoff and increased soil moisture, and the terraces controlled soil erosion and trapped sediment, thereby increasing soil depth. This chapter assesses the agricultural suitability of the soils at this site and measures the possible effects of cultivation on soil fertility. Soil profile descriptions and a suite of physical and chemical laboratory tests were used to characterize the fertility and soil morphological properties important for water-holding properties of the soil.

METHODS

Soil sampling focused on a variety of features suspected of having agricultural potential in Locality 1 (Fig. 1.6). Of the 49 samples collected for analysis, 40 came from 15–cm-deep shovel pits (SP) placed in various features and nearby control areas thought to have remained uncultivated and nine came from two different soil profiles (Fig. 6.1). Soil sampling on the grid features involved two grid rock alignments and adjacent grid interiors from each of four landscape positions of Locality 1, for a total of 16 samples. Six control samples for the grid features (SP 27–29, 30–32)

came from soils and landscape positions similar to the suspected cultivated areas, including three control samples from both the southeastern and northern sectors of Locality 1. The grid features were so extensive that it was difficult to find control areas that were perfectly matched to the suspected cultivated soils; nevertheless, the control areas chosen appeared to be sufficiently similar to make valid comparisons.

We sampled three rock piles and collected control samples from areas next to each rock pile. We excavated a trench (T 1) and six shovel pits to sample the terraces located on the prominent east-facing escarpment in the southern part of Locality 1. All together, we collected nine samples from terrace contexts, including three samples from rock alignments or risers and three from the nearly level areas or treads located immediately above and below each alignment. Three control samples for the terrace samples came from the escarpment east of Locality 1 and Peck Wash, an area with a comparable slope to that of the terraces. We obtained deeper soil profile samples next to two historic prospector pits (PP), including a grid interior in the profile of PP 1 in the central part of Locality 1 and a trench (T 2) excavated between PP 2 and a rock pile in the northern part of Locality 1. Soil profiles entailed identifying soil horizons; recording morphological properties such as depth, color, texture, structure, and consistence; and classifying pedons using standard United States Department of Agriculture (USDA) Soil Taxonomy (Soil Survey Staff 1993, 1998, 1999).

Selection of particular soil analyses was based principally on results obtained by previous studies of prehistoric agricultural features in Arizona (Homburg

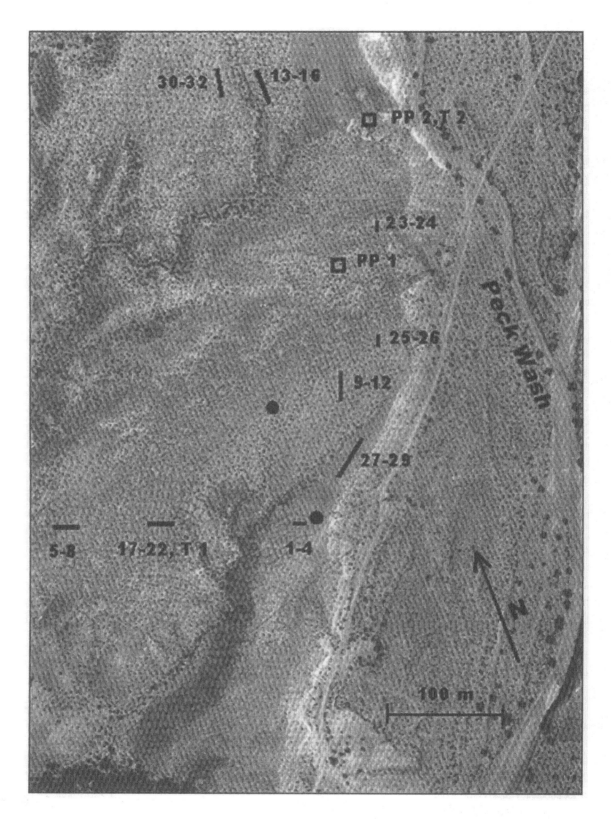

Figure 6.1. Aerial photograph of Locality 1, showing the locations of the soil testing shovel pits (numbers only), trenches (T), and prospector pits (PP). Black circles indicate the locations of panel points laid out 100 m apart for aerial and ground surveys.

1994; Homburg and Sandor 1997) and New Mexico (Sandor and others 1990), with tests focusing on properties that tend to reflect long-term stability. We conducted particle-size and bulk density analyses to obtain data on soil texture, moisture and nutrient retention, and compaction. We completed bulk density analysis for all samples except those that were too weakly aggregated for testing. Chemical analyses included determinations of pH, organic and inorganic carbon, nitrogen, total and available phosphorus, and calcium carbonate equivalent. The particle-size, bulk density, and pH analyses were made in soil labs at Iowa State University, and the organic carbon, total nitrogen, and total and available phosphorus analyses were conducted at the University of Montana under the supervision of Jay Norton. Louis Moran at Iowa State University did the calcium carbonate equivalent analysis. Subsamples for each laboratory test came from bulk samples collected in the field. Initial sample preparation involved air-drying and sifting samples through a 2–mm sieve to remove gravel, roots, and other coarse undecomposed organic debris. Determinations of total carbon, nitrogen, and phosphorus analyses were made on 10–g subsamples that had been mechanically ground fine enough to pass through a No. 100 sieve.

We determined particle-size distributions using the sieve and pipette method (Gee and Bauder 1986, Method 5.4), with carbonates included. Soil samples were pretreated with a 30–percent hydrogen peroxide reagent for organic matter digestion and a sodium hexametaphosphate solution for clay dispersion. We measured bulk density using the clod method, with paraffin-coated peds (Blake and Hartge 1986, Method 13.4). Bulk density samples were analyzed in duplicate and averaged, and if the coefficient of variation exceeded 5 percent, a third sample was analyzed and averaged with the others. After peds were weighed in water, gravel was removed and weighed, so the bulk density of the <2 mm fraction could be determined. Soil pH was measured in a 1:1 suspension (weight basis) of soil and distilled water using a glass electrode (McLean 1982).

For total carbon and nitrogen concentrations, we used a Leco CHN analyzer, and we measured inorganic carbon by titrimetry (National Soil Survey Center 1996). Total phosphorus concentrations were determined using an alkaline oxidation extract (Dick and Tabatabai 1977), and available phosphorus was mea-

sured using the Olsen extraction method (Olsen and Sommers 1982, Method 24–5.5.2).

We evaluated statistical differences between suspected cultivated and uncultivated soils of different contexts using *t*-tests. Statistical analysis was performed using Corel Quattro Pro, Version 7.0 for all quantitative chemical and physical soil tests.

In addition to the above analyses, we undertook granulometric testing to measure the extent to which the natural surface was altered in building possible pebble-mulch features. Relative (or semiquantitative) soil moisture was recorded using a moisture meter with a scale of 1 to 10. Six grids, scattered across six different rock-bordered localities, were selected for these tests and compared to adjacent nongrid areas. Grids ranged from 5 m to 9 m across. A 50 cm-by-50 cm pit was excavated in each of these grids to depths of 5 cm and 10 cm. We sieved the excavated material using graduated screens to separate rocks into size fractions of (1) 0.32–0.64 cm (0.13–0.25 inch); (2) 0.64–1.27 cm (0.25–0.50 inch); (3) 1.27–2.54 cm (0.5–1.0 inch); and (4) 2.54–15.24 cm (1.0–6.0 inches) to collect data on gravel weights by size fraction. Heavy cobbles larger than 15.24 cm were excluded from the sample because: (1) one or two spurious stones of this size would skew total weights; and (2) such a quantification exercise would only show what is visually obvious (that is, nongrid areas were strewn with larger cobbles whereas adjacent grid interiors contained very few and grid borders contained many of these larger stones). We compared these data to similarly excavated material from adjacent nongrid areas to determine whether grid surfaces were mulched by adding gravel to the surface or winnowed to remove gravel and cobbles.

SOIL MAPPING DATA

According to the general soil map of Arizona (scale of 1:1,000,00), site AZ CC:1:2 (ASM) is located in the Continental-Latene-Pinaleño association, which is characterized by "deep, gravelly, medium fine-textured, nearly level to steep soils on dissected alluvial fan surfaces" (Hendricks 1985, Plate 1). A more detailed soil map (scale of 1:20,000) shows three soil map units for the site (Gelderman 1970, Map Sheet 7): (1) Bitter Spring-Pinaleño complex, 0–5 percent slopes, in the far western part of an agricultural complex where

Table 6.1. Previous Soil Testing Results Obtained by the University of Arizona

Sample ID	Lab No.	pH[1]	Electrical Conductivity (mmho/cm)	Soluble Salts (ppm)	Sodium (meq/L)	Potassium (meq/L)[2]	ESP[3]	Nitrate-N (ppm)[4]	Soluble Phosphorus (ppm)[5]
#1 – 982	1027	6.95	0.75	525	0.74	0.28	-0.66	4.83	1.23
#2 – 976	1028	7.85	0.45	315	0.91	0.22	-0.23	2.80	0.59
#3 – 981	1029	7.70	1.40	980	0.16	0.04	-1.18	39.14	0.59

1. Paste with distilled water.
2. Water soluble potassium.
3. Estimated exchangeable sodium percentage.
   (Note: We assume that the negative ESP values indicate that these samples were below levels of detection. Also, the units for the electrical conductivity values were not provided, but we assume they are in mmho/cm).
4. From carbon dioxide extraction. Technicon reduction of nitrate reported as N.
5. Carbon dioxide extraction and orthophosphate determination (Technicon).

Locality 1 is located; (2) Pinaleño-Cave complex, 0–5 percent slopes, throughout most of the site; and (3) Pinaleño cobbly loam, 2–5 percent slopes, in the northeastern part of the site.

All three soil series are sparsely vegetated, calcareous, and they are in the Aridisol soil order. At the family level of the USDA soil taxonomy (Soil Survey Staff 1998), the Bitter Spring series is classified as Loamy-skeletal, mixed, superactive, thermic Typic Calciargids; the Cave series as Loamy, mixed, superactive, thermic, shallow Typic Petrocalcids; and the Pinaleño series as Loamy-skeletal, mixed, thermic Typic Haplargids. These soil series have little to no hazard of water and wind erosion, low to fair moisture holding capacity, medium to rapid runoff, and very slow to moderate permeability. Native vegetation is typically dominated by creosote bush, with some ocotillo, cholla, barrel cactus, annual grasses and forbs, and occasional shrubs of mesquite, wolfberry, and whitethorn and catclaw acacia. Rooting depth, estimated to be approximately 60 cm to 90 cm for the Bitter Spring and Pinaleño series and 13 cm to 60 cm for the Cave series, is limited by a weakly to strongly cemented zone of calcium carbonate. From a modern mechanized agricultural perspective, these soils are not regarded as suitable for cultivation because of their droughty nature, high gravel content, restricted rooting depth, low organic matter content, and low to medium natural fertility. It is noteworthy, however, that many archaeological projects throughout Arizona have documented widespread evidence of ancient farming activity on soils similar to those at the site. It is a testament to the skills and perseverance of the ancient farmers that they managed to farm successfully in so many harsh environments.

Previous Soil Testing Data

In 1984, Larry H. Humphrey and Gay M. Kinkade, archaeologists with the Safford District Office of the Bureau of Land Management, collected a few soil samples from the site for analysis. Three soil samples came from grid interiors and were submitted for routine soil analysis at the Soils, Water, and Plant Tissue Testing Laboratory, Department of Soils, Water, and Engineering, University of Arizona. Results of these soil tests are presented in Table 6.1, with nutrient concentrations determined in the solution phase. The laboratory concluded that soils from within the grids are suitable for cultivating corn, beans, and squash.

Review of Soil Tests

Soil reaction, or pH, is defined as the degree of alkalinity or acidity of a soil, and is a measure of the positively charged hydrogen ions. As such, it provides information on the availability of nutrients to plants. For noncalcareous soils, the optimal pH range for nutrient uptake is between 6.5 and 7.5 (Baize 1993). Nitrogen availability is greatest between pH 6 and 8 (Foth and Ellis 1988), and phosphorus availability is greatest between pH 6 and 6.5 (Tisdale and others 1985). A soil pH of 6.5 is considered optimal for cultivation of most varieties of maize. Organic carbon, a measure of organic matter, is one of the most useful characteristics for assessing soil fertility. Several beneficial properties are associated with soils having high organic matter content, including increased water- and nutrient-holding capacities and improved tilth (Brady and Weil 2002; Wild 1993).

Soil organic matter is difficult to measure precisely, so it is commonly estimated by multiplying the organic carbon concentration by a conversion factor known as the Van Bemmelen factor, a variable that depends on the degree of humification. A Van Bemmelen factor of 1.724 is typically used for plowed topsoils (Baize 1993; Nelson and Sommers 1982). Topsoils with less than one percent organic matter content have the lowest productivity, and soils exceeding three percent organic matter produce the most consistently high crop yields (Young 1982).

Runoff agriculture provides a mechanism for adding organic matter to soils in the absence of artificial fertilizer additions (Sandor 1995). For example, the Tohono O'odham counter naturally low organic matter contents and losses due to crop uptake by placing fields on alluvial fans to intercept organic debris and minerals carried by runoff (Castetter and Bell 1942: 172). Nabhan (1984) discovered that nutrient-rich debris that washed onto Tohono O'odham fields averaged four percent organic matter, an amount significantly higher than natural soil levels.

Nitrogen is usually the most limiting nutrient for agricultural production in Arizona soils (Doerge 1985). Nitrogen deficiencies are so severe in many desert soils that sustainable agriculture is impossible without fertilizer additions, naturally deposited organic debris, or nitrogen-fixing plants such as legumes, including beans (*Phaseolus* spp). Most nitrogen is associated with organic matter that protects its release by microbial activity. The nitrogen cycle is extremely complex because many biological processes are involved and because nitrogen occurs in many forms during its cycle. Nitrogen absorbed by plants is usually in the form of nitrate-N (NO_3-N) and ammonium-N (NH_4-N), both of which are major constituents of inorganic nitrogen. Lower pH levels favor NO_3-N uptake and neutral pH levels favor NH_4-N uptake (Tisdale and others 1985: 120).

The ratio of organic carbon to nitrogen (C:N) provides an index of the stage and rate of organic matter decomposition by microorganisms. As microbes convert organic carbon to gaseous carbon dioxide, carbon is released to the atmosphere, nitrogen is combined into new protein molecules, and the C:N ratio narrows through time. High C:N ratios indicate that the soil contains high amounts of incompletely decomposed organic matter. Maize stalks have C:N ratios of about 40:1 (Hausenbuiller 1972, Table 3.1), and agricultural soils usually have ratios between 8:1 and 15:1. Undistrubed topsoils that have reached equilibrium with environmental conditions often have ratios between 10:1 and 12:1 (Tisdale and others 1985), and ratios are usually lower in the soils of warm and dry climates than in those of humid and cool regions (Brady and Weil 2002). Many modern cultivated soils have narrower ratios than comparable uncultivated soils (Jenny 1941; Sandor and others 1986).

Phosphorus is a plant macronutrient that is added to soil by natural chemical weathering and biological processes. Unlike soluble macronutrients, phosphorus usually occurs as a highly stable compound that is not easily mobilized, so it is an especially useful indicator of ancient cultivation effects. Because of its strong affinity with oxygen, virtually all soil phosphorus is in the form of phosphate. Small quantities of soluble phosphate are leached from the surface, but most phosphate is quickly fixed in compounds of low solubility (for example, calcium phosphates above pH 7 or aluminum phosphates below pH 6). Consequently, most phosphorus is unavailable to crops, even in heavily fertilized soils where phosphorus accumulates to high levels.

Calcium carbonate in the soil originates from one or more sources, including the soil parent material, atmospheric inputs (that is, dust), and biogenic precipitates. Carbonate-enriched soils are represented by several stages of formation (Gile and others 1966) and they are widespread in the Southwest (Gile and others 1981; Machette 1965). Calcium carbonate equivalent (CCE) is a measure of the acid-neutralizing capacity of a liming material, and it is expressed as a weight percentage of pure calcium carbonate (Tisdale and others 1985).

Calcium carbonate is significant agriculturally because of the strong effect it exerts on soil chemistry, especially on pH and the availability of phosphorus and micronutrients such as iron, zinc, copper, and manganese (Fuller and Ray 1965; Yaalon 1957). The importance of calcium carbonate in buffering soil pH in the alkaline range is highlighted by the fact that approximately 10 tons of sulfuric acid per acre is required to neutralize every one percent calcium carbonate.

Bulk density is defined as the "mass of dry soil per unit bulk volume" (Soil Science Society of America

1987: 4). This soil property strongly influences aeration, permeability, moisture retention, seedling emergence, and root penetrability. Depending on soil texture, bulk densities in the range of 1.55 to 1.80 g/cm³ may impede root growth (Wild 1993: 117). Bulk densities are often highly variable, even for comparable soil horizons with similar textures, because of differences in size, shape, connectivity, and tortuosity of pores.

Clay, clay loam, and silt loam topsoils commonly have bulk densities between 1.0 and 1.6 g/cm³, and sands and sandy loams have values typically between 1.2 and 1.8 cm³ (Brady and Weil 2002). Bulk density and aggregate size usually increase with depth as the weight of overlying soil horizons increases, and organic matter content, root biomass, and faunal burrowing activity decrease.

Cultivation can cause either increased or decreased bulk densities (Hausenbuiller 1972: 81). Compaction is usually more severe in mechanized agricultural systems, but cultivation by no-tillage systems can still cause long-term compaction if organic matter is depleted, especially when native grasses and weeds fail to recover after fields are abandoned (Sandor and others 1990).

Soil texture is defined as the relative proportion of particles smaller than 2 mm, including the clay (<2 μ), silt (2–50 μ), and sand (0.05–2.0 mm) fractions. Particle-size distribution is a significant soil property because all physical and chemical processes depend on size of particulate matter (Murphy 1984). Twelve textural classes are defined in the USDA system (Soil Survey Staff 1993).

Soil texture is one of the most useful properties for evaluating agricultural potential because it strongly affects soil permeability, cohesiveness, erodibility, cation exchange capacity, and the ability to maintain nutrients and water in the rooting zone (Glinski and Lipiec 1990; Homburg and Sandor 1997; Jeffrey 1987). Sandy soils tend to have low nutrient- and water-holding capacities, but are prone to wind erosion; silty soils have an intermediate nutrient-holding capacity, but are easily eroded and are subject to problems associated with surface sealing; clayey soils have a high nutrient- and water-holding capacity, but have a low permeability. Overall, loams, sandy loams, and silt loams are the most productive agricultural soils in terms of fertility and available water capacity.

SOIL MORPHOLOGICAL PROPERTIES AND THEIR AGRICULTURAL IMPLICATIONS

All six soil profiles are described in Appendix A, including morphological soil data for: (1) the PP 1 in a grid interior and T 2 next to PP 2 and a rock pile; (2) T 1 across two terraces and a rock alignment; and (3) a 40–cm deep shovel pit in a grid interior (Fig. 6.1). The profile descriptions, combined with observations of exposures on the eastern edge of Locality 1 above Peck Wash, indicate that a petrocalcic horizon (a Bkm, or carbonate-cemented layer that is completely indurated) characterizes most of Locality 1, including most areas where agricultural features were built. The top of the petrocalcic horizon is about 30 cm deep in PP 1 and other areas (Fig. 6.2), but it was encountered at a depth of 40 cm to 45 cm in the terraces of T 1 (Fig. 6.3). It is approximately 1 m thick at a minimum, and it is capped by thin laminae. These laminae form due to carbonate precipitation after soil pores have been plugged. Such an advanced stage of carbonate accumulation (stage IV in the system of Gile and others 1966) is significant for agricultural soils because water infiltration and root penetration is effectively blocked. The soil of the grid interior exposed in the profile of PP 1, where the petrocalcic horizon was documented in the greatest detail, was classified to the family level as Loamy, mixed, superactive, thermic Typic Petrocalcid.

Areas with subsurface petrocalcic horizons are strongly associated with creosote bush (*Larrea tridentata*), the plant dominating the landscape of the site. Creosote bush is better adapted than, and tends to dominate, other plants growing in thin, drought-prone, alkaline soils, which accounts for its widespread distribution in the western deserts of the United States (Solbrig 1977). Creosote bush can grow in soils as thin as 10 cm to 25 cm, where their rooting system is confined above a petrocalcic horizon (Barbour and others 1977). Its roots are an important source of biogenic carbonate in soils, and they contribute to petrocalcic development (Gallegos and Monger 1997).

In parts of Locality 1, especially the lower landscape positions of the fan terrace, an argillic horizon (a Bt horizon with significant alluvial clay accumulation) was encountered at very shallow depths of 3 cm to 4 cm. Well-developed argillic horizons occur in areas with less gravel in the soil than where the petrocalcic

Figure 6.2. Jonathan Sandor points to a thick petrocalcic horizon exposed in Prospector Pit 1. (Photograph by Jeffrey A. Homburg.)

Figure 6.3. Shallow petrocalcic horizon below terraces and rock alignments in Trench 1. (Photograph by Jeffrey A. Homburg.)

Figure 6.4. Argillic horizon in Prospector Pit 2, surrounded by desert pavement. (Photograph by Jeffrey A. Homburg.)

horizons formed. Argillic horizons were at least 1 m thick in PP 2 (Fig. 6.4), where they are coterminous with a calcareous zone (a Btk horizon) marked by carbonate filaments, masses, and gravel coatings. Interestingly, a buried argillic horizon marking a lithological discontinuity was identified in PP 2. This soil is likely associated with the more reddish colored basin fill (Tbf unit B; see Chapter 3) upthrown along a normal fault in the area. The soil of PP 2 was classified to the family level as a Fine-loamy, mixed, thermic Calcic Paleargid. In the shovel pit placed in a grid interior, the argillic horizon was only 7 cm thick, overlying a Bk horizon. Some evidence of clay illuviation (though not enough to qualify as an argillic horizon) was noted in the Btkm horizon found only in T 1, in the upper terrace position immediately below the rock alignment. It is noteworthy that creosote bush and other plants grow more profusely along these alignments than elsewhere, presumably due to lateral water seepage from the mulching properties of the rocks (see Chapter 7).

Argillic horizons are significant agriculturally because they effectively impede infiltration and maintain moisture in the overlying rooting zone, thereby enhancing available water capacity. Observations throughout the Southwest indicate a widespread pattern of dryland fields associated with subsurface argillic horizons (Homburg 1994, 1997; Homburg and Sandor 1997; Sandor 1995; Sandor and Homburg 1997).

Topsoils (or A horizons) are generally thin throughout Locality 1, at less than 5 cm, but they thicken to approximately 15 cm in the lower terrace fill deposits of Trench 1 (see Chapter 5). This difference between terrace soils and other soils is important because of the thickening of the rooting depth and suggests that terraces could have served an agricultural function distinct from other features, perhaps with different crops.

Gravelly and cobbly to extremely gravelly and cobbly soils are characteristic of most of Locality 1 and the rock-bordered grids in general, both surficially and in the subsurface. Desert pavement covers much of the surface of Locality 1, and most exposed rocks have coatings of desert varnish. Desert varnish forms mainly due to microbial activity at pH levels below 9.0. It consists of microscopic layers of clay minerals, oxides and hydroxides of iron and manganese, admixed with detrital silica, calcium carbonate, and organic matter (Dorn and Oberlander 1981). These coatings are thought to take hundreds to thousands of years to form (Dorn and DeNiro 1984; Elvidge 1982). Thicker coatings mark the most stable landscape positions, because such traces would have been removed if the surface had been highly eroded, disturbed by human activity, or if deposition was still active. Desert pavement and varnish are most strongly expressed in the vicinity of PP 2 (Fig. 6.4). Many of the cobbles that were used to build agricultural features have coatings of varnish, but with irregular and inconsistent orientations. The variability expressed in these orientations suggests that people had indeed deliberately moved rocks to construct these enigmatic landscape features. Cation ratio ($K^+ + Ca^{2+}/Ti^{4+}$) and radiocarbon dating have been used to determine when desert varnish formed, and thus when the rocks were first exposed (Dorn and others 1986). It was originally thought that these methods might help establish the age of the rock-bordered grids through analysis of varnish formed on the fresh rock surfaces exposed after construction. The reliability of these methods for dating purposes, however, was subsequently refuted with the discovery that varnish formation does not occur within a closed system. Exogenous windblown carbon from outside of the system (such as nearby Pleistocene playas) may be deposited on the rock surface and then incorporated within the varnish. Such a process can produce erroneous radiocarbon dates unrelated to the age of surface exposure.

Desert pavement protects soil similar to a suit of armor. It dissipates the energy of raindrop impacts,

thereby countering erosional processes. The rocks forming the pavement can also serve a number of functions pertinent to agricultural production. For example, they provide the raw material for building various agricultural features. Lithologically, the rocks of the bordered grids and terraces are identical to those of the local alluvium, clearly indicating that they were obtained on-site (see Chapter 3). Also, the rocks can function to increase the depth of wetting after rainfall events by concentrating infiltration to soil between the rocks, thus reducing evaporative loss and improving agricultural productivity (Alderfer and Merkle 1943; Choriki and others 1964; Fairbourn 1973; Homburg and Sandor 1997; Lightfoot 1993a, 1993b; Mehuys and others 1975; Saini and MacLean 1967). In addition, because the rocks retain heat, they warm the soil at night, thereby reducing the potential for frost damage to crops. Although the rocks provide several advantages for agricultural production, they also limit agricultural production in certain ways. An increased volume of rocks in the soil proportionally reduces the capacity for water and nutrient storage, as well as the volume available for root exploration and foraging. Despite these potential negative effects, overall the rocks served essential functions that the ancient farmers could have taken advantage of in this semiarid climate.

PHYSICAL AND CHEMICAL SOIL TESTING DATA

Soil chemistry, bulk density, and particle-size data are summarized in Tables 6.2 and 6.3 for the soil profiles, and in Tables 6.4 and 6.5 for the soils associated with rock features (grids, terraces, and piles) and their controls. Mean soil test values for the suspected agricultural soils are presented graphically as histograms in Figure 6.5. Tables 6.6 and 6.7 show all of the mean values and standard deviations, and Table 6.8 summarizes the *t*-test probability values for pair-wise comparisons of soils in suspected cultivated and uncultivated contexts.

Most of the uncultivated soils in Locality 1 are moderately alkaline, with pH levels in the range of 8.0 to 8.5, reflecting the calcareous nature of the soils. At these levels, the availability of some nutrients is limited, especially phosphorus and most micronutrients (iron, manganese, zinc, copper, cobalt, and boron), but nitrogen, potassium, calcium, magnesium, sulfur, and

Table 6.2. Soil Chemistry and Bulk Density Data for Soil Profiles

Soil Horizon	Depth (cm)	pH	Organic C (g/kg)	CCE (%)	N (g/kg)	Total P (mg/kg)	Avail. P (mg/kg)	Bulk Density (g/cm³)
PP1								
A	0-2	8.1	9.8	7.2	0.96	756	14.2	
ABk	2-12	8.7	6.2	9.8	0.76	649	11.9	1.30
Bk	12-30	8.4	9.0	14.4	1.01	635	11.5	
PP2								
A	0-4	9.1	0.7	9.5	0.22	628	4.8	
Btk1	4-17	8.5	3.3	14.6	0.41	705	8.8	1.35
Btk2	17-40	8.5	0.7	24.0	0.36	911	6.5	1.51
Btk3	40-59	8.5	1.6	33.4	0.37	1428	6.8	1.39
2Btk1	59-77	8.4	0.7	42.9	0.27	1390	8.7	1.35
2Btk2	77-100	8.6	0.7	37.1	0.20	1043	7.0	1.69

NOTE: CCE = calcium carbonate equivalent; bulk density values are missing for samples with weakly aggregated peds.

Table 6.3. Particle Sizes by Percent in Sediments of Soil Profiles

Soil Horizon	Depth (cm)	Very Coarse Sand	Coarse Sand	Medium Sand	Very Fine Sand	Fine Sand	Total Sand	Coarse Silt	Fine Silt	Clay
PP1										
A	0-2	5	6	8	10	28	56	24	9	11
ABk	2-12	5	5	8	11	28	57	23	11	10
Bk	12-30	7	5	7	2	33	54	21	15	9
PP2										
A	0-4	5	4	7	5	31	53	23	17	7
Btk1	4-17	3	4	4	2	15	28	17	26	29
Btk2	17-40	5	4	4	2	15	30	11	26	33
Btk3	40-59	3	5	6	2	19	35	14	31	20
2Btk1	59-77	0	3	4	2	13	22	13	27	38
2Btk2	77-100	0	2	2	0	18	22	21	15	42

NOTE: Percents do not always add up to 100 due to rounding.

molybdenum are readily available (Homburg 1994, Fig. 11.9). Although micronutrient availability is reduced at these pH levels, it is worth noting that micronutrient deficiencies are rare in soils throughout the Southwest (Doerge 1985). In T 2 in the northern part of Locality 1, next to PP 2, the surficial uncultivated soils were very strongly alkaline, with pH levels of 9.1 to 9.3. Soils with a pH above 8.5 nearly always have exchangeable sodium percentages of 15 or more (Fireman and Wadleigh 1951), and at these levels, serious problems can be caused by reductions in water uptake by plants and dispersal of soil aggregates. Although reduced agricultural productivity would result from pH levels above 8.5, such soils appear to be limited in areal extent in Locality 1, so they probably did not pose serious problems to the ancient

farmers. However, some highly calcareous and possibly very alkaline soils occurred in some clast-free grids in the large grid area just east of Peck Wash and Locality 1.

An important finding is that in all of the suspected cultivated soils, compared to their controls, pH levels are consistently reduced to levels that improve overall nutrient availability. The largest pH reductions were found in the soils of the rock alignments and the grid interiors, with decreases averaging 0.7 and 0.5 pH units for these features, respectively (Table 6.6), and these differences are statistically significant (Table 6.8). The lower pH of these soils is consistent with their lower calcium carbonate equivalent. For the terrace features, the greatest pH reductions existed within and immediately below the alignments, suggest-

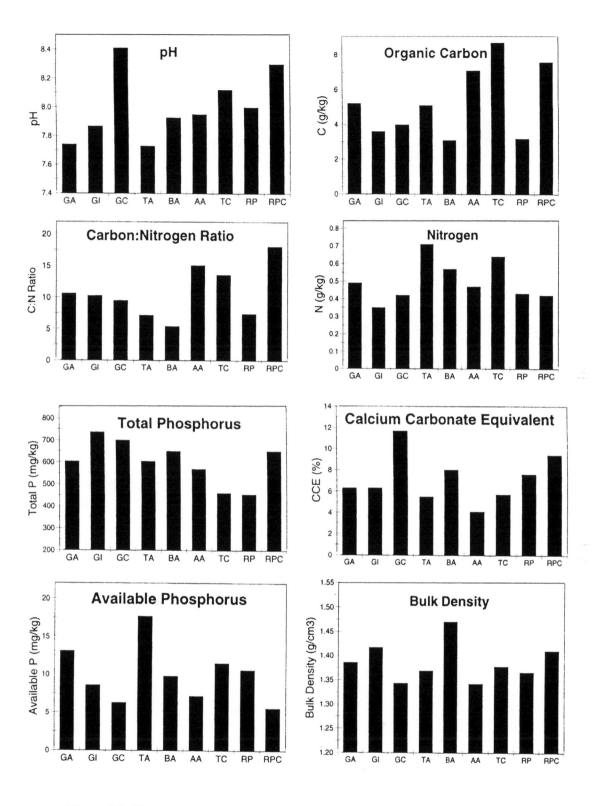

Figure 6.5. Histograms of soil data (means) by sample context. GA, grid alignment (N is 8); GI, grid interior (N is 8); GC, grid control (N is 6); TA, terrace alignment (N is 3); BA, below terrace alignment (N is 3); AA, above terrace alignment (N is 3); TC, terrace control (N is 3); RP, rock pile (N is 3); RPC, rock pile control (N is 3).

Table 6.4. Soil Chemistry and Bulk Density Data for Grid Features, Terraces, Rock Piles, and Their Control Areas

Sample Type and Location	pH	Org. C (g/kg)	CCE (%)	N (g/kg)	C:N Ratio	Total P (mg/kg)	Avail. P (mg/kg)	Bulk Density (g/cm3)
Grid Alignment								
SP 1	7.7	5.9	8.0	0.62	9.6	626	20.2	1.42
SP 3	7.7	6.0	4.7	0.52	11.5	666	26.1	1.39
SP 5	7.4	3.9	5.8	0.41	9.6	559	11.5	1.36
SP 7	7.7	5.6	3.8	0.54	10.2	496	10.4	1.43
SP 9	7.5	5.3	5.7	0.51	10.6	662	11.4	
SP 11	7.9	3.9	6.2	0.35	11.3	529	8.6	1.28
SP 13	7.9	5.3	6.9	0.41	13.0	691	10.6	1.43
SP 15	8.1	5.5	9.2	0.59	9.4	597	6.2	
Grid Interior								
SP 2	8.0	4.6	1.9	0.42	10.9	723	9.4	1.45
SP 4	8.1	5.0	4.0	0.42	11.9	965	9.8	1.47
SP 6	7.5	3.3	2.1	0.32	10.4	484	13.8	
SP 8	7.8	4.8	3.5	0.41	11.8	691	9.1	1.36
SP 10	7.5	2.3	5.9	0.27	8.3	640	5.9	
SP 12	7.7	1.6	9.1	0.24	6.9	699	10.5	1.42
SP 14	8.2	3.9	11.6	0.40	9.7	865	5.2	
SP 16	8.2	3.3	12.0	0.35	9.3	833	5.2	1.38
Grid Control, SE Locality 1								
SP 27	8.3	1.4	9.2	0.34	4.1	587	4.9	1.50
SP 28	8.4	2.5	11.0	0.41	6.0	715	5.2	1.48
SP 29	8.5	7.5	15.1	0.57	13.0	750	5.3	1.49
Grid Control, West of PP 2								
SP 30	8.5	3.3	9.3	0.40	8.3	746	9.7	1.17
SP 31	8.4	4.0	10.7	0.42	9.6	787	7.2	1.12
SP 32	8.4	4.7	12.5	0.41	11.4	613	5.2	1.30
Below Terrace Alignment								
SP 17	8.1	3.0	11.7	0.58	5.2	657	10.2	
T 1a	8.1	3.4	6.2	0.41	8.2	596	5.9	
SP 20	7.6	3.0	6.20	.71	4.2	699	13.3	1.47
Terrace Rock Alignment								
SP 18	7.8	5.1	5.5	0.45	11.3	510	11.3	
T 1b	7.6	5.5	6.0	0.60	9.2	591	15.4	1.45
SP 21	7.8	4.6	5.1	1.08	4.3	710	26.5	1.29
Above Terrace Alignment								
SP 19	8.0	5.5	4.4	0.42	12.9	584	5.3	1.40
T 1c	7.7	8.6	4.1	0.45	19.1	647	9.2	1.49
SP 22	8.2	7.3	3.7	0.53	13.8	477	7.0	1.14
Terrace Control								
SP 33	8.2	11.7	5.8	0.59	19.9	432	11.6	1.32
SP 34	8.2	9.5	6.2	0.64	14.7	457	10.5	1.38
SP 35	8.0	5.0	5.2	0.69	7.2	493	12.4	1.43
Rock Pile								
T 2	9.0	2.5	6.0	0.40	6.3	372	5.4	1.45
SP 23	7.7	4.1	9.1	0.42	9.6	560	8.9	1.28
SP 25	8.1	3.0	7.7	0.46	6.5	432	17.5	
Rock Pile Control								
T 2	9.3	9.3	12.4	0.42	22.4	672	5.9	1.41
SP 24	8.3	8.9	10.2	0.42	21.3	632	3.7	
SP 26	8.2	4.5	5.6	0.42	10.7	651	7.1	

NOTE: CCE = calcium carbonate equivalent; bulk density values are missing for samples with weakly aggregated peds.

Table 6.5. Particle Sizes by Percent in Sediments of Grid Features, Terraces, Rock Piles, and Their Control Areas

Sample Type and Location	Very Coarse Sand	Coarse Sand	Medium Sand	Very Fine Sand	Fine Sand	Total Sand	Coarse Silt	Fine Silt	Clay
Grid Alignment									
SP 1	4	4	6	16	14	44	19	14	23
SP 3	4	5	8	18	18	53	20	10	17
SP 5	3	4	4	11	18	41	25	15	19
SP 7	5	3	3	2	25	38	27	16	19
SP 9	7	6	7	11	18	49	26	11	13
SP 11	4	5	5	14	19	47	26	13	14
SP 13	5	5	6	11	19	47	22	15	16
SP 15	7	6	5	10	12	41	20	17	22
Grid Interior									
SP 2	2	3	5	14	17	41	23	13	23
SP 4	3	3	5	12	20	43	23	15	19
SP 6	5	4	5	12	18	43	25	13	19
SP 8	3	4	6	14	18	45	22	18	16
SP 10	7	6	9	17	18	58	22	11	10
SP 12	6	5	6	15	21	53	25	10	11
SP 14	9	6	7	14	18	54	21	13	11
SP 16	3	3	6	10	20	42	24	19	14
Grid Control, SE Locality 1									
SP 27	3	5	7	11	25	48	21	15	16
SP 28	3	4	7	13	19	46	17	19	18
SP 29	4	3	6	18	14	44	17	21	18
Grid Control, West of PP 2									
SP 30	5	5	6	15	21	51	32	6	11
SP 31	5	5	6	16	21	54	24	14	8
SP 32	5	5	5	14	22	51	25	14	10
Below Terrace Alignment									
SP 17	9	'7	7	4	25	51	26	13	10
T 1a	12	7	6	8	20	53	28	10	8
SP 20	5	6	7	9	24	51	29	12	8
Terrace Rock Alignment									
SP 18	8	8	8	11	17	53	24	12	11
T 1b	5	5	5	7	20	42	33	14	11
SP 21	5	6	6	0	28	45	32	14	9
Above Terrace Alignment									
SP 19	5	6	6	4	27	48	29	14	9
T 1c	4	4	4	0	28	40	36	15	9
SP 22	5	5	6	0	29	45	32	13	10
Terrace Control									
SP 33	5	5	5	2	25	43	27	12	17
SP 34	5	6	6	2	26	46	26	11	18
SP 35	5	5	6	12	16	44	29	12	15
Rock Pile									
T 2	4	4	6	16	12	42	18	21	19
SP 23	3	6	11	27	11	58	16	14	12
SP 25	5	6	8	8	33	59	21	10	9
Rock Pile Control									
T 2	2	4	4	0	18	28	14	31	27
SP 24	4	4	6	0	36	49	16	19	16
SP 26	3	5	6	17	21	53	25	12	9

NOTE: Percents do not always add up to 100 due to rounding.

Table 6.6. Means (X) and Standard Deviations (σ') for Soil Chemistry and Bulk Density Tests

Sample Context	pH X	pH σ'	Organic C (g/kg) X	Organic C (g/kg) σ'	CCE % X	CCE % σ'	N (g/kg) X	N (g/kg) σ'	C:N Ratio X	C:N Ratio σ'	Total P (mg/kg) X	Total P (mg/kg) σ'	Avail. P (mg/kg) X	Avail. P (mg/kg) σ'	Bulk Density (g/kg) X	Bulk Density (g/kg) σ'
Grid Alignment	7.7	0.0	5.2	0.8	6.3	1.7	0.49	0.10	15.8	1.2	603	70	13.1	6.6	1.39	0.06
Grid Interior	7.9	0.3	3.6	1.2	6.3	4.1	0.35	0.07	22.5	1.7	738	14	8.6	3.0	1.42	0.04
Grid Control	8.4	0.1	4.0	2.1	11.7	2.2	0.42	0.08	20.0	3.3	700	8	6.3	1.9	1.34	0.17
Below Alignment	7.9	0.3	3.1	0.2	8.0	3.2	0.57	0.15	13.9	2.1	650	5	9.8	3.7	1.47	0.00
Terrace Alignment	7.7	0.1	5.1	0.5	5.5	0.5	0.71	0.33	10.9	2.6	604	10	17.7	7.9	1.37	0.12
Above Alignment	8.0	0.3	7.1	1.6	4.1	0.4	0.47	0.05	16.9	3.4	569	86	7.2	2.0	1.34	0.18
Terrace Control	8.1	0.1	8.7	3.4	5.7	0.5	0.64	0.05	12.7	6.4	461	30	11.5	0.9	1.38	0.05
Rock Pile	8.0	0.7	3.2	0.8	7.6	1.6	0.43	0.03	18.6	1.9	455	96	10.6	6.2	1.37	0.12
Rock Pile Control	8.3	0.6	7.6	2.7	9.4	3.5	0.42	0.00	19.8	6.5	652	20	5.6	1.7	1.41	0.00

Table 6.7. Means (X) and Standard Deviations (σ') for Particle-size Analysis

Sample Context	Coarse Sand X	Coarse Sand σ'	Very Coarse Sand X	Very Coarse Sand σ'	Medium Sand X	Medium Sand σ'	Fine Sand X	Fine Sand σ'	Very Fine Sand X	Very Fine Sand σ'	Total Sand X	Total Sand σ'	Coarse Silt X	Coarse Silt σ'	Fine Silt X	Fine Silt σ'	Clay X	Clay σ'
Grid Alignment	5	1.5	5	1.1	6	1.6	12	4.7	18	3.8	45	5.1	23	3.4	14	2.5	18	3.6
Grid Interior	5	2.5	4	1.4	6	1.4	14	2.1	19	1.4	47	6.5	23	1.7	14	3.3	15	4.7
Grid Control	4	1.1	4	0.9	6	0.6	15	2.5	20	3.7	49	3.7	23	5.8	15	5.4	13	4.2
Below Alignment	6	3.8	6	0.4	6	0.4	6	2.7	22	2.7	46	1.2	30	1.5	13	1.5	10	0.8
Terrace Alignment	8	1.6	6	1.7	7	1.4	7	5.5	23	5.7	52	5.5	28	4.9	12	1.3	9	1.0
Above Alignment	5	0.9	5	0.8	5	1.1	1	2.0	28	0.7	44	4.0	32	3.3	14	1.0	9	0.6
Terrace Control	5	0.2	5	0.6	6	0.6	5	5.9	22	5.4	44	1.3	27	1.6	12	0.8	17	1.7
Rock Pile	4	0.6	5	0.9	8	2.6	17	9.5	19	12.4	53	9.4	19	2.8	15	5.2	13	4.9
Rock Pile Control	3	1.0	4	1.0	6	1.1	6	9.9	25	9.4	43	13.6	18	5.8	21	6.5	17	8.9

Table 6.8. *t*–Test Probabilities of Pair-wise Comparisons of Suspected Cultivated and Uncultivated Soils

Sample Comparison	pH	Organic C	CCE	N	Total P	Average P	Bulk Density	Sand	Silt	Clay
Grid Features										
GA vs. GI	0.36	0.01[b]	0.99	0.00[b]	0.04[a]	0.10	0.34	0.41	0.99	0.25
GA vs. GC	0.00[b]	0.09	0.00[b]	0.10	0.03[a]	0.03[a]	0.58	0.13	0.78	0.05[a]
GI vs. GC	0.00[b]	0.50	0.02[a]	0.11	0.59	0.12	0.39	0.61	0.74	0.41
Rock Piles										
RP vs. RC	0.55	0.05	0.46	0.64	0.03[a]	0.25	0.45	0.37	0.23	0.53
Terrace Features										
BA vs. TA	0.36	0.00[b]	0.25	0.53	0.51	0.19		0.18	0.38	0.08
BA vs. AA	0.93	0.01[a]	0.10	0.34	0.23	0.35		0.04[a]	0.05[a]	0.34
BA vs. TC	0.37	0.05[a]	0.28	0.47	0.00[b]	0.47		0.00[b]	0.82	0.00[b]
TA vs. AA	0.28	0.10	0.01[a]	0.27	0.23	0.09	0.87	0.62	0.50	0.20
TA vs. TC	0.01[a]	0.14	0.64	0.74	0.08	0.25	0.87	0.54	0.36	0.70
AA vs. TC	0.39	0.50	0.00[b]	0.02[a]	0.11	0.03[a]	0.77	0.99	0.06	0.00[b]

[a] significant at α = 0.05; [b] significant at α = 0.01.

NOTE: no *t*–tests were performed for some bulk density comparisons due to missing data.

GA, grid rock alignment; GI, grid interior; GC, grid control.

RP, rock pile; RC, rock pile control.

BA, below terrace alignment; TA, terrace rock alignment; AA, above terrace alignment; TC, terrace control.

ing these were favorable planting locations. The rock pile soils have reduced pH, but not at significant levels. The lack of statistical significance in this apparent trend may be a function of small sample size.

Mean organic carbon levels in uncultivated soils vary among the sets of control samples, with the terrace and rock pile controls averaging 8.7 and 7.6 g/kg (or approximately 1.5 percent and 1.3 percent organic matter, respectively, based on the Van Bemmelen factor), which is nearly double that of grid controls. There is no statistical difference between either the grid interiors or rock alignments and their controls, but organic carbon content is significantly higher in the alignments than the interiors. This finding suggests that organic carbon is conserved by the rock alignments forming the grids and that the alignments are favorable planting locations. In comparing the terrace features, the rock alignments and terrace positions immediately below the alignments, where creosote bush is concentrated, have significantly less organic carbon than their controls, possibly due to cultivation effects. Moreover, the rock pile soils have reduced organic carbon levels, but the difference is not statistically significant.

Overall, organic matter levels estimated by the Van Bemmelen factor are low at the site, usually less than 1.0 percent in the soils suspected as having been cultivated. The naturally low organic matter content is due to aridity, low biomass production, and high temperatures that promote rapid oxidation and decomposition of organic debris. It is noteworthy that the Hopi successfully farm soils with organic matter contents similar to those of this site, through their management practices and possibly through the use of varieties of maize with relatively low nutrient requirements (Sandor and others 1990). In semiarid regions of Arizona, natural organic matter levels are usually between 1.0 and 1.5 percent, which is consistent with the uncultivated terrace and rock pile controls at the site. Organic matter levels in cultivated soils at the site vary widely, from about 0.3 to 2.1 percent, with most measuring between about 0.5 and 0.9 percent; these levels, though not ideal, are sufficient for growing many crops, especially with wide spacing between plants.

No statistical differences were noted in nitrogen levels between agricultural soils and their controls, with one exception; the terrace position above align-

ments had significantly reduced nitrogen levels compared to the controls. The only other statistical difference is the elevated nitrogen levels in the rock alignments constituting the grids as compared to the control areas. Soils associated with the rock features have similar or slightly elevated nitrogen levels compared to uncultivated soils, suggesting that rocks act to conserve nitrogen stores. Alternatively, the elevated nitrogen levels may be a result of post-cultivation vegetation associations with the rock features. Nitrogen and organic carbon trends parallel one another for the rock alignments, grid interiors, and control areas. These trends did not appear in the other agricultural contexts, possibly because of differences in organic matter decomposition or production, or simply a function of small sample size.

There is little difference in the mean carbon:nitrogen ratios among the rock alignments, grid interiors, and the control areas, but the control areas have higher ratios than the soils of rock piles and those within and below the terrace alignments. C:N ratios of possibly cultivated soils are mainly in the range of 6:1 to 11:1, indicating that most organic debris is highly decomposed, a form in which much of the organic matter is available to plants. C:N ratios between 8:1 and 10:1 are typical for desert soils in the Southwest, due to rapid organic matter decomposition rates (Fuller 1975: 25).

Many suspected agricultural contexts, including rock alignments forming grids and the terrace positions above rock alignments on slopes, have significantly lower total phosphorus levels than their control areas. In addition, the rock alignments comprising the grids have significantly reduced total phosphorus levels compared to the grid interiors. Because total phosphorus levels are slow to change in the soil, reductions in these suspected agricultural contexts likely reflect cultivation effects. More important to agricultural production, however, is the amount of plant-available phosphorus, and soils of all rock features have elevated levels compared to their respective control areas. These differences are statistically significant for the rock alignments, both grids and terraces. Phosphorus requirements for crops are not well understood for many Arizona soils, but available phosphorus levels less than 2 mg/kg (or 2 ppm) are usually considered low, and values above 5 mg/kg are considered sufficient (Doerge 1985). Consequently, all of the soils associated with suspected agricultural features are sufficient in available phosphorus.

No statistical differences were noted in bulk density values, so there is no indication that cultivation caused significant long-term compaction. Even so, it is possible that soils were compacted during cultivation but have since recovered. There is now considerable overlap in the bulk density values of soils suspected of having been cultivated and those that were not cultivated. The bulk densities are mainly between about 1.30 and 1.45 g/cm³, and none of the samples exceed levels of 1.55 g/cm³, the level at which root growth can be restricted (Wild 1993: 117). The extensive petrocalcic horizons, however, strongly limit root growth at the site.

Surface soil textures consist mainly of loams and sandy loams, which are good textural classes for holding high amounts of plant-available moisture. The high sand content (generally between 40 and 60 percent of the <2 mm fraction) promotes good aeration and rapid water infiltration into the rooting zone. The clay fraction has an especially profound effect on soil moisture retention and uptake of water and nutrients by plant roots; clay levels near the surface of the site are mainly between 10 and 23 percent, which is a range that is productive agriculturally. Vertical textural variability on the alluvial fan terrace of the site, caused by both soil horizonation (that is, soil formation) and sedimentary stratification, promotes both moisture retention and lateral water flow in the rooting zone. Subsurface gravel-cobble content is high, usually between 20 and 70 percent. As noted in the previous section on soil morphology, coarse rock fragments lower the water- and nutrient-holding capacity of the soil, but they effectively increase the depth of wetting in the soil after a runoff event and serve an important mulching function.

Few statistical differences appeared between the sand, silt, and clay contents of soils suspected of having been cultivated and those that remained uncultivated. Clay content was significantly higher in the rock alignments forming the grids than in their control areas, and terrace positions above and below rock alignments had significantly less clay than their control areas. Significantly more sand and less silt occurred below terrace alignments compared to above the alignments. Sand content was consistently higher in the rock pile soils than in their control areas, probably due

to the rocks trapping windblown sand. This difference, however, is not statistically significant, probably due to the small sample size. If aeolian sand has indeed been entrapped, this process may be a postcultivation effect of the rock piles.

GRANULOMETRIC TESTS

If grid surfaces were mulched with rock materials, there should be noticeably more gravel within the grids than outside the grids (see Fig. 1.3). In fact, however, grid interiors at the site averaged 24 percent less gravel (by weight) than adjacent areas outside of the grids, and averaged 70 percent fewer of the larger cobbles (2.54–15.24 cm) within the upper 5 cm of the 50 cm-by-50 cm test pits (Table 6.9). Few larger cobbles (>15.24 cm) were encountered in the test pits dug within grid interiors, yet many such cobbles were used in constructing the rock alignments that formed the grids. Furthermore, for every size fraction there is a greater quantity in the upper 5 cm than in the 5-to-10-cm level, except for the 2.5–15.0-cm fraction, where there is 64 percent less of this size material (yet 5 percent more of this fraction in the upper 5 cm outside of the grids; Table 6.10). This finding demonstrates intentional cultural modification of the surface layer of soil within grid interiors, where there is less gravel as a whole than outside of grids, and particularly fewer cobbles larger than 2.5 cm due to removal during construction of grid borders. Rather than being mulched, the surfaces of grid interiors were apparently winnowed in an effort to thin out coarser gravel and move the cobbles to grid borders. This finding not only agrees with the construction proposition first offered by Hough (1907) and Russell (1908), and subsequently assumed by others that inspected these grids, but con-

Table 6.9. Percent Change (+ or −) in Weight of Rock Material Within Grids Compared with Rock Material Outside of Grids

Size Fraction (cm)	Depth 0–5 cm	5–10 cm	Mean
2.54–15.24	−70.0	−12.0	−42.0
1.27–2.54	−22.0	−22.0	−22.0
0.64–1.27	−0.8	−26.0	−13.0
0.32–0.64	+8.0	−17.0	−4.0
Total	−29.0	−18.0	−24.0

Table 6.10. Percent Change (+ or -) in Weight
of Rock Material in the 0–5 cm Level
Compared with the 5–10 cm Level
Within and Outside of Grids

Size Fraction (cm)	Within Grid	Outside Grid
2.54–15.24	–64	+5
1.27–2.54	+27	+27
0.64–1.27	+29	+4
0.32–0.64	+25	+3
Total	*–3*	*+10*

Table 6.11. Relative Measures of Moisture Content
Within and Outside of Grids
(Expressed as mean readings on a scale of 1 to 10).

Depth (cm)	Within Grid	Outside Grid	Magnitude of increase within versus outside grid
0–5	2.8	1.1	2.6 X
5–10	3.8	2.2	1.8 X
All (0–10)	3.3	1.6	2.0 X

firms it. The interiors of the rock-bordered grids at site AZ CC:1:2 (ASM) were not mulched, meaning that a more or less uniform layer of gravel or cobbles was not prepared across the planting surface, unless the principal planting surface was to be the grid borders. In the process of clearing the gravel and cobbles from fields, the clasts were placed to form linear grid borders, and they contributed to the retention of moisture across the entire surface of the rock-bordered grids (Chapter 5).

SOIL MOISTURE: THE COBBLE-MULCH EFFECT

Control of evaporation is one of the most important goals of soil management aimed at improving the supply of water to crops (Heinonen 1985). The amount of moisture in the soil at the time of planting significantly affects the survival and success of crops, especially in semiarid and arid soils. In areas like the exposed terraces on which the rock-bordered grids were built, the gravelly surfaces and heavy cobble borders promoted retention of soil moisture (Benoit and Kirkham 1963; Homburg and Sandor 1997; Lightfoot and Eddy 1994). The size of the grids may even have been limited by reduced soil moisture away from cobble borders in large fields; if grids are made too big, their centers will be significantly drier because of greater evaporative effects away from the borders.

Relative soil moisture tests supplied data for comparing six individual rock-bordered grids from different localities (the same ones sampled for granulometric analysis) with adjacent nongrid areas to determine if the rock alignments forming the grids aided crop growth by retaining moisture. Precipitation data provided by Russell S. Vose of the Office of Climatology,

Arizona State University, indicate that precipitation in the months preceding fieldwork in mid-March 1997 were typical for the study area. A total of 55 mm (2.17 inches) of rain was recorded in the two and a half months before moisture data were collected, including 34 mm in January, 14 mm in February, and 7 mm in March. A total of 18 mm of rain fell approximately two weeks before fieldwork, so soil moisture in the upper 5 cm had some time to dry through losses to drainage, evaporation, and transpiration.

Soil moisture data were collected from the centers of each grid and from areas just outside the rock borders. An average two-fold increase in moisture was recorded inside the grids compared to adjacent areas outside the grids (2.6-fold increase in the upper 5 cm and 1.8-fold increase in the 5–10 cm level (Table 6.11). Several additional grids were randomly sampled in the upper 5 cm at the center, just inside the upslope and downslope borders, and at random points inside each grid. These measures of soil moisture were then compared to readings collected from surfaces outside of the rock-bordered grids. There was no significant difference in moisture levels from point-to-point within the grids but, just as in the more controlled tests, moisture readings inside the grids were double those taken outside the grids. Much like the topographic and hydrologic evidence discussed in Chapter 5, these data validate earlier, but untested, assumptions that the rock-borders served as water retention-water control features (Gilman and Sherman 1975; Stewart 1939, 1940a).

Several terraces and associated rock alignments were also sampled at random in the upper 5 cm. Moisture readings immediately upslope of the features were similar to those taken inside of grids, and readings on adjacent unterraced slopes registered approximately half that of terraces upslope of rock alignments. These data show that terraces built on steeper slopes offered moisture retention benefits similar to those of rock-bordered grids built on more gently sloping terrain. If agricultural, rock mulch associated with both the terrace and grid areas would have lowered crop stress and increased crop yields.

FINDINGS AND MEANINGS

Soils at site AZ CC:1:2 (ASM) consist chiefly of gravelly loams and clay loams dominated by shallow petrocalcic or argillic horizons, both of which strongly impede or block water infiltration and hold moisture in the rooting zone within or above these zones. Compared to uncultivated soils, soils suspected of having been cultivated generally have reduced pH levels that would have been beneficial for crop production due to increased plant availability for many essential nutrients. Nitrogen and available phosphorus content are consistently high in the soils of the rock alignments forming grids and terraces and the upper portions of terrace treads, immediately below terrace risers. Unless these elevated nutrient levels are the result of changes since site abandonment, improved soil fertility is most likely a function of cultivation. This finding, therefore, provides at least tentative support for Proposition 3, as outlined in Chapter 1, that the grids were used for agricultural production. Reduced total phosphorus levels further support this hypothesis. Compared to the soils of uncultivated control areas, the soils of areas suspected of having been cultivated tend to have simi-

lar or slightly reduced organic carbon levels. Importantly, soils of the rock alignments forming grid borders have significantly elevated organic carbon, nitrogen, and available phosphorus levels compared to the grid interiors. The precise cause of these chemical soil differences is uncertain; they may reflect either direct cultivation effects or postcultivation vegetation associations with agricultural features. Bulk density tests do not indicate soil compaction. Accordingly, there is no indication that ancient farming, if it was practiced at this site, seriously degraded the soil, and that is especially true for rock-bordered grids. Soil nutrient levels are sufficient to have supported maize agriculture within the grids, but the thin rooting zones, high temperatures, low rainfall, and low runoff throughout most landscape positions of the field suggest that crops such as agave or other drought-tolerant plants were likely the focus of agricultural production.

In sum, Proposition 4f (Chapter 1), rocks comprising the grid borders provided mulch that reduced evaporation and soil moisture loss, is accepted. And Proposition 3b, crops were grown among the rocks comprising the grid borders, and by extension the rock piles and the terraces, is similarly supported over Propositions 3a and 3c, both of which involve cultivation of crops within the grid borders. This is not to say, however, that crops were never cultivated within the grids. The interiors were winnowed to remove gravel, and soil moisture content within the grids was high. The important question is: exactly what crops were grown on these rock features?

CHAPTER SEVEN

Growing Conditions and Crops: The Field Evidence

Suzanne K. Fish, Paul R. Fish, Arthur MacWilliams,
Guadalupe Sánchez de Carpenter, and Karen R. Adams

Although the geologic, cartographic, hydrologic, and edaphic evidence from site AZ CC:1:2 (ASM) all strongly suggest an agricultural function for the rock-bordered grids, terraces, and rock piles, are we able to provide evidence of the cultivation of specific crops? One strategy to obtain such evidence is an assessment of present-day vegetation growth patterns on the rock alignments compared with adjacent, relatively rock-free areas. Such an assessment should either confirm or refute the proposal put forth in Chapter 6 that the former settings are enhanced microenvironments that could have facilitated crop production. A second strategy involves an analysis of ancient pollen extracted from the same pits and trenches that were excavated for soil analysis, with the expectation that evidence of crops as opposed to wild plants exclusively could be identified among the grids.

A third strategy is an assessment of charred plant remains extracted by flotation from soil collected during the excavation of four roasting pits found adjacent to the grids. Evidence from elsewhere in southern Arizona indicates that such features were used to process plant resources, and they often contain remains of cultivated plants.

Finally, a fourth strategy involves an assessment of artifacts collected on the surface of the site. If the site and the features that characterize it were agricultural, it is likely that some of the associated artifacts are tools made for, and used exclusively in, ancient farming pursuits.

MODERN VEGETATION RESPONSES

Modern desert vegetation growing on the site offers potentially powerful insights into the effectiveness of rock-bordered grids and related features as agricultural constructions. The configuration of present-day vegetation can be conceptualized as an integrated response to the effects of these cultural interventions in conjunction with a multiplicity of natural factors, including climate, soil, topography, and hydrology, thereby providing a measure more intricate and inclusive than any single-variable analysis. As the cumulative outcome of all these factors, the relative density and vigor of present-day vegetation is an ideal proxy for spatially delineating enhanced growth conditions in the past.

Admittedly, the intended effects of these features may have diminished through the intervening years since they were built for an agricultural purpose. In particular, the successful functioning of grids, terraces, and other features to impede surface runoff would have triggered sedimentation (see Chapters 5 and 6) and eventually geomorphological equilibrium, thereby decreasing their subsequent capacity for capturing water, suspended nutrients, and topsoil. Thus, any enduring benefit to present-day vegetation from ancient features constitutes a singular affirmation of their original efficacy.

It is clear to anyone who visits this site that vegetation growing on the rock features is different from that

Figure 7.2. Herbaceous annual plants blooming in a rock pile but not in surrounding rock-free areas at Locality 1. (Photograph by William E. Doolittle.)

Figure 7.1. Herbaceous annual plants growing more profusely in a rock grid border than in a grid interior at Locality 1. (Photograph by William E. Doolittle.)

growing in relatively rock-free areas. This difference is particularly visible shortly after a heavy rain following a long dry period, when herbaceous annuals bloom (Figs. 7.1, 7.2). Because of the extreme seasonality of these plants, a strategy involving plants that could be measured during any season was preferable. We selected creosote bush (*Larrea tridentata*) as the species most amenable for assessing advantageous growing conditions that might still be offered by grid borders and terraces. It is the prominent and most widespread perennial of the low-diversity, shrub-dominated vegetation on and around the site. As such, creosote bush should register long-term rather than transient or seasonal effects, although brief periods of improved conditions could also contribute to germination and initial growth rates. To illustrate, photographs taken in 1960 and 1997 (Figs. 7.3, 7.4) both show creosote bush as the dominant plant growing on and between grid borders. The low heights, indicative of juvenile status, in 1960 may well be a function of clearing a few years earlier, perhaps by a naturally occurring fire. The greater bush heights evident in 1997 illustrate the long life and slow growth of this perennial species. Indeed, several individual plants can be identified in both photographs.

The research design for this vegetation study was based on the premise that the low rainfall of the study area would not have permitted cultivated or tended plants to grow uniformly across the considerable surface area encompassed by rock-bordered grids and terraces. Rather, plantings would have been necessarily circumscribed in relation to those constructions that provided differentially concentrated moisture. The soil moisture-conserving effects of rocks is well documented (Evenari and others 1971; Nobel and others 1992), as is the augmented growth of modern vegetation in the immediate environs of prehistoric agricultural features comprised of rocks in arid regions (S. Fish and others 1985; S. Fish and others 1992; Lightfoot 1993a; White and others 1998). The effects of the microenvironments along stone alignments in grid borders and terraces were examined, assuming that their construction in itself imparted localized moisture benefits in addition to any benefits from associated topographic modifications that might have directed and concentrated the flow of surface runoff.

The number of creosote bushes growing along transects measuring approximately 100 m was tabulated for five sets of rock alignments and adjacent control areas. We selected three sets of grid borders, two sets of terraces, and the adjacent control areas from three localities. We extended a measuring tape along each rock alignment and counted the number of bushes overhanging it. Bushes tabulated according to this criterion were not always rooted directly in an

Figure 7.3. Creosote bush growing on and between rock-bordered grids in December, 1960. Richard B. Woodbury provided this photograph; it was taken at the southernmost tip of Locality 1 looking toward the west. Compare with Figure 7.4. (Photographer and person in the picture remain unknown.)

Figure 7.4. Creosote bush growing on and between rock-bordered grids in March, 1997. Compare with Figure 7.3. Person in the photograph is Suzanne Fish. (Photograph by William E. Doolittle.)

alignment, but grew sufficiently close to it that the canopy intersected its path, a proximity permitting root contact with the soil along and under the rocks. Control-area transects differed between grid borders and terraces. In the case of grids, control transects extended diagonally between opposing corners. In the case of terraces, control transects extended longitudinally at the midpoint between adjacent alignments, running lengthwise along the terrace tread (the intervening space between terrace risers).

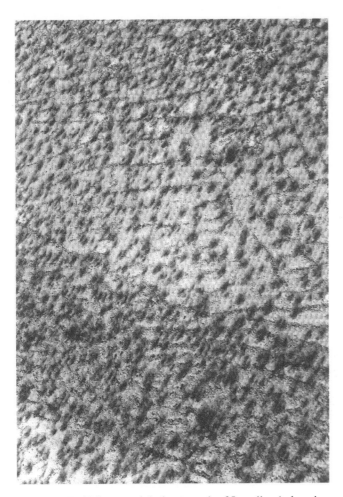

Figure 7.5. Oblique aerial photograph of Locality 4 showing creosote bush growing on grid borders rather than in grid interiors. (Photograph by James A. Neely.)

Table 7.1. Comparison of Creosote Bush (*Larrea tridentata*) Distribution on Rock Alignments and Control Areas

Location	Alignment Transects (m)	Control Transects (m)	Number Bushes in Alignments	Number Bushes in Controls	Alignment: Control Ratio
Locality 1					
Grids	100	102	49	17	2.9:1
Terraces	100	100	71	22	3.2:1
Locality 4					
Grids	100	100	35	7	5.0:1
Terraces	100	100	33	8	4.1:1
Locality 5					
Grids	98	103	28	17	1.6:1
Total	*498*	*505*	*216*	*71*	*3.0:1*

The results of comparing creosote bush density as an indicator of an enhanced growth environment are both consistent and convincing (Fig. 7.5, Table 7.1). In every case, substantially more bushes were growing along rock alignments than in intervening relatively rock-free control areas. For all transects, bushes in this sample were more abundant along grid borders and terraces than along control transects by a factor of three. Rock alignments in some areas appear to be more effective than in others, although all show higher densities; the ratio of bushes along rock alignments compared to control areas varies from 1.6:1 to 5.0:1. Clearly, ancient farmers would have obtained the best returns by concentrating crop production on or immediately adjacent to the rock features.

Results of this study have further implications for understanding grid borders and terraces in the Safford Valley and agricultural features elsewhere. The use of nonirrigated terraces in the arid zones of the Americas is relatively well described ethnographically and ethnohistorically (Donkin 1979; Wilken 1987) and, hence, well understood. In contrast to this wealth of knowledge, little is known about rock alignments. The high creosote bush densities along both grid borders and terraces, in comparison to the control areas at the site, suggest functional equivalence for these two types of constructions. Although the sample size is small, in neither of the localities where both grid borders and terraces were sampled did one type of feature perform better than the other. The effectiveness of grid borders for enhancing crop growth appears to be equal to that of terraces.

The only difference we recorded in creosote bush distributions other than between rock alignments and control areas was that both types of features had higher densities in Locality 4 than in Locality 1. Presumably differences in geology, topography, or soils, or some combination of the three, underlie this tentative finding.

Although shrub densities demonstrate the enduring capacity of rock alignments to promote heightened plant growth, these findings, *per se*, do not resolve the question concerning the prehistoric production of crops. It remains unclear if the increases in densities of creosote bush, the most drought-tolerant of desert species, can be equated with minimum requirements for even the hardiest varieties of maize, beans, squash, or cotton. The time of year in which soil moisture is available for these annual domesticates of tropical origin is also critical. The consistent patterning in creosote bushes is unequivocal, however, in indicating significant benefits for indigenous perennials such as agave or cacti that, like creosote bush, could withstand seasonal moisture shortfalls.

POLLEN ANALYSIS

Pollen samples came from a variety of proveniences associated with archaeological features as a means of reconstructing the crops and prehistoric agroecology of the site. We collected pollen samples in relation to rock features such as grid borders, terraces, and rock piles, and from test pits excavated in relatively rock-free areas to obtain materials for soil analyses (see Chapter 6). Control samples were collected from matching topographic situations and at similar depths to provide contrasting pollen assemblages from locations without features. We also examined present-day surface samples as analogs for interpreting past vegetational conditions. Additionally, an excavated two-room field house (see Chapter 8) was sampled as a probable location of crop processing and storage. Table 7.2 lists both scientific and common names of pollen taxa. Tables 7.3 and 7.4 present taxa for 55 samples as a percentage of total pollen in 200–grain tabulations.

The notable result of this extensive analysis is the failure to recover any pollen of an unequivocal cultigen. Maize pollen is the most frequently reported cultigen in prehistoric Southwestern samples. It is not invariably recovered in analog samples from present-day cornfields (Berlin and others 1977; S. Fish 1984; Martin and Schoenwetter 1960; Raynor and others 1970; Raynor and others 1972), but it is commonly encountered and has been reported from prehistoric agricultural contexts in the region on numerous occasions (Berlin and others 1977; S. Fish 1984, 1985; Martin and Byers 1965; Winter 1978). Maize pollen almost certainly should have been present in the large number of samples we processed if maize had been a crop in the grids. Although significantly more rare than that of maize, the pollen of squash, beans, and cotton has also been identified in the sediments of prehistoric fields.

In a previous study of 34 samples from archaeological contexts in the Safford area, several instances of maize and cotton pollen were reported in the sediments of rock-bordered grids, rock piles, and nearby roasting

Table 7.2. Names of Pollen Taxa in Samples

Latin Name of Genus	Common Name
Artemisia	Sagebrush or related species
Ambrosia-type	Bursage or related species
High spine Compositae	Sunflower Family
Liguliflorae	Dandelion type, Sunflower Family
Cheno-am	Chenopod, amaranth
Tidestromia	Tidestromia
Gramineae	Grass Family
Boerhaavia	Spiderling
Sphaeralcea	Globe mallow
Kallstroemia	Arizona poppy
Onagraceae	Evening primrose Family
Eriogonum	Wild buckwheat
Euphorbia	Spurge
Erodium	Heron-bill
Gilia	Gila
Plantago	Indian wheat
Solanaceae	Potato Family
Cylindropuntia	Cholla
Larrea	Creosote bush
Prosopis	Mesquite
Cercidium	Paloverde
Leguminosae	Pea or bean Family
Rosaceae	Rose Family
Rhamnaceae	Buck-thorn Family
Acanthaceae	Acanthus Family
Ephedra	Mormon tea
Pinus	Pine
Quercus	Oak
Juniperus	Juniper
Alnus	Alder
Salix	Willow
Celtis	Hackberry
Fraxinus	Ash
Picea	Spruce
Eucalyptus	Eucalyptus

pits (Cummings and Puseman 1997). It is possible that these locations provided the opportunity for diverting sufficient supplemental water to satisfy the requirements of these relatively moisture-dependent crops or that the pollen reflected other sources in the vicinity. In view of the greater number of samples in the present analysis, the failure to recover these pollen types underscores the conclusion that such crops were not grown among the rock features at this site.

The absence of agave pollen has little bearing on the possibility of the plant being cultivated at the site. Agave is typically harvested prior to the development of the flowering stalk (and the concomitant production

Table 7.3. Values for Major Pollen Taxa in Site AZ CC:1:2 (ASM)

Location	Context	Artemisia	Ambrosia-type	High spine Compositae	Cheno-am	Gramineae	Boerhaavia-type	Sphaeralcea	Eriogonum	Euphorbia-type	Solanaceae	Onagraceae
SP4	Grid center	1.5	48.0	13.5	9.0	5.0	1.5		4.5			
SP3	Grid alignment	3.0	40.5	6.0	15.5	2.0	9.0		4.5			
SP3, 4	Modern surface	1.0	45.0	4.5	10.0	4.5	+		3.5	1.0	0.5	
SP2	Grid center	+	43.0	19.5	6.5	3.5	4.5		2.0	0.5	1.0	
SP27	Control, no grids		51.5	11.0	7.5	7.0	1.0					
SP28	Control, no grids	INSUFFICIENT POLLEN										
SP12	Terrace center		60.5	12.5	5.0	1.5	8.0*		6.5			
SP11	Below terrace alignment	1.0	49.5	18.5	8.5	0.5	1.5		7.0			
SP10	Terrace center		54.0	12.5	7.0	3.0	6.5		5.0			
PPA	Control, no terraces	0.5	51.0	14.0	9.5	5.0			2.5			
SP23	Within rock pile		52.0	7.0	10.0	1.5	8.0		4.5	1.0		
SP24	Control, no rock piles		53.5	14.5	4.5	5.0	1.5		3.5			
SP25	Within rock pile	1.0	55.0	2.5	16.5	+	1.0		7.5	0.5	0.5	
SP26	Control, no rock piles		46.5	18.0	6.0	3.5	2.0		2.5			
ST2	Within rock pile	2.5	34.0	10.5	33.5*	3.0	2.0		1.0			
PrP2	Control, no rock piles	INSUFFICIENT POLLEN										
SP13	Below terrace alignment		41.5	21.0	9.0	4.0	4.5		3.0	2.0		
SP14	Terrace center		51.5	6.0	7.0	0.5	10.5		8.0			
SP15	Within terrace alignment	0.5	44.0	13.5	5.5	3.5	7.0	0.5	5.5			
SP31	Hilltop control	3.0	52.0	7.5	8.5	2.0	6.5		9.0			
SP32	Hilltop control	1.5	56.5	14.0	4.0	6.0	1.0		2.5			
ST1	Above terrace alignment	2.0	39.5	18.5	8.0	5.0	16.5		0.5			
ST1	Below terrace alignment	1.5	47.0	27.0	3.5	2.0	4.0		1.5			
SP19	Above terrace alignment	0.5	50.0	10.5	7.5	1.0	13.0		4.5			
SP21	Within terrace alignment		48.5	12.0	9.0	2.5	10.5	+	3.0			
SP22	Above terrace alignment	1.5	46.5	19.0	6.0	3.5	5.0			0.5		
SP20	Below terrace alignment	0.5	51.0	14.5	11.5	4.0	9.5		2.0		+	
SP6	Grid center	0.5	53.5	16.5	8.0	1.5	8.0		3.0			
SP5	Above grid alignment		49.0	20.0	6.5	3.0	12.0		1.0			
SP7	Within grid alignment	1.0	52.5	10.5	8.5	2.5	7.5		2.5			
SP8	Grid center	1.5	60.5	12.5	11.0	2.5	6.5				0.5	
PP6	Above checkdam alignment		34.0	11.5	17.5	4.0	12.5*	1.0	5.0			
PP4	Above checkdam alignment	0.5	33.5	13.0	25.0	4.5	9.0*		4.0			
PP5	Above checkdam alignment		24.5	13.5	16.5	6.0	19.0*		3.5		1.5	1.0
PP7	Above checkdam alignment	+	40.0	9.0	24.0	8.5	7.5	0.5	3.0		0.5	
PP3	Above checkdam alignment	+	32.5	17.0	16.0*	3.0	11.0		2.0	+		0.5
PP2	Above checkdam alignment		38.0	8.5	18.0	6.0	2.0	+	0.5	1.5	1.0	
PP1	Above checkdam alignment		36.5	13.0	26.5	4.5	9.5*	1.0	2.5		+	+
N of F4	Above grid alignment	0.5	43.0	19.5	9.0	2.5			6.0			
N of F4	Above grid alignment		39.5	20.0	8.5	8.0	4.0	1.5	7.0			
SP33	Control, no terraces	1.5	48.5	22.5	7.0	4.5	3.5				0.5	
SP34	Control, no terraces		52.0	17.0	4.5	11.0						
NW Loc. 6, Above grid alignment		1.0	42.5	23.5	4.5	2.0	6.5		7.5			
	Above grid alignment	+	46.0	18.5	7.5	1.5	4.5		5.0	0.5		
	Modern surface	0.5	53.0	13.0	10.0	3.5			2.0			
Big Spring Wash, modern surface		1.0	19.0	4.0	32.5	7.5	0.5		4.5			0.5
	Above grid alignment		27.0	4.5	47.5	7.5	9.0		0.5			
	Above grid alignment		8.5	5.0	70.0	1.0	7.5*	0.5	1.0			1.0
Field House 1												
	Room 2, 0-5 cm, Level 1	+	51.5	11.5	7.0	2.0			4.0			
	Room 2, 5-10 cm, Level 2	5.0	51.5	12.0	6.5	3.5	3.0	0.5			1.5	
	Room 2, 10-15 cm, Level 3		16.5	21.5	26.5	8.0	9.0		0.5	0.5		
	Room 2, 15-20 cm, Level 4	0.5	18.5	9.0	36.5	3.0	9.5	0.5	4.0		0.5	
	Room 2, 20-25 cm, Level 5	+	30.5	11.0	27.0	9.5	3.5				2.0	
	Room 1, 0-5 cm, Level 1	1.0	49.0	15.5	7.5	4.0	+		1.5	1.0		
	Room 1, 5-10 cm, Level 2		16.0	22.5	22.0	4.0	11.0	1.5	10.5			2.0
	Room 1, 10-15 cm, Level 3		20.0	13.0	34.5	6.5	3.5					
	Room 1, 15-20 cm, Level 4		19.5	17.0	42.5*	6.0	3.0		2.5	+		

+ Pollen type observed only in scanning of additional material after tabulation of the 200-grain standard sum.
* Pollen type occurring in aggregates of 6 or more pollen grains.

Table 7.3. Values for Major Pollen Taxa in Site AZ CC:1:2 (ASM), *Continued*

Larrea	Prosopis	Cercidium	cf. Leguminosae	Ephedra	Pinus	Quercus	Juniperus	Salix	Indeterminate	Minor Taxa (Table 7.4)	Location	Context
	0.5			6.0	2.5	1.0	1.5		5.5		SP4	Grid center
		4.5		6.0	4.5				4.0	0.5	SP3	Grid alignment
0.5	1.0		2.0	12.5	5.0	1.0	1.0	1.0	3.5	2.5	SP3, 4	Modern surface
	+			8.5	3.0	+	1.0		7.0		SP2	Grid center
				0.5	6.5	1.0	4.0		9.5	0.5	SP27	Control, no grids
				INSUFFICIENT POLLEN							SP28	Control, no grids
				1.0	0.5		+		4.5		SP12	Terrace center
	0.5			4.5	+		1.0		7.5		SP11	Below terrace alignment
			0.5	3.0	2.0	1.0	2.5	+	3.0		SP10	Terrace center
			0.5	3.5	3.0	2.0	0.5		8.0		PPA	Control, no terraces
			0.5	1.5	4.0	1.0			8.0	0.5	SP23	Within rock pile
				5.0	3.5	4.5	2.0		2.5		SP24	Control, no rock piles
	1.0			6.0	1.0	1.5		1.5	4.0	0.5	SP25	Within rock pile
				7.0	3.5		0.5		11.5		SP26	Control, no rock piles
0.5				3.5	1.5		0.5		7.5		ST2	Within rock pile
				INSUFFICIENT POLLEN							PrP2	Control, no rock piles
1.5				2.0	4.5	2.5	2.0		2.0	0.5	SP13	Below terrace alignment
				6.5	5.5	0.5			3.5	0.5	SP14	Terrace center
				4.0	3.5	1.0	3.0		7.5	1.0	SP15	Within terrace alignment
				1.0	4.0		1.5	0.5	4.0	0.5	SP31	Hilltop control
				3.5	6.0	+	+		0.5		SP32	Hilltop control
				6.0	1.5	0.5	2.5		4.5		ST1	Above terrace alignment
2.5				1.5	+	3.5	1.0	2.0	3.0		ST1	Below terrace alignment
				5.0	2.5	+			5.5		SP19	Above terrace alignment
0.5				4.0	1.0	1.5	1.0		6.0	0.5	SP21	Within terrace alignment
				3.5	4.0	1.0	4.5		5.0		SP22	Above terrace alignment
			1.0	2.0	1.5	0.5			1.5	0.5	SP20	Below terrace alignment
				6.0		0.5	1.0		1.5		SP6	Grid center
+				3.0	2.0	1.0			2.5		SP5	Above grid alignment
	0.5			4.5	3.0	0.5	2.0		4.0	0.5	SP7	Within grid alignment
2.0				0.5	1.0	+		0.5	0.5	0.5	SP8	Grid center
1.0	+		0.5	1.0	7.0	+	3.5		1.5		PP6	Above checkdam align.
			2.0		4.5	1.0			3.0		PP4	Above checkdam align.
2.0				3.0	3.0		2.0		4.5		PP5	Above checkdam align.
				4.0	2.0			0.5	5.0		PP7	Above checkdam align.
		0.5		5.0	4.5	1.0	1.0		5.5	0.5	PP3	Above checkdam align.
1.5	1.0			4.5	8.0	1.0	0.5	1.0	7.0		PP2	Above checkdam align.
				1.5	3.0	+	+		1.5	0.5	PP1	Above checkdam align.
				3.5	2.5		0.5	2.0	11.0		N of F4	Above grid alignment
	1.0		2.0	2.5		+		0.5	5.5		N of F4	Above grid alignment
0.5				3.0	3.5				5.0		SP33	Control, no terraces
				8.0	3.0	1.5			2.5	0.5	SP34	Control, no terraces
1.0			0.5	3.5	2.0		0.5		5.0		NW Loc. 6,	Above grid alignment
				4.0	1.5	3.0		0.5	7.5			Above grid alignment
			1.0	2.0	1.5	4.0	2.0	1.0	3.0	3.5		Modern surface
1.0	2.0	3.5		8.5	4.0	2.0	2.5		6.0	1.0	Big Spring Wash, modern surface	
	0.5					0.5			2.5	0.5		Above grid alignment
				0.5	0.5				4.0	0.5		Above grid alignment
											Field House 1	
2.5				5.5	5.0	1.5	1.0	0.5	8.0			Room 2, 0-5 cm, Level 1
1.0		1.0		7.5		2.0	0.5		4.5			Room 2, 5-10 cm, Level 2
	0.5			11.0					6.0			Room 2, 10-15 cm, Level 3
				4.5	2.0	1.5	2.5		7.5			Room 2, 15-20 cm, Level 4
2.0		1.0	0.5	1.5	3.0		1.5	1.5	5.0	0.5		Room 2, 20-25 cm, Level 5
				7.0	4.5	1.0	1.0		6.5	0.5		Room 1, 0-5 cm, Level 1
				5.5	+	0.5	1.0		3.5			Room 1, 5-10 cm, Level 2
2.5				9.0	2.5	2.0			6.5			Room 1, 10-15 cm, Level 3
0.5			1.0	4.0		1.0	2.0		3.5			Room 1, 15-20 cm, Level 4

+ Pollen type observed only in scanning of additional materials after tabulation of the 200-grain standard sum.

* Pollen type occurring in aggregates of 6 or more pollen grains.

Table 7.4. Minor Taxa in Pollen Spectra

Location	Context	Pollen Taxa
SP3	Grid alignment	0.5 *Fraxinus*
SP3, 4	Modern surface	0.5 *Alnus*, 0.5 *Eucalyptus*, 1.5 *Erodium*
SP27	Control, no grids	0.5 Liguliflorae
SP23	Within rock pile	0.5 Liguliflorae
SP25	Within rock pile	0.5 *Celtis*
SP13	Below terrace alignment	0.5 Rosaceae
SP14	Terrace center	0.5 *Alnus*
SP15	Within terrace alignment	0.5 Cylindropuntia, 0.5 *Plantago*
SP31	Hilltop control	0.5 Rhamnaceae
SP21	Within terrace alignment	0.5 *Erodium*
SP20	Below terrace alignment	0.5 *Kallstroemia*
SP7	Within grid alignment	0.5 *Tidestromia*
SP8	Grid center	0.5 *Plantago*
PP3	Above checkdam alignment	0.5 *Kallstroemia*
PP1	Above checkdam alignment	0.5 Liguliflorae
SP34	Control, no terraces	0.5 *Picea*
NW Location 6	Modern surface	3.5 *Erodium*
Big Spring Wash	Modern surface	0.5 *Celtis*, 0.5 *Fraxinus*
Big Spring Wash	Above grid alignment	0.5 *Celtis*
Big Spring Wash	Above grid alignment	0.5 *Gilia*
Field House 1 Room 2	20–25 cm, Level 5	0.5 Acanthaceae
Field House 1 Room 1	0–5 cm, Level 1	0.5 *Alnus*

Table 7.5. Comparison of Weedy Pollen Types in Upper Slope Samples

Location	No. of Samples	Average % Cheno-Am	Average % *Boerhaavia*-type
Modern Surface	2	10.0	4.0
Rock Features	33	11.7	7.2
Controls	9	6.4	1.9

of pollen), an event that occurs only once, near the end of the plant's life cycle. Carbohydrates stored in the plant are depleted by the flowering process, and it thereafter has no value as an edible resource.

Groups known to gather agave often monitor, select, and even manipulate wild plants to insure timely retrieval before the stalk emergence (Castetter and others 1938). Because agave cultivation involves a greater investment of effort than gathering, it is unlikely that prehistoric farmers would have failed to harvest their plantings prior to the flowering stage. Even in the event of flowering, insect and bat-pollinated agaves disperse so little pollen that it is virtually never detected in surface samples from vegetation zones containing these plants. No agave pollen was recovered, for example, from a composite surface sample collected beneath a colony of *Agave murpheyi* (Bozarth 1997: 192, 199). In sum, the absence of agave pollen is not a reliable indication of the absence of these potential cultivars at the site.

Pollen assemblages also provided no clear evidence of other native or drought-adapted plants that might have prospered in the enhanced moisture regimes of the rock-bordered grids and related features. The list of probable cultivated, transplanted, or tended plants of this sort has expanded with current research (Bohrer 1991; S. Fish and Nabhan 1991) and includes diverse species such as little barley (*Hordeum pusillum*), a source of edible seeds, and cholla (*Cylindropuntia* spp.), prized for its fleshy buds. Cholla pollen was recovered only once in a field sample, a record that cannot be distinguished from the low natural occurrence that would be expected for this type because of the general presence of this cactus in study area vegetation. Similarly, the grass pollen category, which encompasses the nonseparable pollen of little barley, appeared in most samples, but without exhibiting a quantitative bias that could be linked to heightened local densities near rock features.

Although pollen analysis did not reveal the identity of cultigens, the distributional profiles of samples collected from rock features appear to register the vegetational hallmarks of prehistoric cultivation (Table 7.5). Herbaceous chenopods and amaranths are common species of disturbed habitats. In pollen samples from other Southwestern archaeological sites, this combined pollen category is typically elevated over levels in samples from natural vegetation as a result of soil disturbance and enrichment from organic residues. The average frequency in two present-day surface samples collected on the upper slopes of the site is 10 percent, probably reflecting a degree of current soil disturbance from many years of grazing. The average percent of cheno-am pollen from 33 samples collected in rock features at a depth approximating that of the former field surfaces is only slightly higher at 11.7 percent. This figure contrasts, however, with the average of 6.4 percent in nine control samples collected at similar depths in comparable slope locations without rock grids, terraces, and rock piles.

More agriculturally specific weedy indicators are a set of three pollen types composed of spiderling (*Boerhaavia*-type), globe mallow (*Sphaeralcea*), and Arizona poppy (*Kallstroemia*). These taxa often occur in elevated percentages in the sediments of Hohokam fields, reflecting the disturbed and moisture-enhanced conditions of cultivation (S. Fish 1984, 1985, 1994). Spiderling, the most abundant of these weedy pollen types, averages 4 percent in the present-day surface samples, but only 1.9 percent in the control samples. Samples from rock features average a higher 7.2 percent, in conjunction with the only occurrences of globe mallow and Arizona poppy.

A present-day surface sample and two grid samples came from a suspected prehistoric agricultural field at the edge of the floodplain of Big Spring Wash (Fig. 4.1*b*). The better-watered surroundings and riparian vegetation of this setting are reflected in the pollen assemblages. At 32.5 percent, cheno-am frequencies in the present-day sample are substantially higher than in the upper slope samples. Rock feature samples yielded even higher levels of 47.5 and 70 percent, as well as agricultural weed pollen in the general range of fields on surrounding slopes. Despite the potential for flood-water diversion onto these suspected agricultural plots, no cultigen pollen was encountered.

We also examined samples from both rooms of a two-room field house excavated on the upper slope (see Chapter 8). A stratigraphic series was collected in each case because floor levels could not be clearly defined. Elevated cheno-am pollen occurred in all room fill samples below uppermost postoccupational deposits in each room. No cultigen pollen was present to indicate field crops stored in the structure. Although field house inhabitants probably consumed maize or other cultigens during seasonal occupations, these resources may have been transported to the structures in more portable processed forms that dispersed little pollen.

ROASTING PITS

Roasting pits have been reported in association with rock-bordered grids elsewhere in the Safford Valley (Doak and others 1997) and more widely with rock pile fields and other upland prehistorical agricultural complexes in southern Arizona (Dart 1983; Debowski and others 1976; Doelle 1975; Doelle and others 1985; S. Fish and others 1985; S. Fish and others 1992; Masse 1979). These pits figure prominently in the interpretation of crops and the organization of production.

Reconnaissance

Extensive reconnoitering within the direct confines of rock features at the site failed to reveal roasting pits. In the Hohokam area, roasting pits are commonly positioned in the channels of ephemeral washes that are interspersed among rock pile fields on dry basin slopes (S. Fish and others 1992), probably because of conveniently soft alluvial soils for pit excavation and the greater immediacy of riparian fuel resources. Accordingly, during a two-day reconnaissance to locate roasting pits associated with adjoining drainages, we covered approximately 25 hectares along Peck Wash, Big Spring Wash, and an unnamed wash to the east. The large floodplains of these washes contain numerous trees and large riparian shrubs. We identified eight roasting pits or roasting areas in Big Spring and the unnamed wash and two additional roasting pits adjacent to the site along a relatively shallow tributary to the larger and more deeply incised Big Spring Wash. Although close to the rock-bordered grids, this tributary did not support species offering substantial woody fuel.

The three best-preserved roasting pits included two along Big Spring Wash and one on its smaller tributary (Fig. 4.1*b*). They consisted of fire-cracked basalt cobbles in low mounds, approximately 25 cm high and 3 m to 4 m in diameter; a central depression measuring 1.50 m to 2.25 m in diameter was filled with fire-cracked rock in a fine-grained soil matrix. Dark, ashy soil and dispersed fire-cracked rock extended several meters in all directions from each of these mounds. The other seven roasting locations were highly disturbed by erosion and consisted of ashy soil and abundant but dispersed fire-cracked basalt cobbles, extending across areas up to 25 m in diameter.

No roasting pits were located in Peck Wash, the largest of the three drainages, probably due to the extensive disturbance of the floodplain by occasional sustained and heavy flows. Dense vegetation also ob-

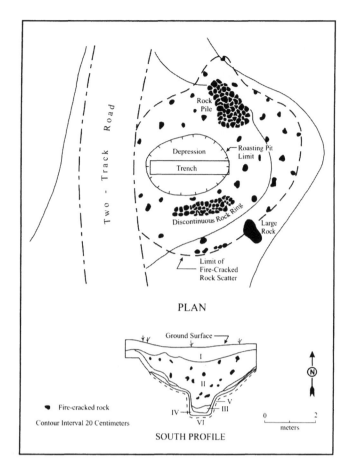

Figure 7.6. Plan and excavation profile of Roasting Pit 1.

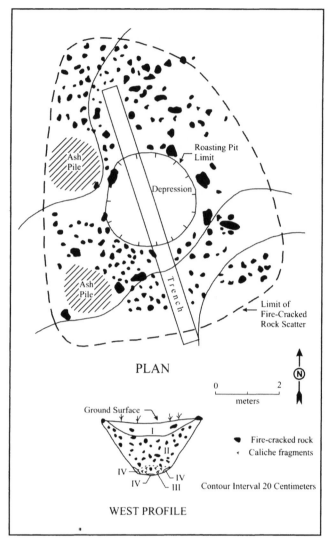

Figure 7.7. Plan and excavation profile of Roasting Pit 2.

scured visibility on many portions of its less disturbed floodplain. Even with better surface visibility along Big Spring and the unnamed wash, identified features undoubtedly represent only a fraction of prehistoric roasting pits. The repetitive occurrence of scattered fire-cracked rocks along these washes probably reflects buried pits or ones obliterated by flooding and erosion.

Excavations

For excavation we selected two of the well-preserved pits on Big Spring Wash (Roasting Pits 1 and 2) and a well-preserved pit (Roasting Pit 3) and a diffuse scatter (Roasting Pit 4) along its tributary. We made surface collections before excavation and drew plan views of the three pits (Figs. 7.6, 7.7, 7.8). Trenches 0.5 m wide were excavated across the widest axis of each intact feature. We screened the contents of the trenches through quarter-inch mesh and recorded artifacts as to depth below datum. Artifacts were limited to

several sherds and flakes in each case. Flotation samples were collected from varying locations in the bottom one-third of each pit fill. Two trenches across the diffuse scatter revealed significant erosional disturbance and the widely scattered contents of a roasting pit that probably had been similar to the others.

Plant Remains

Preliminary identifications of plant remains were based on flotation samples totaling 15 to 23 liters of soil from each of the three excavated roasting pits. Monocot tissue morphologically compatible with agave, but not conclusively definitive, was present in each roasting pit. Fragmentary leaf bases in Roasting

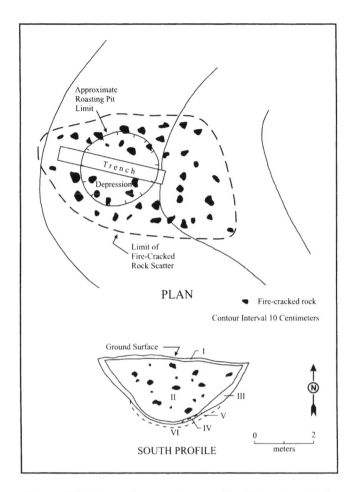

Figure 7.8. Plan and excavation profile of Roasting Pit 3.

Table 7.6. Quantity of Charred Plant Remains from Roasting Pits at Site AZ CC:1:2 (ASM)

Plant Remains	Roasting Pit 1	Roasting Pit 2	Roasting Pit 3
Liters of Soil	15	23	20
Unknown (Seed)		3	1
Trianthema (Seed)	5		
Portulaca (Seed)		1	
Cheno-am (Seed)		1	1
Boerhaavia (Seed)	1		
Gramineae (Seed)		2	
Zea Kernel?		1	
Zea Cupule?		1	
Monocot cf. *Agave* (Leaf Base)	1		1
Monocot cf. *Agave* (Tissue)	X	X	X
Chenopodiaceas cf. *Atriplex* (Wood)	X	X	X
Populus/Salix (Wood)	X	X	X
Prosopis (Wood)	X	X	X

X, presence

Pits 1 and 3 were more structurally distinctive in suggesting this resource. Occasional seeds of a chenopod or amaranth (cheno-am), horse purslane (*Trianthema*), purslane (*Portulaca*), spiderling (*Boerhaavia*), and grass (*Gramineae*) represent species with possible resource uses, but just as likely reflect the unintentional inclusion of seeds of the nonwoody floodplain vegetation. Identifications of a possible maize (*Zea*) kernel and cupule in Roasting Pit 2 are uncertain in view of the highly fragmentary nature of the remains (Table 7.6).

Roasting pit fuel is dominated by species available on the floodplains of the main washes. Mesquite (*Prosopis*) is present in all three facilities and is ubiquitous on the floodplains today. Roasting Pit 3 contained most of the combined *Populus-Salix* (cottonwood or willow) category of riparian species identified; these charcoal types are also present in lesser quantities in the other two pits. The location of Roasting Pit 3, on a smaller

tributary next to rock-bordered grids on the upper slopes, apparently denotes a decision for placement near these features. The placement of Roasting Pits 1 and 2, near the source of fuel on the main wash floodplain, apparently represents a somewhat different choice of location. In neither case, however, would it have been necessary to transport harvested plants or wood more than a few hundred meters.

Dating

Radiocarbon dates were obtained on charcoal from all three excavated roasting pits. Charcoal selected for dating from Roasting Pits 1 and 2 consisted of small mesquite branches thought to closely approximate the actual age of pit use. Charred monocot tissue was dated from Roasting Pit 3. In each case, the sample came from near the pit floor. The dates for Roasting Pits 1 and 2 are unexpectedly early, with calibrated midpoints at A.D. 490 and 500 respectively. The corrected and calibrated midpoint date for Roasting Pit 3 is A.D. 1370 (Table 7.7).

The early radiocarbon dates and a second line of chronological evidence from Roasting Pits 1 and 2 are contradictory. Roasting Pits 1 and 2 are similar in form and separated by approximately 100 m. Both pits contain late corrugated ceramics (about A.D. 1150 to 1450) from deep within their interiors. A single corrugated sherd came from 130 cm below present ground surface in the fill of Roasting Pit 1. Another corrugated sherd was on the surface of Roasting Pit 2

Table 7.7. Radiocarbon Dates of Roasting Pits

Sample No.	Roasting Pit No.	Radio-carbon Years B.P.	Corrected Date B.P.	Dated Material
TX–9215	1	1270 ± 60	1460 ± 60	Small mesquite branches, twigs
TX–9216	2	1240 ± 40	1450 ± 40	Small mesquite branches, twigs
TX–9217	3	390 ± 40	580 ± 40	Monocot (Agave) tissue

Table 7.8. Comparison of Artifact Collections from the Marana Community and Rock-bordered Grids

Collections	Marana Fields	Rock-bordered Grids
Total square meters collected	52,500	15,000
No. of 50-m collection units	21	6
Total number of artifacts	371	567
No. of artifacts per square meter	1/140	1/26.5
No. of tools per square meter	1/276	1/441
No. of formal tools	190	34
No. of unretouched cores	3	74
No. of nonutilized flakes	158	459

and two additional corrugated sherds came from the fill 120 cm below the surface. A similar corrugated sherd was in the fill of Roasting Pit 3, which produced a much later radiocarbon date in line with the age of the pottery. Although no explanation can be offered for the discrepancies between early radiocarbon dates and later ceramics in Roasting Pits 1 and 2, these determinations should be treated with caution.

ARTIFACT COLLECTIONS

Systematic artifact collections were undertaken to seek distinctive assemblages related to crop cultivation, harvesting, and processing. Because stone tools and other artifacts were sparse and widely dispersed across the fields, large areas were comprehensively collected. We recovered all artifacts from six 50-m–square collection units distributed among field sectors containing rock-bordered grids, rock piles, terraces, and other features (Figs. 4.1*a*, *b*) Although analysis of stone tools and debitage are discussed here, light scatters of sherds came from every field collection unit (Chapters 8, 10). Stone artifact densities ranged between one per 17 square meters to one per 60 square meters in the six sample units. One ground stone object (a pestle) and 566 flaked stone artifacts are in the inventory.

Comparison of this lithic artifact assemblage with collections from other complexes of prehistoric agricultural features provides an important line of evidence for crop production at this site. Direct quantitative comparison (Table 7.8) is possible with the Hohokam Marana rock pile fields in the Tucson Basin, where we used comparable field and analytical methods and documented an association with agave cultivation and processing (S. Fish and others 1985; S. Fish and others 1992). Variability in classification, reporting, and sampling in other studies does not permit similarly direct comparison. However, qualitative comparison with artifacts from additional fields with rock-bordered grids and rock piles elsewhere in the Safford Valley (Bierer and Ahlstrom 1997) and rock pile fields near Florence, Arizona (Vanderpot 1992), provides a useful perspective on the likelihood of agave as a crop at this site.

The flaked stone assemblage collected from the site clearly meets the definition of an expedient technology (Nelson 1991). A majority of artifacts are the product of on-site quarrying activities using igneous raw materials immediately available among the gravels and cobbles of the Pleistocene river terrace (see Chapter 3). A preponderance of cores and many flakes exhibit few flake scars and considerable cortex; these are likely the product of prehistoric testing for suitable flaking materials. The 74 cores in the collections average only 1.7 negative flake scars and only 36 percent of all flakes are noncortical and have negative scars on their exterior surface. Differential patination on some of the stone artifacts and a biface of preceramic style suggest that cobble testing and quarrying took place throughout a considerable span of time. In terms of artifacts exhibiting such attributes related to expedient use of terrace gravels, the assemblage at this site contrasts with that of the Marana fields, where suitable raw materials for stone tools were entirely lacking.

High proportions of primary flaking debris and single fracture cores, coupled with a relatively low frequency of tools in the overall assemblage, also appear to be typical of prehistoric rock pile and rock-bordered grids on old river terraces elsewhere along the Gila River (Bierer and Ahlstrom 1997: 5.32;

Figure 7.10. Core scrapers or pulping planes from site AZ CC:1:2 (ASM). *Lower right*, 10.2 cm wide (horizontal dimension). (Photograph by Ken Matesich.)

Figure 7.9. Tabular knives from site AZ CC:1:2 (ASM). *Bottom*, 13.2 cm wide (horizontal dimension). (Photograph by Ken Matesich.)

Vanderpot 1992: 61–67), as well as in a wide range of nonfield locations throughout the Southwest where suitable cobble raw materials are readily accessible (Anderson 1992; Dosh 1988; Keller and Wilson 1976). In these instances, abundant debris related to raw material procurement throughout extended periods could mask the character of the remainder of the stone tool assemblages that reflect agricultural field use or other localized activities.

Without a similar history of raw material acquisition, Marana lithic assemblages are tied more directly to agricultural field activities. Despite the differential availability of stone sources, the morphology and high frequencies of distinctive types of formal tools are remarkably similar between the Marana site and this one, and in a more general way parallel the kinds of

formal tools recovered from two other exemplary agricultural locations with rock piles, terraces, and rock-bordered grids on upper river terraces of the Gila River (Bierer and Ahlstrom 1997: 5.25–5.28; Vanderpot 1992: 6). Significant tool categories in all these field contexts include distinctive core tools and tabular knives. Tabular knives (usually recovered as fragments) are flat implements with chipped and ground edges made of specialized raw materials with a tabular fracture (Figs. 7.9, B.1). The frequency of these tools among all tools recovered at this site exceeds levels at Marana. At this site, and in each comparative case, large primary utilized flakes, which could have been used in a manner similar to tabular knives, also occur regularly in the assemblages (Bierer and Ahlstrom 1997: 5.28; Vanderpot 1992: 70; S. Fish and others 1992: 83). Such large primary flakes account for 8 of the 11 retouched or utilized flakes from AZ CC:1:2 (ASM).

Core tools (steep-edged scrapers or pulping planes, Fig. 7.10) are more frequent in the Marana assemblage than that of this site (Table 7.9), but this disparity may be influenced more by technological and classificatory differences than by differences related to function and

Table 7.9. Frequencies of Formal Stone Tools
in Assemblages from Marana Fields
and Rock-bordered Grids

| | Marana Fields | | Rock-bordered Grids | |
	No.	%	No.	%
Tabular knives	32	16.8	12	35.3
Core tools,				
Pulping planes	56	29.5	6	17.7
Hammerstones	8	4.2	1	2.9
Bifaces	5	2.6	3	8.8
Retouched,				
Utilized flakes	70	36.9	11	32.4
Ground stone	19	10.0	1	2.9

activity. Without similarly immediate access to suitable raw materials, the Marana rock pile farmers were more likely to have curated and refurbished their core tools, using them more intensively and retouching them more often, thus making them more recognizable as tools in analysis. Gila River terraces provided ample raw materials, on the other hand, and farmers there who needed core tools could have easily and expediently manufactured them for a one-time only use.

The Marana artifact assemblage is closely related to the harvesting of cultivated agave and secondarily to the in-field extraction of agave fiber (S. Fish and others 1985; S. Fish and others 1992: 83–84). Tabular knives (Castetter and others 1938) and core tools or pulping planes (Hester and Heizer 1972: 109–111; Kowta 1969: 62–69; Osborne 1965: 47–49; Rogers 1939: 51–53; Salls 1985) similar to those from the Marana fields and this site have been archaeologically and ethnographically associated with agave harvesting and processing. Both tabular knives and large primary flakes with coarse, sinuous edges from field locations are cutting tools; these sorts of knives are distinct from other tabular stone implements, also called knives, that have smooth and polished edges for scraping agave and yucca leaves to remove pulp and expose fibers (Appendix B).

Convergences between stone tool emphases at Marana and this site point to agave cultivation in both instances. In each case, tabular knives and pulping planes account for approximately one-half of all stone tools (46.2 percent for Marana and 52.8 percent for this site). Furthermore, comparable densities of these tools in fields (Table 7.8, Chapter 8) suggest a similar intensity of agave cultivation.

MAGNITUDE OF PRODUCTION

The combined evidence of nearby roasting pits suitable for cooking, agavelike tissue recovered from them, and a distinctive, agave-related tool assemblage in the fields indicate that agave was grown at the site among the rock alignments forming the terraces and the borders of the grids and in rock piles. This finding is supported by the failure of pollen and flotation analysis to identify other likely crop candidates and critical evidence indicating that the soils of the site are not especially suited for other crops requiring greater moisture. The recognition of agave as a primary crop is only a first step, however, in understanding the potential productivity and economic significance of this kind of field. The alignments composing grids and terraces are the key to assessing such parameters, and perceived productivity must have been the incentive for constructing such an extensive network of rock alignments at this site.

In conjunction with the probable spacing of plants, the 89,089 m cumulative length of alignments provides a basis for estimating production. This methodology assumes that agaves were preferentially planted along the alignments to receive the associated benefit of enhanced moisture. Estimates based on the alignments are conservative with regard to overall yield because additional plants undoubtedly were placed in rock piles, although rock piles are a relatively minor component among all field features.

Information on optimal spacing of plants from both ethnographic and experimental sources is in general agreement. Parsons and Parsons (1990: 22) cite a spacing of 2.5 m to 5.0 m for large species grown by traditional farmers to avoid interplant shading and to provide for maximal growth of large species in an arid region of the Mexican highlands. Agaves planted commercially in rows for the mescal-tequila industry are separated by an average of 2 m (Tello-Balderas and Garcia-Moya 1985: 82; Valenzuela-Zapata 1985: 67). These figures pertain to plantings of *Agave salmiana* (baked hearts averaging 65.8 kg; Tello-Balderas and Garcia-Moya 1985: 85) and similar species that are more than ten times larger than *Agave murpheyi* (baked hearts approximately 4 kg; S. Fish and others 1992: 85), which is usually considered the foremost Hohokam cultivar. In experimental plantings of multiple species (*Agave americana, A. desertii, A. murpheyi, A.*

Table 7.10. Comparison of Production Estimates for Site AZ CC:1:2 (ASM) and the Marana Fields

	AZ CC:1:2 (ASM)	Marana Fields
Total Area	82 hectares	485 hectares
Total Plantings	44,545 agaves	102,000 agaves
Plantings per Hectare	543 agaves	210 agaves
Total Annual Yield	4,455 agaves	10,200 agaves
Annual Yield per Hectare	54 agaves	21 agaves
Annual Food Harvest	17.8 metric tons	40.8 metric tons
Annual Fiber Harvest	1.63 metric tons	3.75 metric tons

parryi, A. sisalana, A. vilmoriniana, A. weberi), Nobel and McDaniel (1988: 148) also used spacings between 2 m and 4 m, depending on the size of the species. Experience with current experimental plantings in prehistoric alignments and rock piles near Tucson supports the closest spacings within cited ranges for the relatively small *Agave murpheyi* (S. Fish and others 1992: 85).

With a spacing of 2 m, 44,545 agaves could have been growing along the 89,089 meters of grid and terrace alignments at the site. Annual harvests would have been limited to those plants reaching maturity in a given year. Assuming that plantings reflected an even distribution of sequential plant ages to ensure equivalent yields in succeeding years, an average maturation rate of ten years would result in 4,455 harvestable plants per year. The more conservative 5 m spacing would produce a lower figure, or 1,782 harvestable agaves. If agaves in rock piles were added to either of these estimates, the total harvest would be larger. If an adjustment were made for fewer plants grown along apparently drier uphill alignments, the total harvest would be less. Additionally, Tucson experiments suggest the eventual harvest of clones or offsets that regularly emerge and grow alongside a mother plant as it matures could increase overall harvests by one to several magnitudes (S. Fish and others 1992: 85).

Using the 2 m spacing and 4,455 harvestable plants as reasonable proxies for prehistoric yield, it is possible to evaluate annual productivity and economic significance. At approximately 4 kg of edible baked heart and 365 g of fiber per plant (S. Fish and others 1992: 86), the site would produce 17.8 metric tons of food and 1.63 metric tons of raw material for fiber crafts per year. If agave provided 20 percent of the dietary caloric intake, a maximum contribution accord-

ing to ethnographic studies, the needs of 338 people would have been met (FAO/WHO 1973; Ross 1944). At a more likely 10 percent caloric intake, 676 people would have been supplied. This contribution might have been particularly critical in years when other crops failed. Agave fiber supplied extensive cordage, net, basketry, and textile crafts, with surplus raw materials and manufactured products representing highly portable items for exchange.

How does the estimated productivity of the 82 hectares of fields at AZ CC:1:2 (ASM) compare with that of the 485 hectares of fields at Marana near Tucson, another well-studied agricultural complex devoted to Hohokam agave cultivation (Table 7.10)? The more extensive Marana rock-pile fields produced an estimated 10,200 harvestable plants per year, for a yield of 21 plants per hectare. Site AZ CC:1:2 (ASM) produced an estimated 4,455 harvestable plants per year, but for a notably higher per hectare yield of 54 plants. The yield of food and fiber per unit of cultivated land would have been correspondingly higher at this site as well. These fields appear to represent a more intensive form of dry-slope farming, as measured both by investment in stone constructions and related magnitudes of yields.

FINDINGS AND MEANINGS

The combined evidence from AZ CC:1:2 (ASM) presents a strong case for large-scale agave cultivation. Soil analyses (Chapter 6) indicate that cultivation of annual crops such as maize would have been marginal, at best, within the interiors of the rock-bordered grids. However, a study of creosote bush densities on the site demonstrates that the rock features, grid borders, terrace alignments, and rock piles continue to provide a greatly enhanced microenvironment for the growth of desert perennials (Fig. 7.5).

Analysis of large numbers of pollen samples from across site AZ CC:1:2 (ASM), including one field house, yielded no evidence of maize or other crops. Roasting pit facilities similar to those used to process agave elsewhere were located adjacent to the rock features, in adjoining drainages. Flotation studies of each of three archaeologically excavated roasting pits revealed agavelike fibrous tissue and radiocarbon dates of a pre-European time. An associated distinctive set of stone tools fits Southwestern ethnographic and archaeological correlates of agave harvesting and processing. Finally, no fewer than 44,500 agave plants are estimated to have been growing on this site at any one time.

Although there is now no way of determining conclusively the actual ages of the rock-bordered grids and related features, radiocarbon dates from the roasting pits and artifacts on the surface indicate that the site is of prehistoric age, thereby supporting Proposition 1 as outlined in Chapter 1. Furthermore, the features were clearly of an agricultural nature, and agave, a specialized crop, was grown among the rocks constituting the grid borders, terraces, and rock piles. This finding supports acceptance of Proposition 3b and provides yet additional merit for acceptance of Proposition 4f (Chapter 1).

This site is among a growing number of instances that document the importance of agave for food and fiber across the southern Southwest and northwest Mexico (S. Fish and Fish 2004). The typical locations of large agricultural complexes related to agave cultivation are on dry basin slopes where this drought-adapted plant could make cumulative use of the seasonally bimodal rainfall of the region. The large-scale planting of agave significantly contributed to subsistence by providing an alternative food crop requiring minor maintenance and insuring a low-level productive stability on previously unproductive land, even in times of reduced precipitation. In addition, fibers from leaves supported craft manufacture and furnished raw materials and finished products for trade. Such land-extensive production can be viewed as an arid land version of intensification, adding substantially to the availability and reliability of resources in prehistoric subsistence systems that encompassed mixed farming strategies (S. Fish and others 1992; S. Fish 1995).

CHAPTER EIGHT

Archaeological Perspective

James A. Neely

The 1994 visit to site AZ CC:1:2 (ASM) discussed in Chapter 1 disclosed tantalizing clues, in the form of ceramic sherds, lithic tools and debitage, and field houses, that indicated an archaeological investigation could provide information as to the chronological placement, use, and perhaps function, of the rock-bordered grids. Thus, in addition to the limited survey of the collection units and the excavation of the roasting pits described in Chapter 7, we conducted a more extensive survey and additional excavations.

The larger survey encompassed the approximately 800,000 square meters (80 hectares) of terrace surface covered with rock-bordered grids (Figs. 1.6, 4.1*a, b*). The sparse vegetation facilitated the recognition of features, and we made observations on the distribution of artifacts, features, and structures. However, the large amounts of naturally occurring stone materials on the ground surface (Figs. 1.9, 7.4), constituents of the piedmont alluvium (Qpa; see Chapter 3), made the recognition of artifacts especially difficult. The small size of most of the ceramic sherds rendered them indistinct among the many small stones. Visibility of the plain and corrugated ceramics, as well as some types of decorated sherds, was impeded because of their brown to reddish brown color, which closely matched the color of the surface soil.

Further restricting the identification of ceramics and lithics was a uniform brown patina that covered many of the small objects on the ground surface. Unfortunately, this patina was similar in color to the ground-surface soils. Most artifacts were returned to their find spots once they had been examined, although a few unique and chronologically sensitive pieces were collected for additional study.

THE ROCK-BORDERED GRIDS

There are two general locations of rock-bordered grid fields: on the high terrace and in the vicinity of Big Spring Wash. Fields atop the high terrace are described and discussed in previous chapters. We turn now to grids appearing in three places in Big Spring Wash, which bisects the high terrace through the approximate center of the grids (Figs. 1.6, 4.1*b*), and in a smaller adjacent wash to the east.

Big Spring Wash and Vicinity

The survey along the lower terraces above the channel of Big Spring Wash, and an adjacent wash to the east, recorded the scattered presence of linear borders and grid field areas constructed of unmodified cobbles and small boulders (Fig. 4.1*b*). The lower terraces probably were inundated occasionally when the arroyo flowed, and some of these rock-bordered features may well have occasionally functioned as "channel-bottom weir terraces" (following Doolittle 1980: 333–335, 1988: 48–49) for agricultural pursuits.

One set of these floodplain rock-bordered grids was just east of the bench-terrace and hill slope containing Pit House Locality 1 and its midden (Figs. 4.1*b*, 8.1). This set of grids was most likely associated with that habitation site. The grids were constructed on the alluvial flat, forming an area approximately 20 m to 40 m wide (east-west) and more than 100 m long (north-south) between the foot of the midden-covered slope and Big Spring Wash (Fig. 8.1). The grids were located on both sides of the mouth of a small, intermit-

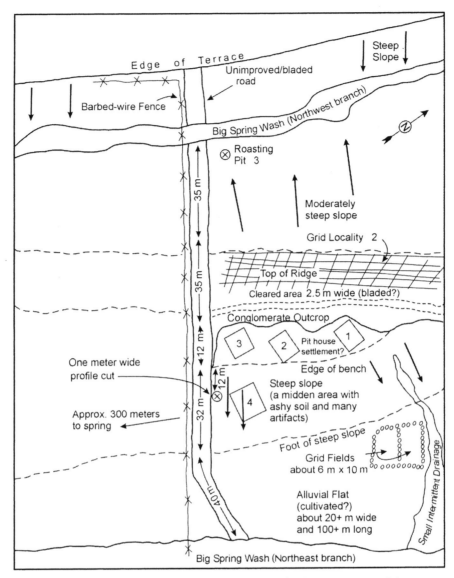

Figure 8.1. Pit House Locality 1 and vicinity (map not to scale).
Numbered squares are 4–m by 4–m survey collection areas.

tent drainage that descends from just east of Locality 2 and empties into Big Spring Wash, some 50 m north of a bladed dirt road and abutting the foot of the slope. The grids averaged about 6 m by 10 m, and at least four were clearly discernable. The placement of these fields apparently was designed to take advantage of runoff waters, as well as alluvial and midden enrichment, from the slope to their west. Heavy flooding in the arroyo to their east may have provided occasional runoff water and alluvial enrichment, but such events may have also brought destruction by washing out the fields or burying the plants.

Boundary Markers Among the Grids and Terraces

Large stones located among the grids and terraces throughout the site are of particular interest. Many of these stones are oblong in shape and were positioned standing on end (Figs. 1.16, 5.9); others are symmetrical and attract attention only because they are larger than the other boulders found on the ground surface. Their distribution is by no means uniform; in some areas they are common, in others only a widely scattered few are evident. Their occurrence and placement in some areas undoubtedly reflect human action. The distribution of these distinctive stones in Grid Locality 1 (Figs. 1.6, 4.1*a*) appears to represent a set of boundary markers defining small segments of the terraced and grid field area.

These stones are generally similar to the elongate stones occurring in rock-bordered grids in the Verde Valley (P. Fish and Fish 1984: 155) and in the open fields associated with the Las Acequias–Los Muertos irrigation system in the eastern portion of the city of Tempe, Arizona (Masse 1987: 76–82, Fig. 5.26). Similar stones were also incorporated in both open and grid fields at the Rocky Point Site (AZ W:10:108 ASM), a short distance to the north in the Point of Pines region (Figs. 1.5, 2.1; Woodbury 1961: 13–14). Sandor and his colleagues (1990) have reported terraced fields in the Mimbres area with these features. Other markers have been previously recorded for the Safford Valley at the Sanchez Copper Project (Fig. 1.5; Doak and others 1997: 4.3). Some of the markers in the Safford grids are like the outer boundary markers reported by Forde (1931) at Hopi and by Cushing (1920: 153) at Zuñi. Others, such as those in our Grid Locality 1 (Fig. 5.9), resemble the Zuñi intraplot markers (Cushing 1920, Plate 2). Some of the stones from AZ CC:1:2 (ASM) are distinguished by the presence of petroglyph markings (Chapter 9). A similar stone with a petroglyph appeared among the fields at the Marana Community, located some 15 km (9.3 miles) north-northwest of Tucson (S. Fish and others 1992: 86).

FEATURES AND STRUCTURES

The surveys of AZ CC:1:2 (ASM) recorded the presence of two types of features and two types of structures. The features are: (1) subterranean roasting pits, evidently used to prepare agave hearts for human consumption, and (2) a large mound of piled cobbles and boulders. The two types of structures identified are: (1) semisubterranean pit houses, and (2) small surface structures.

Roasting Pits Among the Grids

In addition to the roasting pits discussed in Chapter 7, two other roasting pits were atop the terrace forming the southwestern side of Peck Wash. The pits were cut into the surface of a narrow margin of land a few meters north of Shovel Pits 23–24 (Fig. 6.1), between the grids to the west and the steep edge of the terrace forming the southwest side of Peck Wash in Grid Locality 1 (Figs. 1.6, 4.1*a*). If other pits existed here they would have been destroyed, because the face of the mesa has eroded away. These two pits were about 5 m apart, each represented by a single, clearly visible course of small boulders forming a nearly perfect circle about 1.7 m in diameter. The interiors of these circles of stone were shallowly depressed, suggesting that they had been emptied of their contents after a roasting event.

The depressions, and a surrounding area extending 1 m to 3 m out from the circle of stones, were characterized by a fine, dark, ashy soil and many fire-altered rocks. Woodbury (notes on file, Arizona State Museum) may have recognized one of these pits as "a cluster of fire-cracked rocks approximately two meters in diameter." The grid area immediately to the southwest of these pits was included in the "Artifact Collections" section of Chapter 7.

In an apparent variation on the Hohokam theme, the topographic setting of these two pits does not correspond to that of the other pits discovered at AZ CC:1:2 (ASM), nor to the general positioning of roasting pits in the channels of ephemeral washes in the Hohokam area. Within the Safford Valley, the placement of roasting pits includes their occasional occurrence at the edge of relic fields located atop mesas and other more elevated and flat terrain (Neely and Rinker 1997). Verifying this diversity of situating roasting pits, Doak and his colleagues (1997: 4.25) have reported finding roasting pits on and around a nearly level playa at site AZ CC:2:75 (ASM) at the east end of the Safford Valley. As with the roasting pits discussed in Chapter 7, most of these elevated level areas with roasting pits are located near drainages where vegetation for fuel would have been available.

Features commonly referred to as "rock rings" or "circular rock features" have been recorded for the nearby Sanchez Copper Project (Seymour, Ahlstrom, and Doak 1997b) and at other sites in the Southwest (Table 10.1). A "rock ring" was reported for AZ CC:1:2 (ASM) in Locality 1 (Fig. 1.18). Several uses have been attributed to these features and it is likely that some are the remnants of roasting pits.

Rock Mound Feature 1

The survey recorded three features constructed of rock in a general northwest-southeast trending alignment located from about 68 m to 200 m east of the gravel road that runs from the small community of Bryce into Peck Wash and up onto the high terrace (Fig. 4.1*b*). I concur with Gay Kinkade, who, in 1997, tentatively interpreted one of these features as a ceremonial structure. However, the other two features to the southeast most probably were field houses.

The northwest feature appeared roughly rectangular in plan. Its long axis was oriented northeast-southwest, and the feature was about 1.8 m by 2.2 m (3.96 m²). We initially thought it was a field house similar to the other two structures to the southeast. However, subsequent investigation resulted in its redesignation as Rock Mound Feature 1. It consisted of a pile of cobbles and small boulder-size (Wentworth 1922) unmodified rocks that stood to a maximum height of about 45 cm above the ground surface (Fig. 8.2). No wall alignments were visible and no mortar was evident. This feature was different from the rock piles found elsewhere at this site and at other sites in the Safford Valley (Seymour, Ahlstrom, and Doak 1997b). It was larger and less symmetrical than the rock piles identified as agricultural features, and it appeared as a single feature rather than as one of a number of similar closely juxtaposed features. It was composed of somewhat larger rocks than were the two structures located a short distance to the southeast, was slightly mounded in cross-section, and lacked any indications of a central cleared area or depression. A thorough survey of the structure's surface and an area extending 12 m out from the structure's parameter recovered a small collection of lithics (Table 8.1). The one ceramic sherd was diagnostic, a small fragment of a Gila Polychrome bowl (Table 8.2). Based on Crary (1997) and Dean and Ravesloot (1993: 98–101), this sherd dates the use of this feature with a maximum range of about A.D. 1300 to 1450 and a minimum range of about 1340 to 1385 (the Safford phase of the Late Classic period; see Fig. 2.2).

Structures

Of the four clusters of small habitation structures recorded, two were apparently pit house sites and the other two were small stone surface structures that

Figure 8.2. Rock Mound Feature 1, looking northwest. The mound may be a shrine. (Photograph by William E. Doolittle.)

probably had thatch superstructures, commonly referred to as "field houses." We thoroughly surveyed all four of these sites, but excavated only Field House Structure 1.

The term "field house" has various definitions (for example, Ward 1978), but this monograph follows Woodbury's (1961: 14–15) functional interpretation. They were small, one- or two-room surface-masonry structures located on or near fields. They were architectural facilities inhabited temporarily during the planting, growing, tending, harvesting, and processing of crops. Field houses may have been used for storage, and they were sometimes positioned up to several kilometers from a main habitation. They were one component in the local subsistence-settlement system (Streuver 1968; Wilcox 1978; Woodbury 1961).

Field Houses at the South Edge of the Grids

At least two small field houses were located within a few meters of one another, near the south edge of Grid Locality 6, atop the high first terrace just north of the Gila River. These field houses were situated near the edge of the steep south face of the terrace overlooking the Graham-Curtis canal (Figs. 1.6, 4.1*b*). These one-room structures were constructed of dry-laid unmodified cobbles and small boulders that had been piled rather than stacked. The low wall alignments

Table 8.1. Lithics from Pit House Locality 1 and Rock Mound Feature 1 Surface

	Pit House Loc. 1 Surface between collecting areas	Pit House Loc. 1 Collecting Area 1 Surface	Pit House Loc. 1 Collecting Area 2 Surface	Pit House Loc. 1 Collecting Area 3 Surface	Pit House Loc. 1 Collecting Area 4 Surface	Pit House Loc. 1 Midden Profile	Rock Mound Feature 1 Surface
Total M² Collected	184	16	16	16	16	22	676
Total No. of Artifacts	121	183	142	115	272	91	27
No. Artifacts/M²	1:1.52	1:0.09	1:0.11	1:0.14	1:0.06	1:0.24	1:25
No. Formal Tools	31	44	27	34	41	18	4
No. Tools/M²	1:5.94	1:0.36	1:0.59	1:0.47	1:0.39	1:1.22	1:169
Unretouched Cores							
Andesite	1				2		
Basalt	1	2			9	2	
Chert			2	1	4		
Obsidian		1					
Rhyolite	1	2	1	3	3		
Unutilized Flakes							
Andesite	12		2	2	15	3	2
Argilite(?)		3		1			
Basalt	28	32	53	21	138	45	13
Chert	19	59	43	31	35	13	1
Obsidian	3	3	3	4	1	2	
Olivene?					1		
Quartz	10			2	12	2	
Rhyolite	15	37	8	16	11	5	7
Tabular knives: Basalt	1		2		1		
Core tools, Pulping planes							
Andesite	1						
Basalt	1		1	1	1		
Chert	1		1		3		
Rhyolite				1		1	1
Hammerstones							
Andesite	1						
Basalt	2						
Chert							
Rhyolite					1		
Bifaces							
Chert			[c]1				
Obsidian	[a]1						
Retouched, Utilized Flakes							
Andesite	5			1	3	1	
Basalt	4	10	6	5	8	7	2
Chert	1	12	7	16	12	5	1
Obsidian	5	3	2	3	3	2	
Quartz				1	1		
Rhyolite	7	19	3	4	4		
Ground Stone							
Andesite				[b]1		[b]2	
Basalt			[b]1		[d]4		
Pink Granite			[b]3				
Red Granite	[b]1				[b]1		
Totals							
Andesite	(6) 20		2	4	(2) 20	6	2
Argilite?		3		1			
Basalt	(8) 37	(9) 44	(10) 63	(4) 27	(25) 161	(12) 54	(3) 15
Chert	(7) 21	(12) 71	(8) 54	(11) 48	(15) 54	(8) 18	(1) 2
Granite, pink and red	1		3		1		
Obsidian	(4) 9	7	(3) 5	(2) 7	(2) 4	(2) 4	
Olivene?					1		
Quartz	(1) 10			3	(3) 13	2	
Rhyolite	(4) 23	(4) 58	(3) 12	(4) 25	(4) 18	(3) 6	(1) 8
Concretions			3				

NOTE: Preceding numbers in parentheses are items with a striking platform and bulb of percussion.

a, Small preform; b, One-hand mano; c, Small triangular side-notched projectile point; d, 2 one-hand manos, 2 grinding slabs.

Table 8.2. Ceramics from Survey and Excavation at Site AZ CC:1:2 (ASM)

	Pinaleño/Galiuro Red-on-brown	Galiuro Red-on-brown	Cerros/Three-Circle Red-on-white	Encinas Red-on-brown	San Carlos Red-on-brown	Mimbres Style I Black-on-white	Mimbres Style I/II Black-on-white	Sweetwater Red-on-gray	Sacaton Red-on-buff	Sacaton Red-on-buff (Safford Var.)	Reserve Black-on-white	Tularosa Black-on-white	Snowflake Black-on-white	Maverick Mountain Black-on-red	Gila Polychrome
Survey															
Grid															
Locality 1					X							X			
Locality 2*	X		X	X		X				X				X	
Locality 3		X								X					
Locality 4					X										
Locality 5															
Locality 6					X							X	X	X	
Locality 7															
Locality 8															
Locality 9*				X			X						X		
Locality 10															
Big Spring Wash															
Terrace					1j										
Rock Pile															
NNE of SP 29															
SE of SP 23–24															
SSW of SP 23–24															
Survey and Excavation															
Roasting Pit 1															
Roasting Pit 2															
Surface															
Level 2															
Roasting Pit 3*															
Roasting Pit 4															
Surface															
E. Trench															
Pit House Locality 1															
Terrace Surface	1b			1b											
Collection Area 1	4b/2j	1j		1b			1j	2b	2j	2b					
Collection Area 2**	4b	4b		1b			1b		1b						
Collection Area 3*	2b/1j	2b		3b						1b/2j					
Midden Surface															
Collec. Area 4		2b/1j	1b	2b						1b				3b/1j	
Midden Profile*				2b		1b				1j					
Pit House Locality 2															
Surface		1b		6b											
Rock Mound Feature 1															
Surface															1b
Field House Str. 1															
Surface					1b	4j				2j	1j	21j		1j	
Room 1, Level 1															
Room 1, Level 2	NO CERAMICS IN THIS LEVEL														
Room 1, Level 3															
Room 1, Level 4					2b							1j			
Room 1, Level 5												1j			

NOTE: X, present; b, bowls; j, jars.
* These locations also contained one spindle whorl; ** contained two spindle whorls.

Table 8.2. Ceramics from Survey and Excavation at Site AZ CC:1:2 (ASM), *Continued*

	Reserve Indented Corrugated	Tularosa Indented Corrugated	Safford Indented Corrugated	Safford Obliterated Corrugated	Brown Clapboard Corrugated	Red Clapboard Corrugated	Unknown Neck Corrugated	Brushed Surface Brown Ware	Polished Red Ware	Deep-red Slipped Brown Ware	Upper Gila(?) Red Ware	Gila Plain	Upper Gila Buff Ware	Tan Ware	Brown Ware
Survey															
Grid															
Locality 1			X	X											X
Locality 2*				X		X			X	X					X
Locality 3										X					X
Locality 4			X												X
Locality 5				X											X
Locality 6		X				X									X
Locality 7				X	X										X
Locality 8			X	X											X
Locality 9*	X					X			X		X				X
Locality 10				X	X										X
Big Spring Wash															
Terrace			2j			1j								1b	
Rock Pile															
NNE of SP 29			7j												
SE of SP 23–24			3b												
SSW of SP 23–24		1b	5b												
Survey and Excavation															
Roasting Pit 1		1b													
Roasting Pit 2															
Surface						1b									
Level 2					2b										
Roasting Pit 3*															
Roasting Pit 4															
Surface						1j									2j
E. Trench															3j
Pit House Locality 1															
Terrace Surface															1b
Collection															
Area 1			2b/4j		1b/1j	2j	1j		10b/2j		9b/7j	1j	1j	2j	53b/104j
Collection															
Area 2**			1j						17b/10j	18b/15j		2j	3j		47b/127j
Collection															
Area 3*			1b/5j			1j		1j	9b/6j	13b/3j			2b/3j		38b/56j
Midden Surface															
Collec. Area 4			1b/1j			1j			5b/1j	20b/8j			1j	1j	31b/74j
Midden Profile*									4b/2j	10b/7j				1b	30b/21j
Pit House Locality 2															
Surface									1b						
Rock Mound Feature 1															
Surface															
Field House Str. 1															
Surface	1b										4j			1b	5b/5j
Room 1, Level 1															1b
Room 1, Level 2						NO CERAMICS IN THIS LEVEL									
Room 1, Level 3											1b				1j
Room 1, Level 4														1b	
Room 1, Level 5														1j	1b

NOTE: X, present; b, bowls; j, jars.
* These locations also contained one spindle whorl; ** contained two spindle whorls.

(about 10 cm high) outlined well-defined cleared central areas. The structures measured about 2.0 m by 2.0 m, with the central areas measuring approximately 1.2 m by 1.3 m (about 1.56 m²). A rapid survey of this site disclosed a thin scatter of flaked stone fragments, but no tools and no ceramics on the ground surface. There was a geoglyph with associated petroglyph (Chapter 9) a few meters north of these field houses.

Field Houses Among the Grids

Southeast of Rock Mound Feature 1, the survey discovered what have been interpreted as two field house surface structures constructed of stone.

Structure 2. Along a transect from Rock Mound Feature 1, Structure 2 was in the center of the three features. Located about 34 m to the southeast of Rock Mound Feature 1 and approximately 80 m northwest of Field House Structure 1, Structure 2 was slightly rectangular in plan, with its long axis oriented northeast by southwest, and was about 2.0 m by 2.1 m (4.2 m²). This one-room structure had vaguely distinguishable low, elongated wall alignments formed by haphazardly piled, dry-laid unmodified cobbles and small boulders (Fig. 8.3). These alignments stood to a maximum height of about 35 cm above the present ground surface. The wall alignments surrounded a centrally located cleared area, measuring roughly 1.3 m by 1.4 m (about 1.82 m²). The surface of this central cleared area consisted of a fine, nearly rock-free soil. A thorough survey of the structure's surface and an area extending 12 m out from the structure's parameter revealed no ceramics and produced only a small collection of lithic artifacts (Table 8.3).

Structure 1. The southeast Structure 1 was about 80 m southeast of Structure 2. It was rectangular in plan, about 3.25 m by 5.25 m (17.1 m²), with the long axis oriented northeast-southwest. The wall alignments of this two-room structure were clearly visible on first examination. Walls were dry-laid piles of cobbles and small boulder-size unmodified rocks (Fig. 8.4). The wall alignments were piled in a haphazard fashion like those illustrated by Doyel (1984, Fig. 3) for a similar structure in the New River drainage north of Phoenix. The elongated piles of rock forming the walls stood to a maximum height of about 40 cm above the present

Figure 8.3. Field House Structure 2, looking northeast. The central cleared area is well defined. (Photograph by William E. Doolittle.)

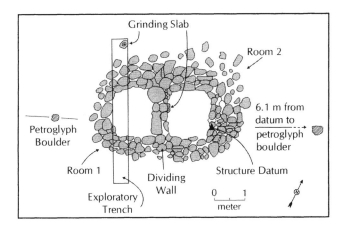

Figure 8.4. Plan of Field House Structure 1.

ground surface, and they outlined two well-defined cleared areas. Before excavation, each of these cleared areas measured approximately 1.2 m by 1.4 m (about 1.68 m²). A thorough survey of the structure's surface and an area extending 12 m out from the structure's parameter produced a relatively large collection of ceramic (Table 8.2) and lithic (Tables 8.3, 8.4) artifacts. Two small boulders contained pecked designs, one 6.1 m to the east (Fig. 9.3) and the other 5.2 m to the west (Fig. 9.4) of the structure's datum. Both examples, each facing away from Structure 1, appeared to be the Gila style of presentation generally attributed to the Hohokam (Chapter 9). The chronological placement of this structure is discussed in Chapter 10.

Table 8.3. Lithics from Field House Structure 1 and Structure 2

	Structure 1 Room 2 Level 1	Structure 1 Room 2 Level 2	Structure 1 Room 2 Level 3	Structure 1 Room 2 Level 4	Structure 1 Room 2 Level 5	Structure 2 Surface
Total M² Collected	[a]2.10	[a]2.10	[a]2.10	[a]2.10	[a]2.10	678.6
Total No. of Artifacts	2	5	5	4	2	24
No. Artifacts/M²	1:1.05	1:0.42	1:0.42	1:0.53	1:1.1	1:28.3
No. Formal Tools				2	1	7
No. Tools/M²				1:1.05	1:2.1	1:96.9
Unretouched Cores						
Andesite						
Basalt						1
Chert						
Obsidian						
Rhyolite						
Unutilized Flakes						[d]3
Andesite						
Argilite(?)						
Basalt			2	1		10
Chert			1		1	
Obsidian						
Olivene?						
Quartz						
Rhyolite	2	5	2	1		3
Tabular knives: Basalt						
Core tools, Pulping planes				[b]1		
Andesite						
Basalt						
Chert						
Rhyolite						1
Hammerstones						
Andesite						
Basalt						
Chert						
Rhyolite						
Bifaces						
Chert						
Obsidian						
Retouched, Utilized Flakes						[d]2
Andesite						
Basalt						1
Chert				1		
Obsidian						
Quartz						
Rhyolite						2
Ground Stone						[e]1
Andesite					[c]1	
Basalt						
Pink Granite						
Red Granite						
Totals						[d](2) 5
Andesite					1	
Argilite?						
Basalt			(1) 2	1		12
Chert			1	1	1	
Granite, pink and red						
Obsidian						
Olivene?						
Quartz				1		1
Rhyolite	2	(2) 5	(1) 2	(1) 1		(1) 6
Concretions						

NOTE: Preceding numbers in parentheses are items with a striking platform and bulb of percussion.

a, 5 cm deep; b, Red quartz; c, Grinding slab; d, Jasper; e, Quartz "phallus"?

Table 8.4. Lithics from Field House Structure 1

	Surface	Room 1 Level 1	Room 1 Level 2	Room 1 Level 3	Room 1 Level 4	Room 1 Level 5	Exploratory Trench
Total M² Collected	790	[b]1.89	[b]1.89	[b]1.89	[b]1.89	[b]1.89	[e]2.63
Total No. of Artifacts	43	2	7	4	6	3	10
No. Artifacts/M²	1:18.4	1:0.95	1:0.27	1:0.47	1:0.32	1:0.63	1:0.26
No. Formal Tools	9		2		2		5
No. Tools/M²	1:87.8		1:95		1:0.95		1:0.53
Unretouched Cores							
Andesite							
Basalt	1						
Chert							
Obsidian							
Rhyolite							
Unutilized Flakes							
Andesite							
Argilite(?)							
Basalt	13	2	2	2	3	2	4
Chert	4		1	1		1	1
Obsidian							
Olivene?							
Quartz				1			
Rhyolite	16		2				
Tabular knives: Basalt	[a]1		1				
Core tools, Pulping planes							
Andesite							
Basalt	1						
Chert							
Rhyolite	2						
Hammerstones							
Andesite							1
Basalt							
Chert							
Rhyolite							
Bifaces							
Chert							
Obsidian							
Retouched, Utilized Flakes							
Andesite							
Basalt			1				2
Chert	3						
Obsidian							
Quartz							
Rhyolite	2						
Ground Stone							[f]1
Andesite					[c]1		[g]1
Basalt					[d]1		
Pink Granite							
Red Granite							
Totals							
Andesite					1		2
Argilite?							
Basalt	(2) 15	2	4	2	(1) 4	2	(2)6
Chert	(1) 7		1	1		1	1
Granite, pink and red							
Obsidian							
Olivene?							
Quartz				1			1
Rhyolite	(7) 21		2				
Concretions					1		

NOTE: Preceding numbers in parentheses are items with a striking platform and bulb of percussion.

a, Rhyolite; b, 5 cm deep; c, Pecking stone; d, Sphere; e, 25 cm deep; f, Quartz "phallus"?; g, Grinding slab.

Pit Houses

Despite the limited amount of archaeology conducted in the Safford Valley, it is evident that, as elsewhere in the American Southwest, there is a long tradition in the construction of semisubterranean "pit house" structures. These domestic pit houses, partially excavated into the earth and with a perishable superstructure, are securely documented in the Safford Valley during the Early Formative and Late Formative periods. A subsequent version known as the "pit room" was constructed well into the Classic period (Crary 1997).

Survey of Pit House Locality 1 with its Associated Midden

Some 620 m northeast of the two-room field house was a pit house settlement, situated about 300 m east-northeast of the spring that has given its name to Big Spring Wash. On top of the ridge remnant located between the northeast and northwest branches of Big Spring Wash (Fig. 8.1, see Fig. 4.1*b*) is an area approximately 35 m wide covered with rock-bordered grids (Grid Locality 2). At the southeast edge of the grids is an outcropping of stone with an 8–m to 15–m wide eastward-facing terrace or "bench" into which the pit houses had been excavated. East of this narrow terrace or bench a midden area with about a 30–degree downward slope, approximately 32 m long, terminated on the terrace of the northeast branch of Big Spring Wash. About 35 m eastward from the toe of the slope is the channel of the wash.

Visible indications that these features were pit houses include: slight depressions on the ground surface; concentrations of artifact materials; concentrations of darker, ashy soils; and slightly more luxurient vegetation. The pit houses appear to have been excavated into the level narrow terrace or bench extending eastward from the east edge of a low outcropping of bedrock, which may well have served as portions of the pit houses' walls (following Neely 1974).

The terrace is about 8 m to 15 m wide (east-west) by 40 m long (north-south) and is about 1.0 m below the top surface of the bedrock outcropping. An estimated three or four pit houses had been excavated into this bench. At the time of the survey, the midden debris to the east of the pit houses appeared to be

heavier to the south, where the bladed dirt road cut through the midden and lighter to the north, which would have indicated that the first pit house was excavated into the southern extreme of the bench. However, a count of the sherds (Table 8.2) and lithics (Table 8.1) showed that the largest quantity of artifacts came from Collecting Area 1 and diminished to the south.

The surface survey of this site consisted of collecting all artifacts, regardless of size, from four collecting areas, each 4 m by 4 m. Collecting Areas 1–3 (Fig. 8.1) are on the bench in locations that appear to have slight depressions and where the artifact scatters were the densest. Collecting Area 4 covered a portion of the midden that had a dense artifact scatter and was relatively clear of vegetation. We also collected diagnostic artifacts from portions of the bench outside of the three 4–m by 4–m collection areas.

A second procedure involved cleaning with shovels and trowels a small area (1.0 m wide by 1.5 m high) of the midden profile provided by the bladed road. Unfortunately, no stratigraphy was discernable, but artifacts were collected from the newly cleaned profile. The artifacts collected from Pit House Locality 1 are considered in Tables 8.1 and 8.2 and in Chapter 10.

Survey of Pit House Locality 2 with its Associated Midden

A second pit house site was discovered about 30 m west-southwest of Big Spring and about 230 m northeast of Field House 1. Grid Locality 9 is located between Pit House Locality 2 and the three aligned surface features to the southwest (Fig. 1.6). As indicated by the artifact scatter, the site extends across the slope and terrace above the channel of Big Spring Wash. We found no indications of structures, but the density and clustering of ceramics and flaked stone fragments were such as to indicate the presence of a midden and at least one pit house, probably more. These artifacts are discussed below and in Chapter 10.

EXCAVATION OF FIELD HOUSE STRUCTURE 1

The small two-room Structure 1 sat atop the high terrace just north of the Gila River, a few meters south of a poorly preserved portion of the rock-bordered grid system (Grid Locality 9; see Figs. 1.6, 4.1*b*). This is the farthest southeast of three rock structures constructed in a general northwest-southeast alignment.

The complete excavation of this structure confirmed that it had two small rooms (Fig. 8.4). Initial clearing and the subsequent trench excavated through the walls verified that the walls were linear piles of unmodified cobbles and small boulders. There was no evidence of mortar or the stacking or coursing of rocks. The limited amount of rocks in and around the structure and the haphazard nature of the wall construction may mean that the upper walls of the structure were constructed of perishable vegetation. The precise function of this structure is not clear, but several factors suggest that it served as a temporary field house: small size; absence of formal floor features such as postholes, hearths, pits, or mixing basins; and the haphazard construction of the walls.

Excavation began with removal of brush from around the structure for a distance of about 12 m in all directions. Vegetation was then removed from the 40-cm-high piles of stone that formed the structure's walls and from within the two cleared areas surrounded by the walls. Care was taken not to disturb the walls or the soil in this process.

For mapping and determining artifact proveniences, we placed a reference datum with an arbitrary elevation of 30 cm in the east corner of the piled wall of Room 2 (Fig. 8.4). We used a line level to measure all vertical levels from this datum. The lowest point of the ground surface within the structure was 60 cm below the datum, in the west corner of Room 1. Thus, the first 5-cm level within that room was 60 cm to 65 cm below the datum. In Room 2, the lowest point of the ground surface within the room was 50 cm below the datum, in the west corner. Thus the first 5-cm level within Room 2 was 50 cm to 55 cm below the datum.

After clearing the vegetation, we carefully removed the loose dirt and stones from the south and east walls in an attempt to better define the size of the rooms and the nature of the stone wall alignments. We quickly determined that construction was of unmodified large cobbles and small boulders that had been dry-laid. This work failed to define more precise wall alignments, so a more drastic and direct approach was taken. We excavated a 50-cm-wide exploratory trench from east to west across Room 1. The trench began a meter east of the eastern edge of the east wall and continued a meter past the western edge of the west wall, and was positioned so as to help define the inner edges of the room's east, south, and west walls. The fill of the trench consisted of a medium brown, loamy soil containing scant cultural debris. The trench was excavated to a depth of 25 cm below the ground surface appearing to the east, within, and to the west of the structure. Between 20 cm and 23 cm below the ground surface we encountered a culturally sterile petrocalcic layer characterized by a hard, white-to-buff colored stratum, with a blocky-fracture, containing pebbles and small cobbles; it probably represented one of the facies of the piedmont alluvium (Qpa, see Chapter 3).

The trench verified the fact that the walls of this structure were not stacked alignments, but haphazardly piled lines of dry-laid rock. Field houses in other regions of Arizona (P. Fish and Fish 1984: 155) exhibit similar construction. The interior edges of the room's east, south, and west walls were irregular, but distinguishable. No floor surface was evident. A small grinding slab was partially buried at the northeast corner of the exploratory trench (Fig. 8.4).

We then shifted focus to the interior of Room 1. Rocks lying on the ground surface were removed and we took a pollen sample at ground surface near the center of the room. We excavated the interior to a level that was 5 cm below the lowest point within the room. Rocks imbedded in the leveled surface were left in situ, to be removed in the 5-cm level in which they lay. We recovered pollen samples from a freshly scraped area in the approximate center of the room as each new 5-cm level was started (Chapter 7). Materials removed during excavation of five 5-cm thick levels were sieved through ¼-inch hardware cloth. A sterile petrocalcic layer was encountered from 1 cm to 3 cm below the bottom of the fourth level. The upper surface of this petrocalcic deposit apparently formed the floor of the field house when it was in use. We found no floor features. After excavation, the better-defined floor dimensions of this room measured about 1.40 m by 1.50 m (2.10 m^2), with the long axis northwest-southeast. Small numbers of both ceramic sherds (Table 8.2) and lithic artifacts (Table 8.4) came from this room.

Using the same techniques, we excavated five 5-cm thick levels in Room 2 of the structure. The sterile petrocalcic layer was encountered at a depth ranging from 73 cm to 75 cm below the datum. The upper surface of this petrocalcic deposit apparently formed the floor of the field house when it was in use. No floor features were evident. After excavation, the floor dimensions of this room measured about 1.40 m by 1.50 m (about 2.10 m²), with the long axis northwest-southeast. We recovered only a few lithic artifacts from this room (Table 8.3) but no ceramics. Based on the absence of ceramics, Field House Structure 2 and Room 2 of Field House Structure 1 may have served as storage locations rather than as habitations.

THE ARTIFACTS

For an agricultural site, AZ CC:1:2 (ASM) contained a large number of artifacts. Many of them came from the survey of one of the two clearly distinguishable pit house habitation areas located among the grids. These materials provide information on the earlier use of this landscape. Although other survey data play a role, the survey and excavation of a single two-room field house provide most of the artifactual materials to complete the picture for the later use of the grids.

Ceramics

Diagnostic pottery in the ten grid localities and the habitation sites located among the rock-bordered grids at AZ CC:1:2 (ASM) has facilitated the chronological placement of the agricultural features (Table 8.2). Although precise dating of the grids cannot be determined, much better chronological control is available for this site than for other similar sites. The chronological history of the various segments of the site is considered in Chapter 10.

Ceramics may have played an important, but as yet undetermined, role in agave production or processing at some sites. There are small sites with large quantities of associated ceramics (Van Buren and others 1992) and large sites with very few associated ceramics (Seymour, Ahlstrom, and Doak 1997b). Site AZ CC:1:2 (ASM) appears to fit somewhere between these extremes. In the Safford area, site AZ CC:1:2 (ASM) had a great deal more pottery (Table 8.2) than the agave production and processing sites investigated by the Sanchez Copper Project (Seymour 1997: 6.4, Table 6.1) at the east end of the Safford Valley (Fig. 1.5).

Ahlstrom and his colleagues (1997: 1.4) note that the area of the Sanchez Copper Project was 3,512 acres (1,422 hectares). However, Seymour (1997: 6.4) reports that only 19 sherds were recorded from that study area, providing a ratio of about one sherd for every 184.8 acres (74.8 hectares). Although a count of all the sherds found in the ten grid localities was not made, the sherds recorded from the proveniences listed in Table 8.2 provide a ratio of about one sherd for every 0.086 hectares (0.21 acres), a strong contrast to the Sanchez Copper Project figures. Undoubtedly the difference in the ratios may be explained at least partially by the presence of habitations at AZ CC:1:2 (ASM), some of which apparently represent long-lived occupations.

Another characteristic of the AZ CC:1:2 (ASM) sherd collection is the diversity of types represented, which is much greater than that at other similar agave field sites. Most of this variation occurs within the vicinity of the habitation sites, where ceramics include more than 90 percent of the decorated diagnostic types. Conversely, more than 90 percent of the sherds among the grids are plain and corrugated wares.

In Table 8.2, jar sherds (551) outnumber bowl sherds (402) by a ratio of nearly 5.5:4. When only habitation localities (both pit house and surface structure) are considered, jar sherds (533) again outnumber bowl sherds (387) by about the same ratio. Pit house localities have a predominance of jar sherds (491) over bowl sherds (373), giving a somewhat smaller ratio of more jars to bowls. Surface structures show an even greater dominance of jar sherds (42) over bowl sherds (14), a ratio of nearly 4:1. However, if only the small collection (10 sherds) from the excavation of Field House Structure 1 is considered, the trend is reversed with bowl sherds (6) outnumbering jar sherds (4). In the grid localities, jar sherds are estimated as outnumbering bowl sherds by about three to one.

Seven shaped and perforated ceramic artifacts made from bowl sherds appear to be spindle whorls: one brown ware (ground surface near Roasting Pit 3, 50 m west of Pit House Locality 1); one Mimbres Style I/II Black-on-white bowl and one Pinaleño-Galiuro Red-on-brown bowl (Pit House Locality 1, Collection Area 2); one deep-red slipped brown ware bowl (Pit House Locality 1, Collection Area 3); one Encinas Red-on-brown (Pit House Locality 1, Midden); one Galiuro Red-on-brown bowl (Grid Locality 2, a few meters northwest of Pit House Locality 1); and one deep-red slipped brown ware (Grid Locality 9, a few meters southwest of Pit House Locality 2). These artifacts are important relative to the function of the rock-bordered grids and the activities conducted at Pit House Localities 1 and 2. Their discovery adds yet another line of evidence suggesting that the grids were used for growing agave, and that at least some of the agave was being processed for its fiber. Paul Fish reported to me in 2002 that house floor assemblages at the Marana Community (S. Fish and others 1992) located a short distance north of Tucson contained agave tool kits. These tool kits consisted of two types of tabular knives and stone or ceramic spindle whorls.

One of the first observations we noted of the sherds from AZ CC:1:2 (ASM), considering both survey and excavation collections, was their small size. With the exception of the surface sherds recorded for the grid localities on Table 8.2, we measured more than 900 sherds from excavation and survey. The average maximum dimension for all sherds was approximately 3.2 cm, and the range of maximum dimensions was 1.0 cm to 7.1 cm. The surface collection of 149 sherds from Pit House Locality 1, Collection Area 3, had the smallest average maximum dimension at 1.9 cm, and the smallest range of maximum dimensions at 1.1 cm to 2.9 cm. Although no measurements were taken on sherds from the grid localities, it was apparent that the average size of sherds away from habitation areas was larger.

In several instances (like Field House Structure 1 and the rock pile proveniences), the survey recovered sherds that joined together to form portions of a single vessel. These instances must reflect the remnants of an in situ pot break or, perhaps more likely, the use of large sherds in the cultivation and processing of agave (Van Buren and others 1992).

One of the most interesting and important discoveries relating to the ceramic collection was the recovery of several sherds indicating early occupation of the two pit house localities, and, therefore, perhaps early use of the area for agave production and processing. Site AZ CC:1:2 (ASM) is certainly one of the earliest sites yet recorded that evidently focused on the production and processing of agave. However, the early occupation of the pit house localities does not necessarily indicate a contemporaneous early construction of the rock-bordered grids.

Table 8.5. Dating of Ceramic Types
(Based primarily on Crary 1997)

Ceramic Type	Range of manufacture (A.D.)	Most abundant manufacture (A.D.)
1. Pinaleño Red-on-brown	700–900	750–850
2. Galiuro Red-on-brown	800–1050	850–1000
3. Cerros/Three-Circle Red-on-white	700–900	750–850
4. Encinas Red-on-brown	950–1150	1000–1125
5. San Carlos Red-on-brown	1150–1400	1175–1300
6. Mimbres Boldface/Style I Black-on-white	800–1050	850–1000
7. Mimbres Style II Black-on-white	950–1100	1000–1075
8. Sweetwater Red-on-gray	600–700	
9. Santa Cruz Red-on-buff	800–1000	875–1000
10. Sacaton Red-on-buff	950–1125	1000–1100
11. Reserve Black-on-white	1000–1300	1050–1150
12. Tularosa Black-on-white	1050–1300	1150–1275
13. Snowflake Black-on-white	1150–1300	1160–1275
14. Maverick Mountain Black-on-red	1050–1350	1275–1325
15. Gila Polychrome	1300–1450	1340–1385*
16. Reserve Indented Corrugated	1025–1275	1100–1200
17. Tularosa Indented Corrugated	1150–1400	1200–1275
18. Safford Indented Corrugated	1150–1400	1200–1350
19. Safford Obliterated Corrugated	1250–1425	1275–1350

*Dean and Ravesloot 1993.
NOTE: The order of presentation of ceramic types corresponds with that used in Table 8.2. The chronological boundaries for the diagnostic types are presented in this table only if the date ranges are known and relatively secure.

Table 8.2 illustrates the distribution of the early ceramics at Pit House Localities 1 and 2. Pit House Locality 1, with an abundance of the broad-line Galiuro Red-on-brown type (Sayles 1945: 42, Plate 22), appears to be earlier than Pit House Locality 2 (Table 8.5). When the small size of some sherds made it impossible to distinguish between Galiuro and the earlier Pinaleño type (Sayles 1945: 42, Plate 21), sherds were lumped together and labeled as Pinaleño/

Galiuro Red-on-brown. These red-on-brown types are similar in decoration to but somewhat later in date than Nantack Red-on-brown reported for the site of Stove Canyon in the Point of Pines region (Figs. 1.5, 2.1; Neely 1974). A single sherd of either Cerros Red-on-white (Sayles 1945: 42, Plate 23) or Three-Circle Red-on-white (Haury 1936a, 1936b), two types that are roughly contemporaneous with the broad-line red-on-browns, could not be specifically identified and was labeled Cerros/Three-Circle Red-on-white. Contemporaneous with, or perhaps slightly later than, the preceding types are sherds identified as Mimbres Black-on-white Style I. Two sherds are listed as Mimbres Black-on-white Style I/II because of their small size and their nondistinctive painted design. The preceding types suggest a founding date perhaps as early as A.D. 750–800 for Pit House Locality 1.

Two small and weathered sherds tentatively identified as Sweetwater Red-on-gray (Gladwin and others 1937: 192–198; Haury 1976: 217–219) may point to an even earlier founding date for the site. Assuming the Sweetwater Red-on-gray identification to be correct, these sherds would support the early radiocarbon dates reported by S. Fish and her colleagues (Chapter 7) for Roasting Pits 1 and 2. The problem of the single late corrugated sherd recovered from within each of these pits during their excavation remains unresolved, although they may represent a later reuse of the pits.

Curiously there was little diagnostic ceramic evidence for the use of the grids during the late Classic period. The few sherds tentatively identified as Maverick Mountain Black-on-red and the single sherd of Gila Polychrome from Rock Mound Feature 1 are the only well-dated late diagnostic sherds recorded. These sherds suggest that Rock Mound Feature 1, and some of the grids, may date as late as about A.D. 1385. Once their chronological placements are more refined and secure, we hope that sherds of late corrugated types will eventually better constrain the later use of AZ CC:1:2 (ASM).

Three diagnostic sherds were identified from among the five recovered from the ground surface of a field located on a floodplain terrace of Big Spring Wash (Table 8.2). Two of these sherds were from jars and appear to be a late, partially obliterated, plain or clapboard corrugated (Crary's 1997 "Safford Obliterated Corrugated," a locally made pottery that is tentatively dated from about A.D. 1250 to 1425, with a

probable date range of 1275–1350 for greatest manufacture). The third sherd has all the basic characteristics of a San Carlos Red-on-brown jar, with the exception of the color of the red painted design. If this sherd is San Carlos Red-on-brown, a date range of A.D. 1150–1400 (with a probable date range of 1175 to 1300 for greatest manufacture, Crary 1997) seems appropriate.

The ceramics labeled "Deep-Red Slipped Brown Ware" came from Grid Localities 2 and 3 and from Pit House Locality 1. The type these sherds represent has not been formally defined, nor has its temporal placement been established, but the location of the sherds (Table 10.1) suggests that the pottery may date to the earlier components of the site. The slip color is generally a magenta (deep purplish red) that most often matches the Munsell Color Chart (1988) "red" (10R 4/6) and "weak red" (7.5R 4/4). The slip is thin to heavy, with thin areas that appear to have worn through to the underlying gray to light orange-tan clay body (paste). This makes the slip appear to be "fugitive" in nature, but it is not. The slip and core contain minute specular particles of mica and iron pyrite. The sherds usually have a dark gray core, and a few have an unslipped tan-gray exterior. The one rim sherd that is large enough to determine form is from a flare-rimmed bowl with out-leaning walls and an everted rim and lip (approximately rim form IB2 in Colton's 1953 rim form classification system, his Fig. 10). The "purplish red" slip color and specular particles in the slip and core are reminiscent of Salado/Roosevelt Red Ware. Based on the aplastic materials (temper) in the core, this pottery apparently was manufactured in two locations: pottery with volcanic inclusions in the clay somewhere north of the Gila River, and pottery with metamorphic granitic inclusions in the clay most likely somewhere south of the Gila River.

Again based on the nature of the core aplastic materials, locally made imitations of foreign ceramics and foreign imports were identified during the work at AZ CC:1:2 (ASM). The most obvious locally made imitations of foreign pottery were Sacaton Red-on-buff (Safford Variety) and a locally made copy of Tularosa Indented Corrugated named "Safford Indented Corrugated" (Crary 1997). A locally made, polished, red-slipped brown ware may be an imitation of San Francisco Red; this pottery was found exclusively in localities with other early ceramics.

Flaked Stone

Quantitatively, flaked stone comprised the largest artifact assemblage from the surface of site AZ CC:1:2 (ASM). Tables 8.1, 8.3 and 8.4 are based on the format used by S. Fish and her colleagues (Tables 7.8, 7.9) for consistency and ease of comparison. I include the numeric breakdown of artifacts based on the rock materials used in manufacture and for each rock material the numbers of artifacts that exhibit the presence of a striking platform and a bulb of percussion. The broad distribution of flakes with platforms and bulbs of percussion indicate that tool production, probably both expedient and formal, was taking place in the fields as well as at habitations.

Ground Stone

Field House Structure 1 contained two small grinding slabs (Tables 8.3, 8.4). One, with maximum dimensions of 19.0 cm by 24.0 cm by 7.5 cm, was made from a roughly rectilinear thick slab of andesite. Its grinding surface shows light use and is only slightly concave in section. The slab was standing on edge against the south wall of Room 2 (Fig. 8.4), with the bottom apparently sitting on the original floor of the structure in Level 5. The second small grinding slab was partially buried and upside down at the northeast corner of the exploratory trench excavated across the southern portion of Room 1. This slab, with maximum dimensions of 18.0 cm by 21.5 cm by 8 cm, was made from a boulder of andesite. In outline it is irregularly oval. The weathered, unmodified exterior surface is convex, and the working surface is weathered and slightly concave. The lightly worn grinding surface is roughly rectangular and parallels the long axis of the stone. What appear to be faint grinding striations also parallel the long axis of the stone. The distribution of these and other ground stone artifacts and the materials from which they have been fashioned are presented in Tables 8.1, 8.3, and 8.4.

Hand-held Stone Hoes

Except for the areas encompassing the field houses and the two pit house localities with their middens, the stone artifact densities and types recorded during the general survey closely paralleled the better controlled

Figure 8.5. A hand-held stone hoe or digging tool found during the survey of Grid Locality 9. The working edge is pointed downward. (Photograph by James A. Neely.)

smaller sample recorded by S. Fish and her colleagues (Tables 7.8, 7.9). The one exception was the scattered occurrence of expedient tools that I have tentatively termed "stone hoes" (Neely 1993b, 1995b, 2002). One complete example (Fig. 8.5) and four fragments of these crudely fashioned tools were in the grids not surveyed by S. Fish and her colleagues (Chapter 7). These digging tools, or perhaps as Doolittle suggested in 2002, brush clearing tools, appear in greater density on the surface of prehistoric relic fields in other parts of the Safford Valley than they do here. For example, their occurrence per acre surveyed in Lefthand Canyon and Marijilda Canyon (Fig. 1.5) was about four times greater than that recorded for this grid site. The single complete specimen came from Grid Locality 9, the area just north of Field House Structure 1 (Fig. 4.1b). Stone hoes evidently date to the Late Formative and Classic periods, and this kind of tool may have been part of prehistoric agricultural tool-kits containing at least five different types of tools (Chapter 2).

Tabular Knives

Of the various artifact finds made while surveying the rock-bordered grid fields, the so-called tabular knife (Figs. 7.9, B.1) was one of the most interesting and prevalent. This artifact form has been ethnographically documented in the American Southwest and Mexico as the tool used to cut and process the leaves of agave for food and fiber production (Castetter and others 1938; Parsons and Parsons 1990) and has been found associated with archaeological fields believed to have been used for agave cultivation (S. Fish and others 1992: 81). The density of these tools among the Safford grid fields is the highest that Paul and Suzanne Fish have seen during their study of many agave cultivation sites. The remaining approximately 800,000–square-meter survey produced a lesser, but still impressive density of these tools (about 25% of the formal tools recorded). Shoberg conducted a use-wear study on a complete specimen recovered from near Field House Structure 1 in Grid Locality 9 (Appendix B). The four other types of tools (hoes, blades, picks, and mattocks) I recorded (Chapter 2; Neely 2001a, 2002) as present in many other ancient dry-farmed and irrigated relic field areas in the Safford Valley were absent or only present in small quantities among the AZ CC:1:2 (ASM) grids. Further discussion of the archaeological findings and the chronological placement of the site and its components are presented in Chapter 10.

FINDINGS AND MEANINGS

The findings of this archaeological survey and these test excavations satisfactorily addressed some of the propositions concerning the nature of site AZ CC:1:2 (ASM) as outlined in Chapter 1 and validated Propositions 1 and 3 regarding the prehistoric origin and use of the rock-bordered grids. Unfortunately, we do not have a direct method of dating the rock-bordered grids. The most obvious of several indirect lines of evidence is the close association of the grids with prehistoric cultural remains, including ceramics, lithics, pit house and surface structures, and roasting pits. Conversely, no cultural remains have been associated with the grids that would suggest they are of historic or modern origin and use. Another convincing line of evidence, one that overlaps with Proposition 3, points toward the cultivation of agave on the grid borders. Agave was cultivated by many ancient inhabitants of the American Southwest and Mexico. Although the plant continues to be used by indigenous peoples in the Southwest, it is not cultivated in the amount and manner indicated by the grid system studied here. Finally, similar findings at the Marana Community (S. Fish and others 1992), a prehistoric agricultural settlement located just north of Tucson, provide strong analogs that indicate the prehistoric origin and use of AZ CC:1:2 (ASM).

Illuminating the nature of field house structures and artifacts in association with the rock-bordered grids casts more light on the use of these features as agricultural fields. Prehistoric lithic tools like tabular knives and pulping planes denote the processing of plant remains. Prehistoric ceramic spindle whorls indicate the spinning of fibers, very likely from agave. There is strong ethnographic documentation that historic groups in the American Southwest and Mexico used spindle whorls for spinning agave fiber. Roasting pits, radiocarbon dated to prehistoric times, that contain burned botanical materials show that agave was being grown and processed in the immediate vicinity. Field house structures associated with agricultural fields elsewhere in the American Southwest provide additional evidence of the agricultural nature of the rock-bordered grids at AZ CC:1:2 (ASM). When combined with the plant survey conducted by S. Fish and her colleagues (Chapter 7) and the GIS study by Lightfoot (Chapter 4), the archaeological data provide an incontrovertible case for the grids as prehistoric fields, most likely for the cultivation of agave in prehistoric times.

CHAPTER NINE

Rock Art

Betty Graham Lee and William E. Doolittle

There are perhaps no vestiges of prehistoric life that have captured the attention and imagination of both professional archaeologists and the general public more than rock art. When it comes to mysteries of the past, pictographs, petroglyphs, and geoglyphs rank among the most intriguing. Speculation still surpasses substance when it comes to understanding these phenomena and some basic questions remain largely unanswered: Who were the artists (Grant 1965)? When did they work (Schaafsma 1975a)? What were they portraying (Cunkle and Jacquemain 1995)? And, why (Martineau 1973)? Indeed, the only things that are known with any certitude about ancient rock art are where and how it was done (Grant 1967; Patterson 1992; Schaafsma 1975b). One place containing prehistoric rock art is at and near site AZ CC:1:2 (ASM).

SITES AND LOCALITIES

Locality 4, Locality 6, and Locality 9 at site AZ CC:1:2 (ASM) contain rock art, and one place immediately adjacent to the site has a sufficient concentration of rock art to merit its own site designation (Gilman and Sherman 1975: 10; see also Rucks 1984: 37, 54, 61). Site AZ CC:1:20 (ASM) is located at the far southwestern tip of Locality 6 (Fig. 1.6). Occupying the entire southeast-facing slope of a narrow spur (Fig. 9.1), this site is small and steep. It measures only approximately 50 m by 30 m and has a gradient of approximately 50 percent. Sometime in the late 19th or early 20th century a wagon road was cut along the ridge of this spur so as to allow easy access from the floodplain of the Gila River below to places on top of the Pleistocene terrace and beyond. Now overgrown, eroded, and nearly indistinguishable, this road has long been abandoned. Its construction and use, however, had direct negative impacts on the integrity of the site.

The rock art at these sites is largely in the form of petroglyphs, wherein the method of manufacture involved pecking rather than incising. The patina was removed to expose the contrasting color of the original rock surface. On these Pleistocene terraces, these petroglyphs appear on individual basalt boulders rather than on bedrock panels (Rucks 1984: 36). Each boulder contains only one, or at most a few, motifs. One of the boulders containing a petroglyph is also part of a geoglyph. We did not record any pictographs at these sites.

Some of the petroglyphs are small, faint, and visible only at certain times of the day, under certain conditions, and from specific angles. Several of these petroglyphs were not found during formal surveys, but instead were discovered accidently, even in areas where detailed work (like soil sampling and archaeological survey) had been conducted for some time. More petroglyphs no doubt await discovery in the area.

The study of rock art here is complicated by four other factors: incompleteness, the juxtaposition of intentional and natural patina removal, *faux* rock art, and damage. Several examples of rock art at these sites seem to be unfinished, and the degree to which any of these works is complete remains a mystery. It may well be that some petroglyphs, although small, are complete, and that others are only a small fraction of what the artists had originally intended. Some works of art were designed to incorporate the natural blemishes of boulders. Artists sometimes used cracks for delineation rather than peck lines and laid out designs so that eyes or dots coincided with natural dimples in the stone.

Figure 9.1. View of site AZ CC:1:20 (ASM) looking northwest. An old wagon road runs along the ridgetop from left to right. Boulders with petroglyphs are along the ridge and on the slope facing southeast. (Photograph by William E. Doolittle.)

Were incompleteness and opportunistic juxtaposition not confusing enough, there are things that look like rock art, but which in fact are not. There is abundant evidence in this area of "natural" pecking, which can be easily confused for rock art. The physical environment in which many of the petroglyphs are located, specifically that of site AZ CC:1:20 (ASM), is highly unstable (Fig. 9.1). Nearly every rock on this slope shows some signs of patina removal from natural causes like rocks colliding with each other while rolling, tumbling, or sliding downslope. The patterns produced on the surface of these rocks can be misleading.

The removal of patina through natural processes not only can result in *faux* rock art, but it can also damage and destroy real rock art. Some boulders containing petroglyphs are also badly weathered, and exfoliation and spalling due to freeze-thaw action is especially common.

Fortunately, there is no evidence of vandalism or malicious damage or destruction of the petroglyphs at these sites, but theft has occurred. A survey of site AZ CC:1:20 (ASM) in 1988 could not relocate at least one glyph-bearing boulder noted previously by the same surveyor in 1976 (notes on file in BLM office, Safford), and five of those recorded in 1988 were not found in 1998.

METHODOLOGY

We first visually inspected individual boulders containing petroglyphs and recorded basic information concerning each boulder and its petroglyphs (Table 9.1). We photographed each boulder-petroglyph in its natural state, without using any photo-enhancing materials such as aluminum powder or chalk. We did not make rubbings because such selective recording injects an undesirable element of bias. Two sketches by a previous recorder are included here (see Figs. 9.12, 9.18); they illustrate both the subtlety of rock art and the subjectivity of viewers.

Analysis of rock art is not a precise science; it can be very subjective in recording and interpreting. Regardless of how well-intentioned and objective viewers might try to be, they typically see certain

Table 9.1. Descriptions of Petroglyphs

	Boulder size WxHxD cm	Boulder situation	Boulder color	Patina color	Design orientation	Design size WxH cm	Design aspect	Motif	Condition	Fig. No.
AZ CC:1:2 (ASM) Locality 4										
1	35 x 30 x 22	In situ	Tan	Light to dark gray	Side	12 x 24	South	Humpback flute player	Good	9.2
AZ CC:1:2 (ASM) Locality 6										
1	30 x 35 x 20	In situ[1]	Tan	Dark gray to black	Top, side	24 x 15	South	Circles encompassing dots connected by a line and possibly a quadruped	Good	9.5
AZ CC:1:2 (ASM) Locality 9										
1	27 x 30 x 15	In situ	Tannish brown	Medium gray	Top, side	12 x 12	East	Circles and lines	Fair to poor, exfoliating	9.3
2	45 x 20 x 30	In situ	Grayish tan	Light to dark gray	Top, side	22 x 12	West	Horizontal zig-zag line with bulbous end and vertical lines	Good	9.4
AZ CC:1:20 (ASM)										
1	60 x 44 x 32	In situ	Reddish light brown	Dark gray to black	Side	27 x 32	East	Five concentric squares encompassing a central dot, with a wavy line on top	Good	9.6
2	50 x 29 x 32	In situ	Grayish brown	Medium to dark gray	Side	7 cm diam.	South	Circle with pecked interior, or perhaps two concentric circles or a spiral	Good, but light and difficult to see	9.7
3	72 x 37 x 52	In situ	Tan to brown	Medium gray	Top, side	6 x 10	West	Interlocking lines	Good	9.8
4	31 x 18 x 25	Surface[2]	Reddish brown	Medium gray	Top	11 x 11	Variable	X or cross	Good	9.9
5	40 x 38 x 23	Surface[2]	Grayish brown	Dark brownish gray	Top / Side	8 x 12 / 40 x 20	Variable / South	Anthropomorph with raised arms / Pit and groove	Good	9.10
6	65 x 65 x 65	Surface[3]	Grayish brown	Medium to dark gray	Top	43 x 30	South	Abstract curvilinear (circles?), and quadruped (big horn sheep or deer?)	Poor, badly weathered	9.11, 9.12
7	40 x 50 x 15	Surface[2]	Reddish tan	Medium brownish gray	Top, side	14 x 20	East	Anthropomorph, X-shaped and walking	Good	9.13
8	45 x 30 x 20	Surface[2]	Reddish brown	Medium brownish gray	Top	20 x 25	Variable	Abstract curvilinear	Poor, faded and undefinable	9.14
9	43 x 40 x 19	Surface[2]	Light brown	Brown to black	Top	20 x 30	South	Circles with lines	Good	9.15
10	38 x 35 x 15	In situ	Reddish tan	Dark gray	Side	17 x 22	South	Animal (bird?) above spiral within a circle	Good	9.16
11	60 x 25, x ?	In situ	Light brown	Dark gray to black	Side	8 x 10	East	Anthropomorph with outstretched arms, long body, no waist or legs, or a bird in flight	Good	9.17
12	70 x 40 x 40	Surface[3]	Tan	Tan	Side	18 x 6	South-east	Quadruped or rake	Good, but faint due to lack of patina on boulder	9.18
13	39 x 60 x 23	Surface[2]	Grayish tan	Brown to black	Top / Side	39 x 23 / 20 x 12	Variable / East	Abstract curvilinear (top and side) / Saluting anthropomorph with headdress	Good	9.19
14	23 x 55 x 15	Surface[2]	Light to medium brown	Medium to dark gray	Side	9 x 4	South	Anthropomorph with down-stretched arms	Poor, lower half of design is broken off and missing	9.20

1. In the center of a cross-shaped geoglyph formed by several smaller boulders oriented true N-S and E-W.
2. Displaced.
3. Possibly displaced.

Table 9.2. Assessment of Petroglyph Boulder
Conditions by Site

	AZ CC:1:2 (ASM)	AZ CC:1:20 (ASM)	
		In situ	Displaced
Situation			
In-situ	4	5	
Displaced			9
Orientation			
Side	1	4	3
Top/side	3	1	1
Top			5
Aspect*			
South	2	2	3.5
Southeast			1
East	2	2	1.5
West	1	1	
Variable			3
Condition			
Good	3	5	6
Fair/poor	1		
Poor			3

*Some petroglyphs have more than one aspect.

things and fail to see others. Although photographs are not perfect, they are the best medium available to reproduce petroglyphs (Martineau 1973: 183, 188) and we provide them here (Figs. 9.2–9.11, 9.13–9.17, 9.19, 9.20).

ASSESSMENT OF CONDITIONS

The petroglyphs and the boulders on which they are located vary considerably in locational characteristics and conditions (Table 9.2). All four of those among the rock-bordered grids at site AZ CC:1:2 (ASM) remain in situ. Three of them are associated with field houses. There is no discernable pattern with regard to their aspects, except that both of the petroglyphs associated with Field House Structure 1 face away from the structure.

Of the 14 petroglyph boulders on site AZ CC:1:20 (ASM), five are in situ and nine show signs of having been displaced. In general, the boulders here are larger than those with petroglyphs among the rock-bordered grids. It is not surprising, therefore, especially since this site is on a steep southeastern-facing slope, that 80 percent of petroglyph boulders in situ have side orientations and southern or eastern aspects. All of the

petroglyphs on in situ boulders are in good condition. Nearly opposite trends are apparent in the petroglyph boulders that have been displaced at site AZ C:1:20 (ASM), some from road building and use. More than 50 percent have top orientations. Those that do have side or top-and-side orientations seem to be more a function of fortuitous downslope movement than deliberate placement. There is no real trend in terms of aspect. Only one petroglyph has a western aspect, which is not surprising on this slope, and there are nearly as many petroglyphs with variable aspects as with southern or eastern aspects. Many of the petroglyphs are in good condition, but the three in poor condition are all on displaced boulders.

INTERPRETATIONS

Rock art is described stylistically as being either *representational* (animate and material things such as animals and the sun) or *abstract* (Grant 1965: 80). Representational art is further dichotomized into *naturalistic*, that is done in a realistic manner (Fig. 9.12), and *stylized*, rendered in a nonrealistic manner and including such things as stick-figure anthropomorphs, supernatural beings, and monsters (Fig. 9.4). Abstract art has little or no reference to the appearance of objects in nature (Grant 1967: 20–27; Heizer and Baumhoff 1962: 77, 83). It can be *curvilinear*, consisting of seemingly aimless meandering lines; dotted patterns, circles, and spirals (Fig. 9.3); *rectilinear*, consisting of straight lines and right angles (Fig. 9.9); or *pit and groove*, consisting of a series of dimples (Fig. 9.10). A few examples of naturalistic representational, abstract rectilinear, and pit and groove petroglyphs are on the two sites, but stylized representational and abstract curvilinear motifs dominate.

Grant (1967: 35–39) and Cunkle and Jacquemain (1995: 22–24) have grouped motifs into six categories according to function: mnemonic, records of events, clan symbols, doodling or graffiti, markers, and ritualistic. Function is often difficult if not impossible to determine; was the artist randomly pecking or structuring a communication (Schaafsma 1980: 9–13). There is a natural tendency to impose religious connotations to ancient rock art (Cunkle and Jacquemain 1995: 24–30), and in many cases there are good reasons for doing so (Grant 1965: 89). Extreme caution must be exercised when interpreting prehistoric renderings (Heizer and Baumhoff 1962: 279–282).

The meanings of most of the petroglyphs at these two sites remain unknown. Some abstractions (Figs. 9.14, 9.19), animals (Figs. 9.11, 9.12, 9.16), and people (Figs. 9.10, 9.20) appear to be mainly expressive graffiti (Cunkle and Jacquemain 1995: 115–117; Jernigan 1992: 63; Mountjoy 1982: 115; Patterson 1992: 33; Schaafsma 1975b: 90, 92, 94–96, 100, Figs. 76, 80, 84). As one rock art authority has noted "many carvings may have been primarily for the pleasure of carving them while tending . . . small garden patches" (Schaafsma 1975a: 58). Others may be records of events or be mnemonic. For example, although fragmentary, the circles and lines of one glyph (Fig. 9.3) are like a "rayed circle within a circle" petroglyph in California that is thought to represent the sun (Rafter 1985: 116–117, Fig. J; see also Schaafsma 1975b: 96). It is unlikely any are clan symbols, because not one is even remotely similar to such motifs identified elsewhere in the Southwest (Grant 1967). A few petroglyphs at these sites, however, are strikingly similar to others recorded elsewhere (Schaafsma 1975a: 59–62) so that reasonable, albeit tentative, interpretations can be proffered here.

Shrines

Two examples of rock art at these sites are probably shrines, one each at Localities 4 and 6 at AZ CC:1:2 (ASM). One of the more unusual, if not truly unique, items in southeastern Arizona is the petroglyph-geoglyph at Locality 6, a cross-shaped geoglyph that is oriented with one axis pointed true north-south and the other due east-west (Fig. 9.5). A similar geoglyph recorded near the confluence of the Gila and Colorado rivers (Johnson 1986: 139, Fig. 92) has been interpreted as a symbolic sign of power of the Mesoamerican sky god Quetzalcoatl (Johnson 1986: 38; Patterson 1992: 15, 76–77).

There is abundant archaeological evidence that all ancient Southwestern people were in regular contact with Mesoamerica. Interregional trade was frequent and regular (Di Peso 1974). The argument has even been put forth that the Hohokam were themselves Mesoamericans who migrated northward (Haury 1976). A Mesoamerican influence on this petroglyph-geoglyph is a reasonable consideration. Less clear is the association between the geoglyph and the petroglyphs. There appear to be two separate motifs portrayed in the petroglyph, a quadruped running from left to right, and above it a line connecting two circles encompassing dots. Whether or not these were made at the same time and are directly related to each other remains unknown. Animals in association with curvilinear abstractions are not unusual motifs in neighboring areas (Schaafsma 1975b: 90, 91, 95, Fig. 80), but unfortunately there are no good explanations for the animal representations. There are, however, two interesting interpretations for the circles-dots-line motif. In western Mexico, such designs are thought to represent the eyes of a god watching the movement of the sun across the sky (Patterson 1992: 86), which would fit with the Mesoamerican sky god explanation. The second interpretation is that of speech or a conference and has its origins on the Colorado Plateau. The two circles may represent heads and the line between them may portray communication (Martineau 1973: 18, 19, Fig. 10). This explanation, too, makes sense as shrines are by definition places were communication takes place, usually with gods.

Concerning an interest in the sky, rainfall was of real importance to people in the Safford Valley. Ancient farmers who went to great lengths building the rock-bordered grids to retain scarce runoff most assuredly pleaded with the gods for rain. The crops they were attempting to grow surely needed it. This concern is equally evident in the second shrine.

The petroglyph at Locality 4, AZ CC:1:2 (ASM), is much simpler than the one at Locality 6, but it is every bit as interesting and its explanation is equally as intriguing. This petroglyph (Fig. 9.2) is nearly a mirror-image duplicate of one near Cochiti Springs in northern New Mexico (Schaafsma 1975a: 8, Fig. 4). The consistent representation across such a long distance reflects the pan-regional identification of this motif. The humpback flute player, sometimes known as Kokopelli, is a sign of fertility, not simply human fecundity (Patterson 1992: 98) but fertility of the land as well (Grant 1967: 60–61) and the crops grown on it (Cunkle and Jacquemain 1995: 47, 51). Furthermore, he has been identified as a rain priest and is hunched over from carrying sacks of seeds as trade items to lands farther to the south (Cunkle and Jacquemain 1995: 46, 49, 51). Rain, seeds, and southern lands ring a familiar note: water, crops, and Mesoamerica.

These are themes echoed in other petroglyph motifs as well.

Water

A scarce and important resource in this exceptionally arid locale, water is hinted at if not explicitly portrayed in certain glyphs. As in Mesoamerica, serpents have long been associated with water among native American people (Mountjoy 1982: 118). One good representation of a snake on a boulder at Locality 9 (Fig. 9.4) contains elements that may represent both falling water and flowing water. The two distinct vertical lines that are immediately beneath the serpent are referred to in motif parlance as "rakes" and are thought to indicate rain (Grant 1965: 77; Schaafsma 1975b: 179, Fig. 155). The snake itself is a "zig-zag line," and such abstractions when oriented horizontally have long been viewed as indicators of streams (Cunkle and Jacquemain 1995: 157, 159, Figs. 314, 315; Grant 1965: 77; Martineau 1973: 100, 101; Patterson 1992: 205; Schaafsma 1975a: 39, 1975b: 61, 91–92). It is possible the line simply represents a snake, because during the course of research on the rock-bordered grids, field researchers encountered more rattlesnakes here than at any other locale; perhaps the glyph was a warning to others.

Motifs other than serpents, and possibly representing water, are in these petroglyphs. The abstract motif in Figure 9.19 is faint and seemingly incomplete and may represent water, but any interpretation is rendered cautiously. More definitive are the interlocking lines in Figure 9.8, sometimes referred to as "frets." They are common in neighboring areas (Schaafsma 1975a: 42, 1975b: 93, 188, Figs. 78, 157) and have been interpreted as signs of water (Patterson 1992: 205).

Concentric circles are some of the most widespread rock art motifs in the Southwest. Opinion among rock art authorities is that these are abstractions of Mother Earth–home, places where people are born or locales that literally give life, where one can pass from one world to another (Munn 1973: 119; Patterson 1992: 67; Schaafsma 1975a: 42). Paradoxically, there are no definitive examples of this design at either AZ CC:1:2 (ASM) or AZ CC:1:20 (ASM). One regional variation, however, is a petroglyph with concentric squares (Fig. 9.6). A review of the southwestern rock art literature revealed only one other example of this motif, and it, too, was from eastern Arizona (Preston and Preston

1985: 127). This glyph is probably a highly localized variation on an otherwise common motif.

This particular glyph has one other element that is impossible to overlook, the zig-zag line adjacent to and paralleling one side. A similar motif in other locales has been identified as an abstraction for springs, places where water emerges from the earth. These spring motifs, however, are not concentric squares or even concentric circles, but spirals, tangent to a zig-zag line (Cunkle and Jacquemain 1995: 155–157, 159, Photo 166, Fig. 316). Although spirals in the Southwest are popularly viewed as having astronomical significance, largely due to one famous spiral in Chaco Canyon (Sofaer and others 1979; Zeilik 1985), they have at least two other connotations. Depending on the point of origin (inside or out) and turning counterclockwise, they can be abstractions for ascension and descent, respectively (Martineau 1973: 18, 19, Fig. 10). The whole idea of going up or down makes sense in terms of passing from one world to another. Accordingly, spirals and concentric circles may have generally similar meanings, especially in specific local contexts.

The notion of regional variations in terms of spirals and concentric circles takes on added meaning when two other factors are considered. First, there exists on at least one Hohokam site farther west, down the Gila River near present-day Phoenix, a petroglyph of a square spiral (Schaafsma 1980: 85, Fig. 54). Second, there are two other petroglyphs at site AZ CC:1:20 (ASM) that may be spirals within circles (Figs. 9.7, 9.16). They are small and faint, but if they indeed represent spirals within circles, they are the only examples of such a motif thus far reported in the literature. Big Spring Wash is named for a water source, and there is good reason to conclude that springs were portrayed in petroglyphs at this site.

Ancient rock artists at these two sites seem to have been expressing or communicating concerns for water. Rainfall, surface flow, and springs were all portrayed, at least abstractly. These people were concerned with the scarcity of rain, the control of runoff, and the dependability of ground water, just as are the present-day inhabitants.

Trade

Ancient farmers no doubt traded some of their produce, but the extent of trade, the distances involved

Figure 9.2.

Figure 9.3.

Figure 9.4.

Figure 9.5.

Figure 9.6.

Figure 9.7.

Figure 9.8.

Figure 9.9.

Figure 9.10.

Figure 9.2. Humpback flute player shrine at Locality 4, site AZ CC:1:2 (ASM). (Photograph by William E. Doolittle.)

Figure 9.3. Circles and lines, possibly a solar motif, situated just east of Field House Structure 1, Locality 9, site AZ CC:1:2 (ASM). (Photograph by William E. Doolittle).

Figure 9.4. A serpent, possibly representing flowing water, situated just west of Field House Structure 1, Locality 9, site AZ CC:1:2 (ASM). (Photograph by William E. Doolittle.)

Figure 9.5. Geoglyph/petroglyph shrine at Locality 6, site AZ CC:1:2 (ASM). The lines of smaller rocks are oriented true north-south and east-west away from the petroglyph boulder. (Photograph by Betty Graham Lee.)

Figure 9.6. Concentric square and wavy line motif, possibly representing a spring, at site AZ CC:1:20 (ASM). (Photograph by Betty Graham Lee.)

Figure 9.7. Circles or spiral at site AZ CC:1:20 (ASM). (Photograph by Betty Graham Lee.)

Figure 9.8. Interlocking lines, possibly representing flowing water, at site AZ CC:1:20 (ASM). (Photograph by William E. Doolittle.)

Figure 9.9. An X motif, possibly an abstraction for trade, at site AZ CC:1:20 (ASM). (Photograph by Betty Graham Lee.)

Figure 9.10. Anthropomorph and pit and groove motifs at site AZ CC:1:20 (ASM). Differences in patina on the top and side of the boulder are visible. (Photograph by Betty Graham Lee.)

Figure 9.11.

Figure 9.14.

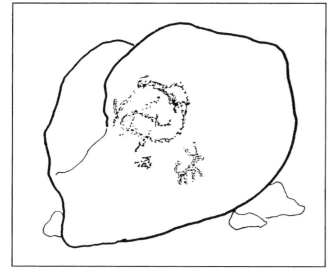

Figure 9.12.

Figure 9.15.

Figure 9.13.

Figure 9.16.

Figure 9.17.

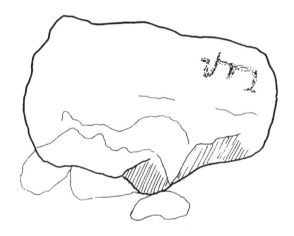

Figure 9.18.

Figure 9.19.

Figure 9.11. Abstract curvilinear and quadruped motifs at site AZ CC:1:20 (ASM). Both petroglyphs are faint, see Figure 9.12. (Photograph by Betty Graham Lee.)

Figure 9.12. Sketch of the petroglyphs photographed in Figure 9.11. (Drawn by Sylvia F. Crisler in 1988, on file in the Bureau of Land Management Office, Safford, Arizona.)

Figure 9.13. X-shaped walking anthropomorph with a load, possibly representing trade, at site AZ CC:1:20 (ASM). (Photograph by Betty Lee Graham.)

Figure 9.14. Abstract curvilinear motif at site AZ CC:1:20 (ASM). (Photograph by Betty Graham Lee.)

Figure 9.15. Circles with lines, possibly an abstraction for trade, at site AZ CC:1:20 (ASM). *Faux* rock art is on the smaller rocks to the left of the petroglyph boulder. (Photograph by Betty Graham Lee.)

Figure 9.16. Animal and spiral within circle motifs at site AZ CC:1:20 (ASM). (Photograph by Betty Graham Lee.)

Figure 9.17. Partial anthropomorph or a bird in flight at site AZ CC:1:20 (ASM). (Photograph by Betty Graham Lee.)

Figure 9.18. Sketch of quadruped or rake motif petroglyph at site AZ CC:1:20 (ASM). (Drawn by Sylvia F. Crisler in 1988, on file in the Bureau of Land Management Office, Safford, Arizona.)

Figure 9.19. Abstract curvilinear and anthropomorph motifs at site AZ CC:1:20 (ASM). (Photograph by William E. Doolittle.)

Figure 9.20. Partial anthropomorph at site AZ CC:1:20 (ASM). (Photograph by William E. Doolittle.)

and the nature of the transactions remain unknown. In all likelihood, food was exchanged on a local level, along with tools and craft items. Trade may be reflected in three of the petroglyphs at site AZ CC:1:20 (ASM).

According to Martineau (1973: 9, 88, Fig. 47), crossed forearms is sign-language for trade, portrayed by an "X" in rock art. One petroglyph at the site is an X (Fig. 9.9), but we need to be aware that the similarity between an X and a cross can lead to confusion between trade and religion interpretations. A second X is more subtle, actually involving lines connecting circles (Fig. 9.15). This rectilinear abstraction (Grant 1967: 27) is like others observed in southern New Mexico (Schaafsma 1975b: 96,110, Table 2, Fig. 84). Because lines connecting circles may be a representation of speech (Martineau 1973: 18, 19, Fig. 10), crossed lines with circles may be an abstract way of portraying trade negotiations. There is better evidence of trade than these two glyphs, however.

The third petroglyph that may represent trade involves an anthropomorph that is both walking and carrying a load on its back (Fig. 9.13). There are no other petroglyphs like this one anywhere nearby. Most anthropomorph petroglyphs made locally (Figs. 9.10, 9.19) and to the east (Schaafsma 1975b: 92) are stick-figures. Most anthropomorph pictographs in the general area are in the shape of an hour-glass. The torso is shaped like an hour-glass, not like a triangle, with the upper portion being larger than the lower portion. The long lines extending from the bottom of the hour-glass are clearly representations of spread legs (Jernigan 1992). The ancient Hohokam, who lived farther to the west, made X–shaped anthropomorph petroglyphs that also involved an hour-glass shape. With upper portions approximately the same size as the lower portions, these hour-glass shapes were made by pecking lines across the top and the bottom of the X. The upper part of the hour-glass represents a torso, the narrow center is the waist, and the bottom part represents hips. In some cases, the X is extended and short lines protruding vertically below the hour-glass result in a design that looks like a woman in a skirt (Schaafsma 1980: 85, Fig. 54). In other cases, long bent legs beneath a small X render a more masculine appearance (Patterson 1992: 120).

The petroglyphs that most closely approximate an X anthropomorph near the rock-bordered grids are Rosa Style men of northwestern New Mexico (Schaafsma 1980: 5–6, 7, Fig. 2). Legs are represented in these petroglyphs by the bottom half of the X. The torso is represented by the upper half, and a line across the top and extending on either side represents broad shoulders and arms (Patterson 1992: 121).

The Rosa Style men appear to be frontal portrayals, backs are not visible and feet point in opposite directions. In contrast, the X–shaped anthropomorph at site AZ CC:1:20 (ASM) is portrayed in side view. There appears to be a pack on its back, and both feet point in one direction. This walking appearance has been interpreted as representing an "easy trail" or a "short-cut" (Martineau 1973: 89, 88, Fig. 47). When combined, the bearing of a load and a favorable route suggest a trade interpretation.

Disclaimers

The interpretations presented here should be accepted with reservation and guardedness. They are offered only as reasonable possibilities and suggestions. Too little is known of rock art to make any definitive interpretations at this time (Schaafsma 1980: 10–13). Despite this note of caution, however, we conclude that none of these glyphs are markers, conspicuous glyphs that point the way to large panels of glyphs (Cunkle and Jacquemain 1995: 3). They are all too small and too inconspicuous to have served such a function. We also conclude that these petroglyphs are probably not maps; they show no signs of indicating way-finding

(Blakemore 1981). Cartographic petroglyphs, pictographs, and geoglyphs are known from surrounding areas (Colwell-Chanthaphonh 2003: 14; Doolittle 1988: 46–47; Grant 1965, Plate 3; Heizer 1958; Moreno 2003: 213; Patterson 1992: 140; Schroeder 1952: 44), but they invariably involve large boulders or panels and they are more complex in the number and design of motifs.

CULTURES AND DATES

Determining who made specific petroglyphs, and when they made them, is always a difficult if not impossible task. A technique once tested for definitive dating of patina and surfaces underneath it (Dorn and Whitley 1984) has now been determined to be unreliable (Beck and others 1998). Interpreters continue to rely on differences in patination, superposition of styles, overgrowth of lichens, deposits covering designs, signs of erosion, association of artifacts, ethnographic analogs, and differences in subject matter, either alone or in some combination, in their attempts to arrive at chronologies (Grant 1967: 45–53; Heizer and Baumhoff 1962: 230–234; Schaafsma 1980: 13–17). These techniques are not yet reliable, and together the use of multiple approaches is not much better than adopting a single strategy.

Two things concerning cultural affiliation are evident from the discussion of petroglyph interpretations at sites AZ CC:1:2 (ASM) and AZ CC:1:20 (ASM): we drew parallels from surrounding areas, and in a few cases we noted local variations on regional themes. The area in which these two petroglyph sites are located, southeastern Arizona, is a land between archaeologically speaking. In prehistoric times, it was a region inhabited by people of a culture influenced by the Mogollon to the east, the Anasazi to the north, the Hohokam to the west, and perhaps Casas Grandes to the south (Wallace 1997), and, not surprisingly, the petroglyphs reflect a number of cultural influences (Rucks 1984:11-23).

There are striking similarities between these petroglyphs and some of those of the Hohokam, especially of the Gila Petroglyph Style (Schaafsma 1980: 83–96; Rucks 1984: 19), and of the Mogollon, especially of the Reserve Petroglyph Style (Schaafsma 1980: 187–196) and Jornada Style (Schaafsma 1980: 199).

Although lacking in chronological precision, these cultural and stylistic affiliations say something about the ages of rock art at these sites.

Some of the petroglyphs may have been made around A.D. 1700, but it is more likely that A.D. 1400 is the most recent date. None of the motifs on these petroglyphs are like those produced by either the Sobaipuri or the Apache, people who lived in the area after 1450 (see Rucks 1984: 2022). Schaafsma (1975a: 42) dated various designs in northern New Mexico to Regressive Pueblo times, or A.D. 1300–1700, but noted that some motifs probably originated earlier (Schaafsma 1975a: 32, 1980: 11, Fig. 11). In another study, Schaafsma (1975b: 61), determined that similar motifs in southern New Mexico dated no later than the end of Mogollon times, or about A.D. 1400. The Mogollon Jornado Style was produced until this time but it started about 1100 (Schaafsma 1975b: 90, 95; 1980: 18–19, Fig. 10). The Mogollon Reserve Petroglyph Style began at approximately A.D. 1000, but its popularity declined around 1300 (Schaafsma 1980: 18, Fig. 10).

The A.D. 1000–1400 dating for petroglyph manufacture is interesting, because it parallels neighboring areas, it matches one of the radiocarbon dates reported in Chapter 7, and it is the interval during which Kokopelli images were the most widely produced (Cunkle and Jacquemain 1995: 47). Flute players were portrayed in the Southwest as early as A.D. 500, but they lacked the humpback that distinguishes Kokopelli (Cunkle and Jacquemain 1995: 49).

The metamorphosis of a flute player into Kokopelli prior to A.D. 1000 is paralleled by the chronology of two other motifs. The petroglyphs involving circles connected by lines are similar to petroglyphs in Canyon de Chelley that have been dated to Modified Basketmaker–Developmental Pueblo times, approximately A.D. 950–1000 (Grant 1979: 161, 164, Fig. 4.10). One anthropomorph at site AZ CC:1:20 (ASM) was compared to Rosa Style men of northwestern New Mexico. That representational style spanned the period from A.D. 700 to 1000. Clearly, some of the rock art at the two Arizona sites may be older than most of the petroglyphs in the Rosa Style. The Gila Petroglyph Style, which terminated about 1400, may have started as early as A.D. 200, and it may have evolved out of the Great Basin Abstract Style that began about 800 B.C. (Schaafsma 1980: 18, Fig. 10).

Boulder 5 at site AZ CC:1:20 (ASM) has two distinct petroglyphs, an anthropomorph on the top and a pit and groove motif on the side (Fig. 9.10). This boulder, however, shows signs of having been displaced, not once, but twice. A clear distinction is visible in the patina from one part of the boulder to another. The patina on what is now the top is much darker than the patina on the side, and the anthropomorph was pecked through the darker surface. The patina on the side is nearly the same color as the boulder itself, meaning that the surface was not exposed to the elements very long before the pit and groove petroglyph was made. Normally, the darker the patina, the older the surface, and hence, the older the petroglyph (Grant 1967: 43–45; Heizer and Baumhoff 1962: 232; Schaafsma 1980: 13–14, Fig. 7). In this case, however, the reverse is true.

Anthropomorphs are early motifs (Schaafsma 1975b: 5–6), but they are not as early as the pit and groove motif. Studies conducted in southern California (Greenwood 1969: 52, 58, Fig. 33) and Nevada (Heizer and Baumhoff 1962: 234) have concluded that pit and groove petroglyphs were made between 5000 B.C. and 3000 B.C. Because this early design appears on a surface with little patina, we conclude that the petroglyph was made before much patina had formed. Sometime later, the boulder must have been displaced so that the glyph was no longer exposed to the elements. A patina then formed on the exposed part of the boulder, and at a later date some artist pecked the anthropomorph. At a still later date, perhaps quite recently, the boulder was displaced again, this time reexposing the pit and groove petroglyph.

FINDINGS AND MEANINGS

As for any relationship between the rock art at sites AZ CC:1:2 (ASM) and AZ CC:1:20 (ASM) and the rock-bordered grids, it would have been in the period extending from about A.D. 750–800 to 1385, thereby confirming Proposition 1 as articulated in Chapter 1. This was the time when all but a few of the petroglyphs were probably made and the time period that corresponds to both the ceramic (Chapter 8) and the radiocarbon (Chapter 7) evidence.

Equally as important as the chronology of the petroglyphs are the motifs. The petroglyphs made after A.D. 1000 invariably involve themes of importance to arid land farmers. Two of the glyphs, one being part of a geoglyph, were shrines. They seem to have been directed toward a sky god and intended as an appeal for rain. Other glyphs portray flowing water and probably reflect a concern for runoff, the conservation of which was the principal function of the grids (Chapter 5). Proposition 4b is accepted.

Finally, there are representations that suggest trade or some type of exchange; whether or not it involved crops supported by the rock-bordered grids remains unknown. However, the estimated productivity of the grid fields (Chapter 7), when viewed in the light of the evidence for trade and a burgeoning population in the Safford Valley (Chapters 2, 8, 10), would suggest that both trade and local consumption may have prompted the construction of the rock-bordered grid fields. The rock art at these two sites seems to be closely related to agriculture, thereby lending yet additional evidence for acceptance of Proposition 3 (Chapter 1).

CHAPTER TEN

Answers and Ideas

James A. Neely and William E. Doolittle

Complete understanding of the rock-bordered grids and the related features constituting site AZ CC:1:2 (ASM) requires systematically answering a number of questions formulated as propositions. These propositions deal with age, construction, purpose, and function.

1. The grids and associated rock piles, alignments, structures, and rock art were constructed in prehistoric times.
2. Grid borders were constructed of rocks from the immediate vicinity, on the terrace surfaces, and not from some remote sources.
3. The grids were used for agricultural production.
    a. Crops were grown in the interiors of the grids.
    b. Crops were grown among the rocks comprising the grid borders.
    c. Certain crops were grown in the grid interiors and others were grown among the rocks on the borders simultaneously.
4a. The grids collected and retained surface runoff.
4b. The grids captured rainfall and retained runoff.
4c. The grids retarded soil erosion.
4d. Grids are the remains of devices used to anchor brush that retarded wind erosion.
4e. The grids collected sediment, thereby resulting in a deeper growing medium.
4f. Rocks comprising the grid borders provided a mulch, thereby reducing evaporation and soil moisture loss.
4g. Grids served no explicit function. The borders are simply the result of clearing rocks from the surface.

AGE

Evidence used in dating the site is admittedly less than perfect and not as secure as we had anticipated. Radiocarbon dates from the roasting pits (Chapters 7, 8, 10), ceramic evidence from the excavation of a structure and from surface collections from across the site (Chapters 8, 10), similarities among lithic artifacts at this site and other known prehistoric sites (Chapters 7, 8, 10), and rock art styles and motifs (Chapter 9) all indicate that the site was used prehistorically. Although the earliest use of the site area may have been about A.D. 500, a more secure date range of around A.D. 750–800 to 1385 is more probable for the construction of the rock-bordered grids. Proposition 1, therefore, is accepted.

CONSTRUCTION

Although the rocks used in the manufacture of the grid borders and other features (rock alignments and rock piles) vary considerably in size from one locale to another, it is clear from the assessments of local geology and soils that rocks were not transported any long distances. They were gathered in situ and re-arranged across a distance of no more than a few meters. In those localities where relatively large rocks were available, they were picked up and moved (Chapter 3). In those places where only smaller rocks were available, with few if any larger rocks, they too were gathered up, presumably in baskets, and arranged in linear piles to form grid borders. Evidence from such settings (Chapter 6) indicates that the grid interiors were winnowed of small rocks for the construction of some grid borders. Proposition 2 is accepted.

PURPOSE

The rock-bordered grids and related features unquestionably served an agricultural purpose. The paucity of permanent dwellings and the small number and scattered distribution of ceramics and artifacts conform to conditions at prehistoric agricultural sites throughout the Southwest. The two best lines of evidence that support an agricultural interpretation are certain crop remains and agricultural features and implements, but the unequivocal nature of the micro and macro remains of crops is less than impressive. The findings related in Chapter 7, although not definitive, are not unexpected considering the edaphic conditions. Soils are not degraded and they have nutrient levels sufficient for maize cultivation (Chapter 6), but they are thin and lack rooting zones deep enough for maize. No evidence of other staple crops was recovered, but the finding of agavelike fibers in roasting pits supports agave cultivation as a likely function. The presence of a few pit houses and field houses (Chapter 8), roasting pits (Chapters 7, 8), and rock piles (Chapters 1, 8, 10), features that have been shown to be associated with agave production elsewhere, lend credence to this inference. Finally, the discovery of a large number and dense distribution of lithic artifacts known as pulping planes and tabular knives (Chapters 7, 8, 10, Appendix B), demonstrated through studies elsewhere to be used in agave cultivation, add to the evidence for an agricultural purpose. By identifying that the rock-bordered grids were used for the cultivation of agave, Proposition 3 is accepted. The corollaries to this proposition are addressed below.

FUNCTION

In discussing the functions of rock-bordered grids, rock alignments or terraces, and rock piles, Propositions 4d and 4g are rejected categorically. There is no evidence that rocks comprising the grid borders anchored brush that might have retarded wind erosion of soil; the chemical and physical analyses point to soils that were not degraded (Chapter 6). Although the grid borders were the result of rock clearance, it was not clearance simply for the purpose of creating rock-free surfaces for the cultivation of maize or some other crop. The soil evidence (Chapter 6) argues against crops having been cultivated in the spaces between grid borders.

Proposition 4a is also rejected, at least tentatively, based on a general survey of the landscape and features and an assessment of surface microtopography at Grid Locality 1 (Chapter 5), which revealed no evidence that rock features of any type played a role in directing the flow of surface runoff any substantial distance. The degree to which this finding may be true for other localities awaits future research. As for the other propositions, distinctions need to be made with regard to specific types of features on the landscape. Detailed study of surface microtopography (Chapter 5) clearly demonstrates that the rock borders retained rainfall that fell directly into the grids, thereby preventing moisture loss to sheetflow runoff. That certain rock art motifs identified with flowing water and rain gods (Chapter 9) have been identified at the site is yet additional evidence in favor of water control. Proposition 4b is confirmed. Considering that even the seemingly "flat" surfaces have some gradient (Chapter 5) and that the soils are thin and rocky (Chapters 3, 6), the rock borders may well have retarded soil erosion. It is doubtful that the rock piles impeded erosion to any extent, but the evidence from rock alignments on slopes (terraces, Chapters 5 and 6) overwhelmingly indicates that these features trapped sediments washing off upslope areas. Proposition 4c is confirmed, at least for one type of feature.

Although some sediment accumulated behind terrace risers, it is doubtful that this was the intended purpose of terraces; they were not built to create deep soils for crop production. The terrace treads (Chapter 5) are too small for any meaningful production of staple crops such as maize. There is no evidence in the way of soils (Chapter 6) or topography (Chapter 5) to indicate that either the rock borders of the grids or the rock piles collected sediment to create deep soils. Proposition 4e is rejected.

All the evidence, geological (Chapter 3), topographical (Chapter 5), edaphic (Chapter 6), botanical (Chapter 7), and archaeological (Chapters 8, 10), points toward cultivation of crops, specifically agave, along the rock borders constituting the grids, on the rock piles, and along the tops of the terrace risers. Therefore, Proposition 3b is accepted and Propositions 3a and 3c are rejected.

As flat as the topography might appear across the area covered with grids and other features, there is some relief. Surface runoff is impeded, and water concentrates along and under the rock features. Underlying petrocalcic and argillic horizons impede infiltration and hold moisture in the rooting zone. Increased soil moisture results in soils that have high levels of organic carbon, nitrogen, and available phosphorus. With more water and better soils, it is not surprising that the rock features today are characterized by more vegetation than occurs in areas and places without dense rock concentrations. In sum, the rocks piled and aligned to make grid borders and terraces, and those stacked into discrete piles, all served to reduce evaporation and soil moisture loss. Proposition 4f is accepted.

LABOR INPUTS

Detailed mapping (Chapter 4) identified 89,089 m of rock alignments (grid borders and terraces) covering 82.2 hectares. With such extensive features, one is prone to ask: How much labor did it take to build these features? The answer is not an easy one to discern, even though the ceramic evidence from survey indicates that the grid fields were constructed throughout a lengthy period of time (Chapters 8, 10), in either a systematic or an incremental manner (Doolittle 1984). More research clearly needs to be done to refine the dating of the grid fields and make it more precise. With the data at hand, we surmise that work on these features involved a small labor force working throughout an extended period of time, rather than a large labor force completing the task quickly.

Close inspection reveals discrete sections of grids within each locality. With abrupt changes in the directions of some grid borders, abrupt changes in the sizes of some grids, and differences in the ways that rocks were stacked or piled in different places, the rock-bordered grids constituting each locality were seemingly built in a piecemeal fashion (Doolittle 1984). Small sections of rock-bordered grids were built and then later subsequent sections were added on, eventually resulting in an extensive network of grids.

Regardless of how these grids were built, an impressive amount of labor was invested in the project. One

study of rock alignment construction in a setting like that of the Safford Valley provides insight about the amount of work expended on the building of the rock-bordered grids and related features. Conducting experiments in the Verde Valley, P. Fish and S. Fish (1984: 156) "found that one person on the average was able to gather nearby rock and construct 1.65 m of alignment per hour." Assuming a six-hour workday, which is typical of subsistence farmers everywhere (Barlett 1980: 150), one worker should have been able to build a 9.9 m segment of rock alignment each day. The 89,089 linear meters of rock alignments, therefore, could have been built in approximately 9,000 person-days. It is highly improbable that construction involved one person working alone, every day for nearly 25 years, or that it involved 9,000 people working only one day. Actual construction time was somewhere in between.

PRODUCTION

Assessment of plant spacings based on evidence from elsewhere (Chapter 7) indicates that 44,500 agave plants could have been cultivated on the rock-bordered grids and related features at this site. This is an impressive plantation, and begs the question: What was being done with all this agave? Probably a certain percentage was consumed locally and the remainder exported. Agave is a slow-growing perennial, unlike staple crops such as maize and beans that are annuals, and it could have been added to a mixed farming strategy as discussed in Chapter 2 and below (see S. Fish 1995). Conversely, it could have been a survival crop that only would have been harvested and consumed when the greater maize crop, which presumably was cultivated under irrigation on the floodplain, failed (Doolittle 1997). Or, agave cultivated on this site could have served both purposes.

AGAVE WITHOUT GRIDS

The geologic (Chapter 3), cartographic (Chapter 4), and soil (Chapter 6) analyses show that there is a remarkably strong correlation between the physical landscape of the region and the location of the rock-bordered grids and related features. Different plants grow best, or at least are their most competitive, in particular environments. The conditions created by rock-bordered grids, rock piles, and terrace risers may be viewed as culturally created environments that mimic those in places where agave grows well naturally. If this is the case, then one can ask: Is there not evidence of agave cultivation at site AZ CC:1:2 (ASM) in localities where there are no rock-bordered grids, alignments, or piles? The answer is yes.

As demonstrated in Chapter 3, a triangular-shaped parcel of land between Grid Localities 3 and 10 (Figs. 1.6, 3.2), underlain by Gila River terrace alluvium, does not contain rock-bordered grids. It is, however, an area where tabular knives have been found in some abundance on the surface, a tool indicative of agave cultivation. Agave grew here without the benefit of artificially constructed rock features that would have facilitated mulching, perhaps because soil conditions were so favorable.

THE ROLE OF GRIDS IN THE PREHISTORIC SAFFORD VALLEY

The archaeological survey and excavations at site AZ CC:1:2 (ASM) have provided important information. Beyond the better understanding of the nature and history of the specific use and development of the area for intensive agave cultivation, this work contributes to the knowledge of the general prehistoric subsistence-settlement system of the Safford Valley.

Archaeological Findings and the Central Place Designation

The observations made by Dale Lightfoot (Chapter 4) that Big Spring and Big Spring Wash represented forms of "central places" for the settlement at AZ CC:1:2 (ASM) are supported by archaeological survey and investigations. Big Spring provided a water source for two small pit house villages nearby (Figs. 1.6, 4.1*b*), some 3.1 and 3.4 km (1.9 and 2.1 miles) north of the current channel of the Gila River.

Lightfoot's suggestion that Big Spring Wash served as a central corridor from the Gila River floodplain to the spring and the center of the grid fields is reasonable. The wash would have been one of the most direct routes into the grid field system, and to its associated pit houses and field houses, from the Gila River floodplain settlements that were on the low terrace

transition zone located between the north floodplain of the Gila River and the base of the high terrace on which the grid fields were situated. The access provided by Big Spring Wash also contemporaneously provided an *en route* location for the placement of roasting pits and for obtaining fuel wood and game. This pattern corresponds with our model of the contemporaneous use of both the dry-farmed grid fields and the irrigated floodplains of the Gila River by the inhabitants (Chapter 2). A similar pattern was identified down river in the Casa Grande area for the Classic period occupation (Crown 1987). Therefore, the symmetry of rock-bordered grids observed by Lightfoot (Chapter 4) seems to have been a function of both cultural and environmental factors.

Cultivation, Processing, and Uses of Agave

Although the collection, cultivation, processing, and uses of agave have been thoroughly discussed for Mesoamerica by Parsons and Parsons (1990) and Patrick (1985), relatively little is known regarding the history of agave use in the American Southwest, and specifically the Safford Valley. Well-preserved artifacts (like cordage and sandals) made from agavelike fiber have been reported by Kelly (1937) and Lee (1975) from the early archaeological investigations at McEuen Cave, located about 36 km (22 miles) north-northwest of the grid fields at AZ CC:1:2 ASM (Fig. 1.5). From recently renewed studies at McEuen cave, it appears possible that agave was collected in the wild around 2,200 B.P. and earlier, as told to us in 2002 by Lisa Huckell and Steven Shackley (see Shackley 2000). Because Lisa Huckell is in the process of analyzing the artifacts and other remains of vegetal materials, she cannot at this time with certainty state that agave, in addition to other similar plants (like yucca), was used by the inhabitants of McEuen Cave. The fibers from McEuen Cave and the cave containing the later Pinaleño Cache (Haury and Huckell 1993), located about 22 km (13.5 miles) to the south-southwest of site AZ CC:1:2 (Fig. 1.5), are so completely processed that it is difficult to determine the species of the plants represented. The earliest radiocarbon-based chronological evidence from the Pinaleño Cache (A.D. 577–664; Haury and Huckell 1993: 115–119) is temporally close to other radiocarbon dates for agave cultivation collected from roasting pits at the Sanchez Copper Project (A.D. 430–660; Seymour, Ahlstrom, and Doak 1997a: 10.4) and by this project in Big Spring Wash (A.D. 490 and 500; Chapter 7). Other radiocarbon dates and ceramic cross-dating provide evidence for agave use from about A.D. 750 to 1385 (Late Early Formative through Late Classic periods), most likely representing the time frame for the initial construction and subsequent augmentations of the rock-bordered grid fields. The Early and Late Classic period dates correspond well with the dating of other fields located to the north of the Gila River (Seymour, Ahlstrom, and Doak 1997b) and in the foothill area along the northern face of the Pinaleño Mountains (Neely 1995a, 1997a, 1997b, 2001a; Neely and Doolittle 1996; Rinker 1998; Rinker and Neely 1998). In these locations, small and large fields may contain one type of agricultural feature or various combinations of features. Rock piles, rock-bordered grids, terraces, linear borders, diversion borders, and "chevrons" have been recorded by Crary (1997) and Neely (1997b, 2001a). These fields were in environmental and topographic locations that would have been favorable for the cultivation of agave, yucca, and related plants.

Several studies (like S. Fish and others 1992), including a project just east of Safford (Seymour, Ahlstrom, and Doak 1997b), have convincingly shown that many, if not most, of the dry-farmed fields that depended solely or predominantly on direct precipitation for moisture were dedicated to the cultivation of agave for the production of edible mescal and other by-products (Parsons and Parsons 1990; Patrick 1985; Shackley 2000). The discovery of roasting pits with agave contents, as well as the recovery of large numbers of pulping planes and some spindle whorls at AZ CC:1:2 (ASM), indicate that agave was being grown there not only for food, but for its fiber as well.

Details concerning agave and the growth of agave in the American Southwest have been presented elsewhere (for example, Castetter and others 1938; Crosswhite 1981; S. Fish and others 1990, 1992; S. Fish and others 1985; Ford 1981; Gentry 1972, 1982). The following comments are restricted to observations on agave growth and cultivation as they relate to site AZ CC:1:2 (ASM).

Because it is adapted to low and unreliable moisture, agave seems to be ideally suited to lands where aridity makes agriculture impossible or risky and where it is not possible to irrigate. Macrofloral evidence for more than one species of agave has been recovered from the roasting pits of the Marana Community, located just northwest of Tucson, but the identity and number of agave species is currently unresolved (S. Fish and others 1992: 83). The most likely species to have been cultivated in the Southwest is *Agave murpheyi* (Crosswhite 1981: 58–59; Fish and Nabhan 1991). Although we personally observed scattered occasional examples of agave in the upper foothills of the Pinaleño Mountains, no true stands or fields of agave have yet been found in the surveyed area.

The agave illustrated in Figure 10.1 was growing on the north-facing upper bajada slopes of the Pinaleño Mountains south of Safford in 1998 (Fig. 1.5). When asked to identify the species of this agave from the photograph, Suzanne Fish replied in November of 2003:

> Without doubt the plants are agaves but conclusively identifying the species without seeing the flowering stalks is difficult. The one with shorter, broader leaves is almost surely *Agave parryi*. The other larger one could be *A. palmeri*, *chrysantha*, or possibly even *murpheyi*. One way to narrow it down is to look in Arizona Flora and Gentry's book to see which ones occur in that area....In any case, it would be best to see what the stalk and flowers are like and I doubt anyone can be certain otherwise.

The two references suggested by Suzanne Fish verify that the smaller, broad leaf species is *Agave parryi* (Gentry 1982: 538–545; Kearney and Peebles 1964: 194–195). However the species identification of the larger agave is not clear. In a brief consideration of the species, Kearney and Peebles (1964: 195) cite *Agave palmeri* as the only species of the three to be present in Graham County. In his extensive treatise on the taxa, Gentry (1982: 426–431, 440–447) does not mention the presence of any of the three species, or any other species in Graham County. With the little that has been said about agave in Graham County, and the Safford Valley specifically, one suspects that the state of knowledge for this plant is currently as poorly known for this area as the archaeology was until recently.

S. Fish and her colleagues (1985, 1992) noted that it is possible that the dry-farmed fields were construc-

Figure 10.1. Agaves growing on the north facing upper bajada slopes of the Pinaleño Mountains. William E. Doolitle is pointing to a small "offset." (Photograph by James A. Neely.)

ed where now extinct stands of agave were once present or that agave was collected as "pups" or "offsets" (Fig. 10.1) from relatively distant stands and then transplanted to prepared fields to mature. Once the fields were established, the perpetuation of the crop could continue by obtaining volunteer offsets from the plants growing in the same fields. As in the Marana Community (S. Fish and others 1992: 73–87), most of the Safford Valley dry-farmed fields identifiable by the presence of water-management features are characterized by large numbers of "rock piles." We presume that these features represent localities for the planting and nurturing of agave plants as they were in the Marana Community. The findings reported in Chapter 7 support this presumption. Because many of the dry-farmed fields in the Safford Valley that have rock piles

also have various combinations of other kinds of features (like rock-bordered grids, linear borders, terraces, and chevrons), it is here proposed that they, too, were dedicated to agave production and possibly other plants as well.

The Role of Agave in the Mixed Subsistence System

The occupants of the Safford Valley developed a long-lived subsistence system based on multiple resources for surviving in the unpredictable and often inhospitable environment. This "mixed" (Welch 1994) or "broad spectrum" (Flannery 1965) and "shifting cultivation" (Spencer 1966; Wilcox 1978) system began in the Archaic period of the region, and it continued until the region's abandonment in the Late Classic period. The subsistence system of the prehistoric inhabitants of the Safford Valley incorporated an adaptively modifiable balance of collecting wild flora in conjunction with cultivating plants (Spencer 1973: 70). Modifications in the balance were occasioned by changes in climate and access to microenvironmental zones. The collection and subsequent cultivation of agave was evidently an integral part of this subsistence strategy, and AZ CC:1:2 (ASM) apparently became a principal locality of formal agave cultivation in the Safford Valley. This long-lived pattern of broad-spectrum subsistence has also been proposed by Crown (1987) for the nearby and well-studied Casa Grande area, downstream on the Gila River, and by Welch (1994) for the Tonto Basin to the northwest.

The increase in number and area of agricultural features (terraces, rock-bordered grids, rock piles) across topographic and environmental zones through time documents an on-going process of agricultural maximization. In addition to the Safford Valley, this process has been recognized in other regions of the Southwest (Crown 1987; P. Fish and Fish 1984; S. Fish and others 1992). During this process of maximization, the agriculturalists must have determined that the additional time and effort to construct rock-bordered grids at AZ CC:1:2 (ASM) were worthwhile so as to provide a more regular and extensive area for planting (see Figure 5.12) compared with the irregular and smaller planting area provided by rock piles (see S. Fish and others 1992, Fig. 7.8). This theory is supported by the estimate provided by S. Fish and her collaborators (Chapter 7) that the per hectare productivity of AZ CC:1:2 (ASM) was more than two and a half times greater than that of the Marana Community. The Marana Community was nearly six times larger in area than AZ CC:1:2, but had no rock-bordered grid field constructions.

Through time there was continuity as well as change in the subsistence strategies used by the early inhabitants of the Safford Valley: change in the emphasis placed on certain foodstuffs and how they were obtained and continuity in the resources utilized and the methods for their procurement. The apparent long-term use of the area around AZ CC:1:2 (ASM) for first obtaining and then cultivating agave serves as a good example. This continuity of cultural practices has been noted for the Casa Grande region and elsewhere in the

Hohokam area (Crown 1987: 148–149) and provides support for the O'odham model (Neely 1997b) briefly summarized in Chapter 2 and below.

Rock-Bordered Grids and Settlement Pattern

The four areas of habitation identified among and at the edge of the grids are all small. Additional settlements, both small and large, have been found away from the grids. The distance of many of these habitations from the grids is not extensive, but their placement enhanced the occupants' access to multiple subsistence resources. Many of these sites are located in the transitional zone, or "ecotone," situated between the irrigated floodplain north of the Gila River and the dry-farmed upper surface of the high terrace above the floodplain. This aspect of the settlement pattern closely parallels findings in the Casa Grande area (Crown 1987).

The site nearest to the grids is in the transitional zone of our study area at the mouth of Peck Wash (Fig. 1.6), appropriately named the Peck Wash Site (Crary 1997). The settlement was large, but, like nearly all of the similarly located sites, is highly disturbed by modern looting, construction, and agricultural activities. Site survey by Gilman and Sherman (1975: 8–9, Fig. 1) recorded a better preserved permanent habitation site (Owens-Colvin, AZ CC:1:19 ASM) approximately 6 km (3.7 miles) west (downstream) of Peck Wash and the grid fields; it was partially excavated (Neily and others 1993; Rule 1993). The Peck Wash Site and Owens-Colvin Site are but two of the many settlements that bordered the Gila River from San José to Bylas, and farther west (Fig. 1.5). Some of these sites were first recorded by archaeologists working in the Safford Valley at the end of the 19th and early in the 20th centuries (Bandelier 1892; Fewkes 1904; Hough 1907). Some 50 years then passed before Donald Tuohy conducted a systematic survey that documented 29 sites (Tuohy 1960, Fig. 1) along both sides of the Gila River in the approximately 65-km (40-mile) airline distance between San José to the east and Bylas to the west. This distance averages about one site for every 2.2 km (1.4 miles) along the river. Ahlstrom (1997: 9.1, 9.2, Fig. 9.1) has published a map showing the locations of seven "major habitation sites" close to the Gila River. These sites, each estimated as having 20 or more rooms, appear to correspond with sites that Tuohy recorded. Only a few of these sites near the Gila River have been tested and excavated (Clark 2002; Fewkes 1904; Johnson and Wasley 1966; Neily and others 1993; Rule 1993; Tuohy 1960).

What has become increasing clear through recent studies by Clark (2002) is that during the Early Formative period (about A.D. 1–300) the inhabitants of the Safford Valley were already exploiting the waters of the Gila River for domestic uses and for agricultural irrigation. Although it is difficult to discern the original settlement pattern because of the extensive and intensive historic modifications of the Gila River floodplain and adjacent terraces through time, there appears to have been a general replacement of the many small settlements located close to the Gila River with fewer, large, aggregated communities located above the floodplain (Chapter 2). The distribution of these larger aggregated communities strongly suggests that they were situated along major canals carrying water from the Gila River. Crary (1997) has noted that these large communities are spaced at 3–6 km (1.8–3.7 mile) intervals along the first terrace above the floodplain of the San Carlos River, as well as along the first terrace above the floodplain of the Gila River between the small modern communities of San Carlos and Geronimo (Fig. 1.5). The 3–6 km intervals noted by Crary closely parallel the intervals between large sites with platform mounds recorded by Crown (1987) for the Casa Grande area down river. Farther east, the Late Formative and later settlements located between the small modern communities of Fort Thomas and San José form a similar distribution along the first and second terraces paralleling both sides of the Gila River floodplain (Ahlstrom 1997; Bandelier 1892; Clark 2002; Fewkes 1904; Gilman and Sherman 1975; Hough 1907; Neely 1997a, 1997b; Tuohy 1960). Note that the distance of approximately 6 km (3.7 miles) between the larger settlements matches the distance between the Peck Wash Site and the Owens-Colvin Site.

There is no direct evidence for the prehistoric antiquity of the channel now known as the Graham-Curtis canal (Figs. 1.6, 4.1a, b). However, there is historic documentation dealing with the town of "Smithville" (now named "Pima") from the Mormon records titled "St. Joseph Stake History, Pima Ward"

and "St. Joseph Stake History, Eden Ward" (Williams 1937: 22) that suggests that the canal may have been prehistoric in origin. The latter document (Williams 1937: 22) states that the Mormons, "had enlarged fifteen to twenty miles of the old ditches (the old ditches were widened from three to four feet to, in many cases, eight to ten feet and deepened proportionally)." The Peck Wash Site and the Owens-Colvin Site would have been located adjacent to this ancient canal system in a manner similar to locations of sites at the eastern end of the Safford Valley that have nearby functioning canals with historic documentation indicating their prehistoric origins (Colvin 1997; Ramenofsky 1984). These site locations relative to major canals in the Safford Valley are similar to those documented by Crown (1987, Fig. 2) for the Casa Grande area down river.

Chronological Placement of Site AZ CC:1:2 (ASM)

Based on the ceramic type distributions (Table 8.2) and dating (Table 8.5), the most likely chronological placement for each locality investigated by survey and excavation during our study of AZ CC:1:2 (ASM) is shown in Table 10.1. The initial date range presented is the maximum possible interval indicated by the ceramic types, and the second date range represents the most likely period of use.

Grid Localities 2, 3, and 9 have beginning dates significantly earlier than other localities. They are adjacent to and near Pit House Localities 1 and 2, which have correspondingly early beginning dates. Considering all ten of the grid localities and associated features and sites, the survey recovered ceramics indicating use of the area from about A.D. 750 until around A.D. 1385.

The ceramics in the rock piles within Grid Locality 1 correspond well with the ceramics recovered elsewhere in Grid Locality 1 that signify a later use of the field. The rock piles in this locality date from about A.D. 1200 to 1350, the middle of the Classic period.

Roasting Pits 1, 2, and 3 within Big Spring Wash contained material that could be dated by radiocarbon (Table 10.1 Note). Roasting Pits 1 and 2, dating about A.D. 490 and 500, respectively, were adjacent to Grid Localities 4 and 6, which have ceramics dating much later. On the other hand, Roasting Pit 3, dating about A.D. 1370 by radiocarbon, was situated between Grid

Table 10.1. Chronological Placement of Site AZ CC:1:2 (ASM)

Location	Maximum range of datable ceramics (A.D.)	Most likely range of occupation or use (A.D.)
Grid		
Locality 1	1050–1425	1150–1350
Locality 2	700–1425	750–1350
Locality 3	800–1125	850–1100
Locality 4	1150–1400	1175–1350
Locality 5	1250–1425	1275–1350
Locality 6	1050–1400	1150–1325
Locality 7	1250–1425	1275–1350
Locality 8	1150–1425	1200–1350
Locality 9	800–1300	850–1275
Locality 10	1250–1425	1275–1350
Big Spring Wash Terrace	1250–1425	1275–1350
Rock Piles in Grid Locality 1		
20 m NNE of SP 29	1250–1425	1275–1350
18 m SE of SP 23–24	1150–1400	1200–1350
19 m SSW of SP 23–24	1150–1400	1200–1350
Roasting Pits		
Pit 1	1150–1400	1200–1275
Pits 2, 3, 4*		
Pit House Locality 1		
Terrace surface	700–1150	750–1125
Collection Area 1	700–1400	750–1350
Collection Area 2	700–1400	750–1350
Collection Area 3	700–1400	750–1350
Midden surface		
Collection Area 4	700–1400	750–1350
Midden profile	950–1125	1000–1100
Pit House Locality 2	800–1150	850–1125
Rock Mound Feature 1	1300–1450	1340–1385
Field House Structure 1		
Field House surface	950–1400	1000–1325
Room 1, Levels 1–3*		
Room 1, Level 4	950–1300	1000–1275
Room 1, Level 5	1050–1300	1150–1275

* Contained no datable ceramics.
NOTE: Material in roasting pits dated by radiocarbon:
  Roasting Pit 1, about A.D. 490
  Roasting Pit 2, about A.D. 500
  Roasting Pit 3, about A.D. 1370

Localities 2 and 9, both of which had surface ceramics dating earlier than that. We cannot explain these disparities except to say that Big Spring Wash was apparently used throughout human exploitation of the area. Perhaps late dating ceramics fell into partially open Roasting Pits 1 and 2 long after they were last used, or they could represent a later reuse of the pits. The early radiocarbon dates from Roasting Pits 1 and 2 have caused some concern (Chapter 7), but they could represent a time during which agave was being collected and do not necessarily indicate that the grids were in place and agave cultivation was established. These early dates are congruent with the radiocarbon date from the roasting pit at the Sanchez Copper Project (Seymour, Ahlstrom, and Doak 1997a: 10.4) and are only slightly earlier than the earliest radiocarbon evidence from the Pinaleño Cache (Haury and Huckell 1993: 115–119).

Based on the ceramics collected from the surface, Pit House Locality 1 is characterized by at least three habitation structures (pit houses) and an associated kitchen midden that may have a range of use from about A.D. 750 to 1350 but more likely from about 750 to 1125. The pit house occupation probably dates to the last half of the Pinaleño phase, to both the Talkali and Two Dog phases of the Late Formative-Preclassic period and to the beginning of the subsequent Eden phase transition to the Early Classic period (Fig. 2.2). Later ceramics (Table 8.2), dating about A.D. 1275–1350, probably represent a secondary use of the location, but not necessarily a reoccupation of the pit houses. The late assemblage of sherds indicates the reuse of the area and adjacent fields during the Bylas and early Safford phases (Fig. 2.2). The most likely time of use of Pit House Locality 2, based on ceramic dating, was from about A.D. 850 to 1125.

The assemblage of sherds in association with Field House Structure 1 suggests a maximum occupation range of about A.D. 950 to 1400. However, considering the ceramics recovered from excavation, a range of about A.D. 1150 to 1275 (the Eden and Bylas phases of the Early Classic period, Fig. 2.2) seems more likely (see Reconstructed History, below).

The latest (most recent) feature dated by ceramics at AZ CC:1:2 (ASM) is Rock Mound Feature 1. Its single sherd of Gila Polychrome gives a maximum probable terminal date of about A.D. 1385. The radiocarbon date from Roasting Pit 3 (TX-9217; cal. A.D. 1370±40) is congruent with a probable abandonment of AZ CC:1:2 (ASM) between about A.D. 1350 and 1385.

Discussion of the Chronological Placements

Two questions that immediately come to mind are: were the habitations and the rock-bordered grids built at the same time, and were the grid fields all constructed contemporaneously or were they expanded outward from the spring and pit house village area through time? For an indication that some of the grids may have originated around the spring area with the founding of the pit house settlements and that the grids were built outward through time, see Table 8.2. A scan of the presence or absence of certain ceramics suggests that both early and late ceramics cluster in Grid Localities 2, 3, and 9, which are close to Pit House Localities 1 and 2, whereas only late ceramics characterize the more distant grids between those localities and the Gila River. The late grids appear to have been associated only with the surface field houses constructed of piled rock.

Two radiocarbon samples (TX–9215 and TX–9216: cal. A.D. 490 ± 60 and cal. A.D. 500 ± 40, respectively, see Chapter 7, Table 7.7) suggest that site AZ CC:1:2 (ASM) was used for plant collecting, and possibly dry-farming cultivation, in the latter part of the Early Formative period at about A.D. 500 (the latter part of the Peñasco phase of the Early Formative-Pre-Classic period, see Fig. 2.2). They do not, however, indicate that the rock-bordered grids were present at that time. A third radiocarbon sample (TX–9217) recovered from a third roasting pit at AZ CC:1:2 (ASM) provided a date of cal. A.D. 1370 ± 40. These temporally widely separated dates appear anomalous, and S. Fish and her colleagues (Chapter 7) state that the two earlier dates "should be treated with caution." These dates could represent the earliest uses of agave growing atop the mesa, however, and not the presence of rock-bordered grids.

These early dates are supported by two other radiocarbon dates from the Safford Valley that may be associated with agave use. The first, with a one-sigma radiocarbon range of A.D. 577 to 664, comes from the Pinaleño Cache (Haury and Huckell 1993). The second, with a two-sigma range of A.D. 430 to 660 (also said to be 450–670 by Doak and others 1997: 4.28), was recovered from a roasting pit excavated during the Sanchez Copper Mine Project in a playa context characterized only by rock piles (Doak and others 1997: 4.25; Seymour, Ahlstrom, and Doak 1997a: 10.4).

But what of the large chronological gap between the early and late dates at AZ CC:1:2 (ASM); could it indicate a hiatus in the cultivation of agave in the Safford Valley? Although it may represent a hiatus at that settlement, there is evidence for agave cultivation from other parts of the Safford Valley in the interim. The excavation of a roasting pit in Lefthand Canyon (Fig. 1.5; AZ CC:1:54 ASM) recovered organic materials that radiocarbon dated (TX–9258) between A.D. 1185 and 1267 (Rinker 1998; Rinker and Neely 1998) and, based on the associated ceramics, represents the Bylas phase of the Early Classic period (Fig. 2.2; Crary 1997). A one-sigma radiocarbon date range of A.D. 1215 to 1300 was obtained from cotton fiber in the Pinaleño Cache (Haury and Huckell 1993: 116, Table 1). A second roasting pit from Lefthand Canyon was radiocarbon dated (TX–9259) between A.D. 1374 and 1452 (Rinker 1998; Rinker and Neely 1998), indicating use during the Safford phase of the Late Classic period. This last date corresponds well with the date of A.D. 1370 from Roasting Pit 3 at site AZ CC:1:2 (ASM). The Sanchez Copper Mine Project (Seymour, Ahlstrom, and Doak 1997a: 10.4) recorded a similar hiatus in their investigations. Their two calibrated two-sigma radiocarbon dates were A.D. 430 to 660 and 1020 to 1260. With so few dates from both AZ CC:1:2 (ASM) and the Sanchez Copper Project, however, it is probable that this hiatus is a result of an inadequate sample size.

There is further evidence that no hiatus existed at AZ CC:1:2 (ASM) in the ceramic distribution (Table 8.2), which shows continuous use of the area after about A.D. 750–800. In the vicinity of Pit House Localities 1 and 2, which includes Grid Localities 2, 3, and 9, the majority of the ceramics are early, but small numbers of late ceramic types indicate the area was used in later times as well.

The survey of Rock Mound Feature 1 and the excavation of Roasting Pit 3 provide ceramic evidence and a radiocarbon date (TX–9217) of cal. A.D. 1370 ± 40 that indicate at least a portion of the extensive system of rock-bordered grids was in use during the Safford phase (Fig. 2.2) of the Late Classic period. Several of the farming localities listed in Table 10.2 that have good evidence for agave cultivation have ceramic evidence for use during times equivalent to the

Safford phase. In summary, the chronological information available from AZ CC:1:2 (ASM) indicates that the area was in use from approximately A.D. 500 to 1385. Unlike some adjacent regions to the north and east (Lekson 2002: 75), these observations, as well as evidence from elsewhere in the Safford Valley, provide support for the continuous occupation of the Safford Valley from at least the Archaic period well into the Late Classic period. In fact, it is conceivable that the Safford Valley may have been a center of population, and perhaps of the Salado tradition, that moved into the essentially "empty" regions defined by Lekson (2002: 75) during the 14th century.

A Reconstructed History of Site AZ CC:1:2 (ASM)

The radiocarbon dates from the roasting pits and the ceramics in association with the grids and related features indicate a maximum range of about A.D. 500 to 1385 for agricultural site AZ CC:1:2 (ASM). This area was used by some of the prehistoric inhabitants of the Safford Valley for a period of about 885 years in a constant, but punctuated, intensification of agricultural pursuits (Neely 1997b).

Beginning in the Early Formative period (about 150 B.C. to A.D. 800), the inhabitants of this region participated in a subsistence system that incorporated a majority of foodstuffs from hunting and gathering, but included some horticultural or agricultural products to augment the diet (Chapter 2). Their lifeway left behind small, scattered sites in all of the ecozones in the area and a preponderance of certain types of tools. Undoubtedly they used parts of the region during this period as localities for the collection of wild agave plants, and in some areas they may have cultivated agave with dry-farming techniques. A period of precipitation variability with a trend toward drought began about A.D. 752 and continued into the early part of the following Late Formative period (Graybill and others 1999; Rose 1994; Van West and Altschul 1994). As drought conditions intensified, the inhabitants of the Safford Valley probably exploited and intensified their collection of agave.

During the subsequent Late Formative period (about A.D. 800 to 1150), this broad-spectrum subsistence pattern continued, most likely to offset the unpredictable nature of moisture in the region (Chapter 2). At the same time, agricultural pursuits intensified. We see more tangible evidence of the growing dependence on agriculture with the increasing size and apparent permanency of communities, along with the expansion of agricultural fields. Permanent infrastructures were built and the distribution and density of tools used for agricultural pursuits increased. It is probable that the continuing climatic variability and drought during the first 117 years (A.D. 808–925) of this period led to the development of the first rock-bordered grids at AZ CC:1:2 (ASM) atop the high terrace north of the Gila River and to other such permanent infrastructures like checkdams, linear borders, chevrons, and rock-bordered grids in other parts of the Safford Valley. The following interval of relatively salubrious climate between A.D. 977 and 1100 probably would not have curtailed the by-then burgeoning agave production, and the subsequent renewal of climatic variability and drought from A.D. 1122 to 1150 may have been expected by the knowledgeable and experienced farmers of the Safford Valley.

The greatest expansion and use of the rock-bordered grids took place during the final period of prehistoric occupation (about A.D. 1150–1385), in the Classic period (about A.D. 1150 to 1450; Crary 1997). There was an increasing focus on agriculture and a greater expenditure of energy in the construction of agricultural features. Contemporaneous similar activities are documented for the middle Gila River region (Crown 1984), the Marana Community (S. Fish and others 1992), and elsewhere in the Southwest. The high degree of climatic variability and low available moisture and drought created an interval with the least agricultural predictability in the 631–year dendroclimatic record of the nearby Tonto Basin (Van West and Altschul 1994: 402–403). And, in spite of the emphasis on the use of canal irrigation of floodplain and lower terrace areas adjacent to the Gila River, for the latter half of this period even canal irrigation was adversely affected by poor climatic conditions (Graybill and others 1999; Huckleberry 1995; Waters and Ravesloot 2000). In addition, it is during this period that interregional trade appears to have increased significantly (Chapter 2; Crary 1997).

With these factors in mind, we suggest that large expanses of cultivable land not situated appropriately for irrigation agriculture were developed to produce vast fields of agave. The agave, drought resistant and hearty, would have flourished to produce foodstuffs and other products for consumption by the local inhabitants as well as for trade. In summary, the sequence of events in the founding and expansion of the grid field system at AZ CC:1:2 (ASM) may be tentatively reconstructed as follows.

1. At about A.D. 500, and perhaps earlier, local inhabitants utilized stands of wild agave in the area of site AZ CC:1:2 (ASM).

2. Perhaps as early as about A.D. 750, people collecting wild agave built pit houses (Pit House Locality 1) near the Big Spring water source.

3. With the founding of this settlement, the inhabitants developed, or adapted from elsewhere, the rock-bordered grid technology. The presence of the naturally occurring lithic materials on the ground surface surrounding the pit houses made this location ideal for the construction of the grids. If the ceramic data are correct, grids in Locality 2 were the first to be constructed.

4. The settlement at Pit House Locality 2 was founded somewhat later (about A.D. 850), perhaps to accommodate a larger population to construct additional grids (Grid Localities 3 and 9, Table 10.1) and to plant, tend, and harvest the by-then recognizably successful agave crop.

5. Ceramic evidence indicates that settlements at Pit House Localities 1 and 2 were abandoned around A.D. 1125.

6. Perhaps as a replacement for the settlements at the Pit House localities, Field House Structure 1 was constructed around A.D. 1150. The workers who occupied this field house on a temporary basis probably came from permanent homes at the Peck Wash Site, AZ CC:1:19 (ASM), or another settlement in that vicinity.

7. Ceramics indicate that the grids at Localities 1 and 6 may have been constructed at approximately the same time as Field House Structure 1.

8. Grids at Locality 4 were constructed around A.D. 1175.

9. Grids at Locality 8 were constructed around A.D. 1200.

10. Grids at Localities 5, 7, and 10 were constructed around A.D. 1275.

11. Ceramics recorded on survey (Table 8.2) indicate that grids at Localities 3 and 9 were not used

after around A.D. 1100 and 1275, respectively, and that Field House Structure 1 was abandoned around A.D. 1275. Curiously, the presence of late ceramics on most of the other grid field localities and at Pit House Locality 1 strongly suggests that some rock-bordered grid fields were in use until at least A.D. 1350.

12. Rock Mound Feature 1 (Table 8.1) appears to have been the last (most recent) construction at AZ CC:1:2 (ASM), perhaps dating as late as about A.D. 1385. Roasting Pit 3 indicates that agave processing was taking place at this time. However, there is no evidence to indicate that the rock-bordered grids were still in use when these features were built.

Social Organization Implications of Site AZ CC:1:2 (ASM)

Some would interpret the extensive infrastructure of AZ CC:1:2 (ASM) as an indicator of a large work force led by elites and organized by means of a ranked society. However, data from AZ CC:1:2 (ASM) and elsewhere in the Safford Valley imply the presence of a small work force and a less complex social organization. A model based on the ethnohistoric O'odham has been presented for the prehistoric social organization of the Safford Valley area (Neely 1997b) and appears to be applicable in this case as well.

In summary, this model proposes that even the most complex and extensive communities and public works of the Safford Valley were constructed and used by peoples organized at a "tribal" level. The model postulates social, political, and religious organization changes, as well as modification in agricultural technology, to accommodate and adapt to stresses occurring between about A.D. 750 to 1400 that resulted from climatic degradation, population increases, and possibly intercommunity conflict (Chapter 2). The model proposes the early presence of an essentially egalitarian society organized by kinship and employing "Chanayov's rule" (Sahlins 1972: 87), an optimizing strategy to "store" labor potential in reserve to be used in emergencies to insure the survival of the household. As stresses built though time, more complex kinship-based organizational integrating mechanisms and religious organizations were adopted. These mechanisms for organization and integration operated as a horizontal form of stratification similar to the "sequential" or "modular" hierarchy described by Johnson (1982,

1989). As noted (Chapter 2), the development of a horizontal form of sociopolitical organization would not have required major reformulations of the system existing since the Early Formative period.

This O'odham-based model could account for the construction of *all* of the rock-bordered grids of AZ CC:1:2 (ASM) as a single major project. However, the apparent construction of the grids in a systematic or incremental manner, as indicated by the surface ceramic collections (this chapter), indicates a small work force and a less complex organization.

Supporting the theory of a small work force and a less complex organization is Parsons and Parsons' (1990) detailed study of maguey utilization in highland central Mexico. Their observations indicate that relatively large fields of agave could be planted, tended, and harvested by members of a household, a level of complexity that is suggested by the boundary markers found at AZ CC:1:2 (ASM). Just how much work was involved in constructing the grids? Using the labor input estimates provided above, the resulting total of approximately 25 person-years is put into perspective by assuming a work force of 10 persons, which results in a construction time of about 2.6 years for the entire 82.2 hectare area of grids. Construction is put into even better perspective when one considers that the grids were evidently built piecemeal and not as a single effort.

Comparison of AZ CC:1:2 (ASM) with Other Agricultural Field Sites

It is helpful to compare the agricultural fields at AZ CC:1:2 (ASM) with other well-documented and reported field systems in southern Arizona. Unfortunately, precise comparisons are not possible because of variations in the collection, recording, and reporting of data. Despite the inherent difficulties, however, reviewing the synthesized data does provide some predictive and cautionary information.

The facts in Table 10.2 come from the written reports and illustrations concerning each field. We chose ten of the eleven fields because of similarities with AZ CC:1:2 (ASM): they were dry-farmed, had some corresponding agricultural features, and many had some form of evidence indicating that they probably served for agave cultivation. Differentially, the eleventh field, chosen specifically because it had rock-bordered grids, was irrigated and evidently used for the cultivation of corn and cotton.

Three fields (AZ CC:2:47, 75, and 127 ASM) within the Sanchez Copper Project area (Seymour, Ahlstrom, and Doak 1997b) are located about 25 airline km (15.5 miles) upstream on the Gila River in the Safford Valley, to the east-southeast of AZ CC:1:2 (ASM). They represent a large, a small, and a rock-bordered grid field, respectively. About 50 km (31 miles) north of AZ CC:1:2 (ASM) in the Point of Pines area is the field site AZ W:10:108 (ASM; Woodbury 1961). Two fields (AZ U:15:46 ASM A and P) in the Casa Grande area (Crown 1984, 1987; Dart 1983; Dart and Deaver 1983; S. Fish 1983) are located approximately 140 km (87 miles) west of AZ CC:1:2, downstream on the Gila River. More distant are the three bajada fields (I–III) adjacent to Tumamoc Hill, AZ AA:16:6 (ASM), located at the western edge of the city of Tucson (Masse 1979). Two fields (AZ AA:12: 205 and 470 ASM) are in the Marana Community area located just north of Tucson (S. Fish and others 1992). The small agricultural site of AZ U:1:111 (ASM) is north of Phoenix in the Cave Creek area (Ayers 1967). The Beaver Creek field (NA 4631), located in the Sacred Mountain region of the Verde Valley some 90 km (56 miles) northeast of the city of Phoenix, was chosen not only because it contained grid fields, but also because these fields were canal irrigated for the cultivation of corn and cotton (P. Fish and Fish 1984).

One important observation evident in Table 10.2 is that although there is a certain similarity in the characteristics of these fields, there is much variability as well. Fields with rock-bordered grids frequently have linear borders and rock piles, but the converse is not always true. There is evidence for the cultivation of agave in fields containing all three forms of agricultural features and of corn and cotton in some of those fields. Apparently only corn and cotton were grown in the Beaver Creek field. Thus, rock-bordered grids, linear borders, terraces, and perhaps other agricultural features, were constructed to serve in the cultivation of several different crops. Pollen is the surest indication of which plants were cultivated, but agave pollen is particularly difficult to find due to the nature of agave cultivation practices (Chapter 7). Therefore, because we now have evidence that agave, corn, and cotton may all have been grown in some fields (Cummings

Table 10.2. Comparison of Selected Prehistoric Field Systems in Southern Arizona

Characteristics (Site ASM) AZ	Safford Grids CC:1:2	Sanchez Copper Project CC:2:47	CC:2:75	CC:2:127	Point of Pines W:10:108	Cave Creek Area U:1:11
Physiography and Environment						
Semi-Arid	X	X	X	X		X
Flat Land	X	X	X	X	X	X
Gentle-Moderate Slopes	X	X		X	X	X
Elevation Range (Feet)	2900-3200	3000-3150	3200-3205	3100-3110	5900 ±	1900 ±
Mean Annual Precipitation (Inches)	8.9	8.9	8.9	8.4	18	13.1
Avg. Growing Season (Days)	200 +	200 +	200 +	200 +	165-170	200 +
Field Size						
Total Area of Fields	600 ha	33.5 ha	3.8 ha	5.04 ha	37.1 ha	3.08 ha
Number of Fields	36	One	One	One	One	One
Average Field Size	16.66 ha	n/a	n/a	n/a	n/a	n/a
Types of Cultivation						
Irrigated (Canals)						
Dry-Farmed	X	X	X	X	X	X
Agricultural Features						
Rock-Bordered Grids	X (82.2 ha)			X (0.5 ha)	X (0.46 ha)	X (0.365 ha)
Terraces	X					
Linear Borders	X	X (One)		X (Two)	X (4.4 ha)	X (0.15 ha)
Checkdams	X					
Rock Piles	X	X (133)	X (8)	X (190)		
Rock "Rings"	?	X (4)		X (12)		
Boundary Markers	X	X (One)		X (One)	X (7)	
Roasting Pits	X	X (7)	X (One)			
Associated Structures						
Pit Houses	X (6 ±)					
Field Houses	X (4 +)				X (11)	
C-Shaped "Windbreaks"					5 +	
Small Habitations						X (4)
Large Habitations						
Artifacts						
Ceramics	X (Many)	X (One)		X (One)	X	X (Few)
Sherd Tools						
Spindle Whorls	X					X (One)
Lithics	X	X	X	X		X
Tabular Knives	X (Many)			X (13)		
Large Flakes	X			X		
Pulping Planes	X (Many)					
Ground Stone Tools	X (Few)	X (2)		X (2)		X (2)
Crops Grown						
Agave	X					
Corn				X		
Cotton		X		X		
Agricultural Weeds	X		X	X		
Field Dating (Years A.D.)						
Quality of Dating	Good	Fair-Good	Fair	Fair	Fair-Good	Poor
Dating Based on Ceramics	X	X		X	X	X
Dating Based on Radiocarbon	X	X	X			
Maximum Date Range	500-1400	1020-1260	450-670	900-1500	1000-1450	1150-1500
Most Likely Date Range	750-1385	1040-1220	550-650	1000-1150?	1150-1450	1150-1500

and Puseman 1997: 7-23–24; S. Fish 1984: 114; Fish and others 1992: 81, 85), the presence of only corn and cotton pollen in similar fields does not obviate the cultivation of agave. To confuse the matter even fur-ther, because of the vagaries of pollen distribution, preservation, and collection, S. Fish (1983: 583) notes that the lack of indisputable agricultural indicators (cultigen or agricultural weed pollen) in samples recovered

Table 10.2. Comparison of Selected Prehistoric Field Systems in Southern Arizona (*Continued*)

Characteristics (Site ASM) AZ	Casa Grande Area U:15:46A	U:15:46P	Tumamoc Hill Bajadas I–III AA:16:6	Marana Community AA:12:205	AA:12:470	Beaver Creek NA 4631*
Physiography and Environment						
Semi-Arid	X	X	X	X	X	
Flat Land	X	X			X	X
Gentle-Moderate Slopes	X	X	X	X	X	X
Elevation Range (Feet)	1550-1600	1550-1600	2360 ±	2030-2200	2030-2200	3800-5500
Mean Annual Precipitation (Inches)	9.3	9.3	10.6	11.2	11.2	11.6
Average Growing Season (Days)	200+	200+	200+	200+	200+	191
Field Size						
Total Area of Fields	42.9 ha	20.0 ha	55.1 ha	0.123 ha	12.13 ha	11.0 ha
Number of Fields	One	One	3	One	One	One
Average Field Size	n/a	n/a	18.37 ha	n/a	n/a	n/a
Types of Cultivation						
Irrigated (Canals)						X
Dry-Farmed	X	X	X	X	X	X
Agricultural Feature						
Rock-Bordered Grids	X (0.9 ha)	X (0.053 ha)	X (0.48 ha)			X (8.31 ha)
Terraces	X (2)				X (56)	X (0.21 ha)
Linear Borders			X (30+)			X (2.27 ha)
Checkdams	X (5)		X (16)		X (36)	
Rock Piles	X (200+)	X (200+)	X (300+)	X (3)	X (532)	
Rock "Rings"						
Boundary Markers			X (One?)			X (20)
Roasting Pits				X (One)	X (4 very large)	
Associated Structure						
Pit Houses						
Field Houses						X (23-25)
C-Shaped "Windbreaks"						
Small Habitations						
Large Habitations						
Artifacts						
Ceramics	X (Few)	X (Few)	X	X (891)	X (Many)	X
Sherd Tools				X (16)		
Spindle Whorls				X? (7)		
Lithics	X	X	X	X (55)	X	X
Tabular Knives			X (One)		?	
Large Flakes	X (2)		X		?	
Pulping Planes				X (6)	?	
Ground Stone Tools	X (One)	X (One)	X		?	
Crops Grown						
Agave				X	X	
Corn					X	X
Cotton						X
Agricultural Weeds						
Field Dating (Years A.D.)						
Quality of Dating	Fair-Good	Fair-Good	Fair-Good	Good	Good	Fair-Good
Dating Based on Ceramics	X	X	X	X	X	X
Dating Based on Radiocarbon				X	?	
Maximum Date Range	800-1350	800-1350	850-1450	894-1148	1150-1350	800-1350
Most Likely Date Range	1150-1350	800-1350	850-1000	1011	1150-1350	1200-1350

* Museum of Northern Arizona site number.

from fields and features does not necessarily provide an argument for a lack of agricultural use. On the positive side, Table 10.2 emphasizes that the probability of the use of rock-bordered grids and rock piles in agave production is greatly enhanced by the discovery of associated features (roasting pits) and artifacts (tabular knives, pulping planes, spindle whorls). Thus, both the presence and absence of a broad constellation of characteristics must be considered to determine the most probable cultigens grown in specific fields.

The practice of constructing rock-bordered grid fields was relatively widespread. A form of grid field has been identified some 475 km (295 miles) to the northeast of AZ CC:1:2 (ASM) in the Rio Chama Valley (Doolittle 2000: 246) of north-central New Mexico, and perhaps there are others even more distant. Such wide distribution of rock-bordered fields (Doolittle 2000: 246–247) surely indicates different crops were cultivated in them. Although some of this variability in the use of specific agricultural constructions may be attributed to variations in local topography and climate, it is apparent that the choice of infrastructure may have been as much culturally driven as it was a result of environmental requirements.

General Observations

Specific types of artifacts may be used to determine not only the presence, shape, and area of ancient fields, but also to deduce what crops were under cultivation in specific fields. Except for the areas encompassing the field houses and the two pit house localities with their middens, the stone artifact densities and types recorded during Neely's general survey closely paralleled the smaller, better controlled sample recorded by S. Fish and her colleagues (Chapter 7, Tables 7.8, 7.9).

The labor-intensive rock-bordered grids and the boundary markers reflect family and group use or ownership, perhaps on a long-term basis. The "boundary marker" stones, especially those having petroglyphs, may have functioned as kinship or corporate group identifiers of tenure or ownership. A future stone-by-stone analysis of the petroglyphs is warranted to determine if any recurring symbols or sets of symbols may be correlated with their positioning within the field system.

The manipulation (cultivation) of a wild plant (agave) at the scale indicated by the fields at AZ CC:1:2 (ASM) suggests that we should look further into the manipulation or tending of other wild plants like mesquite (*Prosopis*) or prickly pear (*Opuntia*). In 2003 Jonathan Sandor reported that he had seen a prehistoric basket filled with charred barrel cactus seeds (*Ferocactus* sp.) in the collections of the Eastern Arizona College Museum in the Safford Valley com-

munity of Thatcher, and he noted that barrel cactus is common in the grids at AZ CC:1:2 (ASM). He, too, supports the possibility of "desert garden" areas, where several wild plant species would have been tended or cultivated.

AFTERTHOUGHTS

The study of agriculture as process, and agricultural maximization as a specific aspect of that process, must be based on both qualifiable and quantifiable data that are available from well-preserved surface remains. This survey has presented results that strongly indicate that these qualifiable and quantifiable data are present in the Safford Valley area. Such studies are crucial in understanding the development of, and regional variations in, prehistoric subsistence.

Certain specific information for much of the American Southwest is lacking in order for us to study agriculture as process and fully comprehend and understand the nature and role of specific agricultural sites such as AZ CC:1:2 (ASM). To accomplish this goal it is necessary to address four factors. First, we need to more thoroughly study all aspects of the technology itself to better determine how it functioned, understand its complexity, and appreciate the effort expended in its planning, construction, and maintenance. Second, we need better and more comprehensive dating of the water management and irrigation features and systems. Third, we need a definition of scale criteria and archaeological studies to determine the actual scale of the features and systems. Fourth, we need a significant increase in the sample size and area coverage to determine ranges of variation in technology.

Furthermore, the difficulties we face in understanding the processes involved and developing an operational model result primarily because all parts of the entire system once present are not yet known. To more fully understand the role and meaning of water management manifestations, we must understand not only the technology, but also the subsistence, economic, settlement, sociopolitical, and ceremonial systems of the prehistoric farmers who built and used them.

We have been too conservative in the formulation of theoretical models and have tended to approach the problem with too much of a single mindedness with the application of primarily hierarchical models. Instead of single, neo-evolutionary models we should generate multitrajectory, alternative models (Chamberlin 1890). Once the archaeological and ethnohistorical data have been augmented, a diversified corpus of models should be applied. Specifically, we should follow Hunt's (1972; Hunt and Hunt 1974; also see Mills 2000: 4) "bottom to top" approach and investigate the problem using several complimentary models (Mills 2000) to more fully investigate leadership as it relates to water management and irrigation and ultimately to economic, sociopolitical, and religious development. The study of leadership strategies in these different, but complimentary, ways would greatly increase our potential for interpreting the variation evident in the data.

Knowledge of water management is vitally important to our understanding of how the ancient inhabitants of the American Southwest conserved and obtained water. It was one of the most important and scarcest of natural resources, and their management of it permitted the intensification of agriculture so as to facilitate the trajectory of human cultural development.

In closing, in part as a self-reminder, we would like to echo the plea for greater detail in the description and illustration of findings. Our ability to more fully understand the similarities, differences, and processes of development of water management technology is dependent on the thoroughness of our reports.

Soil Profile Descriptions

Jonathan A. Sandor and Jeffrey A. Homburg

Profiles were described by Jonathan A. Sandor and Jeffrey A. Homburg, 10–13 March 1997, at site AZ CC:1:2 (ASM), Locality 1 (see Chapter 6). The parent material of all profiles consists of gravelly alluvium derived from the Gila Mountains (see Chapter 3).

PROFILE DESCRIPTION 1
Grid Interior

Classification: Loamy, mixed, superactive, thermic Typic Petrocalcid (Cave series).

Geomorphic setting: Backslope of alluvial fan, elevation 901 m, 3–4% slope.

Local setting: Within grid interior; profile exposed in north wall of PP 1.

A—0–2 cm. Pinkish gray to light brown (7.5YR 6/3) gravelly loam, brown (7.5YR 4.5/3) moist; weak medium and coarse plates plus weak to moderate fine and very fine subangular blocks; slightly hard, friable, slightly sticky, slightly plastic; common very fine and few fine roots; few fine and medium tubular pores; 10% gravel; slightly effervescent; moderately alkaline (pH 8.0–8.5; pH 6.5–8.0 under creosote bush); abrupt smooth boundary. Mantled by 80–85% gravel pavement cover, with gravel typically 0.8–2.0 cm in size; crust varies from 1 cm to 2 cm thick, with an algal crust on the surface, under creosote bush vegetation; some soil is noncalcareous and some thin carbonate coatings noted on parts of the surface.

ABk—2–12 cm. Light brown (7.5YR 6/4) gravelly loam, brown (7.5YR 4/4) moist; weak fine and medium subangular blocks; soft, friable, slightly sticky, slightly plastic; common very fine, fine, and medi-um roots, with some pockets of many fine to very fine and few large roots; few fine tubular pores; 5–10% gravel and 20% cobbles; strongly effervescent; strongly alkaline (pH 8.0–8.5); clear smooth boundary.

Bk—12–30 cm. Light brown (7.5YR 6.5/3.5) to very gravelly sandy loam; brown (7.5YR 4.5/4) moist; weak fine subangular blocks; soft, friable to very friable, slightly sticky, slightly plastic; common very fine and fine roots; few fine tubular pores; 20% gravel and 25% cobbles; violently effervescent; strongly alkaline (pH 8.0–8.5); abrupt smooth boundary.

Bkm1—30–31 cm (2 cm to 3 cm thick in places). Matrix is weakly cemented by white (10YR 8/1) carbonate, pink to pinkish gray (7.5YR 7/3) moist (no texture estimate due to cement, but is gravelly/very cobbly); contains some clayey zones of reddish yellow (7.5YR 6/6) stained by iron oxide(?), strong brown (7.5YR 5/6) moist; 20% gravel; root mat on top; strongly effervescent on top to slightly effervescent below, carbonates noted on all sides of gravel and cobbles, but often thickest on top; moderately alkaline (pH 8.0–8.5); abrupt smooth to slightly wavy boundary.

Bkm2—31–71 cm. Matrix is weakly cemented by white (10YR 8/1) and pinkish white (7.5YR 8/2) carbonate, pink to pinkish gray (7.5YR 7/3) moist (no texture estimate due to strong cement, but is gravelly/ very cobbly); contains some clayey zones of reddish yellow (7.5YR 6/6) stained by iron oxide(?), strong brown (7.5YR 5/6) moist; 35–40% gravel; rare fine and very fine roots; strongly effervescent, carbonate coatings up to 4 mm thick on the bottom of gravel; moderately alkaline (pH 8.0–8.5); clear smooth boundary.

Bkm3—71–118 cm. Matrix is weakly cemented by white (10YR 8/1) and pinkish white (7.5YR 8/2) carbonate, pink to pinkish gray (7.5YR 7/3) moist (no texture estimate due to strong cement, but is gravelly/very cobbly); contains some clayey zones of reddish yellow (7.5YR 6/6) stained by iron oxide(?), strong brown (7.5YR 5/6) moist; 25% gravel and 15% cobbles; rare fine and very fine roots, but occasionally clustered in pockets; violently effervescent carbonate matrix and effervescent clay plus iron(?); moderately alkaline (pH 8.0–8.5); clear smooth boundary.

B'k—118–125 cm. Light brown (7.5YR 6/3) very gravelly sandy loam, pink to pinkish gray (7.5YR 7/3) moist; massive structure; slightly hard, friable, slightly sticky, slightly plastic; few very fine and fine roots, often in clusters; 15% gravel and 10–15% cobbles; violently effervescent, carbonate coatings on all sides of gravel; moderately alkaline (pH 8.0–8.5); clear smooth boundary.

BCk—125–142 cm. Light brown (7.5YR 6/4) very gravelly sandy loam to very gravelly loamy sand, pink (7.5YR 7/4) moist; massive structure; soft, very friable, slightly sticky, slightly plastic; few very fine and fine roots; 25% gravel and 10% cobbles; strongly to violently effervescent, few carbonate coatings on gravel; moderately alkaline (pH 8.0–8.5); abrupt smooth boundary.

2C—142–162 + cm. Pink (7.5YR 7/3) loamy sand, strong brown to reddish yellow (7.5YR 5.5/6) moist; massive structure; soft, very friable, nonsticky, nonplastic; few very fine and fine roots; 5% gravel; effervescent; moderately alkaline (pH 8.0–8.5).

PROFILE DESCRIPTION 2
Next to Rock Pile

Classification: Fine-loamy, mixed, thermic Calcic Paleargid (similar to Pinaleño series; would be classified as a Typic Petroargid if petrocalcic horizon is present in 100–150 cm zone).

Geomorphic setting: Alluvial fan terrace, elevation 899 m, 4% slope.

Local setting: Desert pavement near rock pile feature; adjacent to west side of PP 2.

A—0–4 cm. Light brown (7.5YR 6/4) loam, brown to strong brown (7.5YR 5/5) moist; moderate medium plates; slightly hard, very friable, slightly sticky, slightly plastic; few fine and very fine roots; many fine to very fine vesicular pores; 10–20% gravel, mainly on the surface; effervescent; moderately alkaline (pH 8.0–8.5); abrupt smooth boundary. Contains few filaments and faint spots of carbonate.

Btk1—4–17 cm. Light brown to reddish yellow (7.5YR 6/5) clay loam, brown to strong brown (7.5YR 4/5) moist; moderate fine subangular blocks; slightly hard, friable, sticky, plastic; many moderately thick clay films on ped faces and pores; common very fine and fine roots; few fine tubular pores; 5% gravel; strongly effervescent; moderately alkaline (pH 8.0–8.5); clear smooth boundary. Contains common small (~ 1 mm) masses of carbonate, and the matrix consists of 5–10% carbonate filaments.

Btk2—17–40 cm. Light brown to reddish yellow (7.5YR 6/5) clay loam; strong brown (5YR–7.5YR 5/6) moist; moderate fine subangular blocks; slightly hard, friable, sticky, plastic; many moderately thick clay films on ped faces and pores; few very fine and fine roots; few fine tubular pores; 5% gravel; strongly effervescent; moderately alkaline (pH 8.0–8.5); gradual smooth boundary. Contains common to many soft powdery masses, with few moderately hard masses; several are 5–10 mm across and some are cylindrical in shape.

Btk3—40–59 cm. Light brown to reddish yellow (7.5YR 6/5) loam, strong brown (7.5YR 5/6) moist; moderate fine and medium subangular blocks; hard, firm, sticky, plastic; common thin clay films on ped faces; few very fine and fine roots; few very fine tubular pores; 5% gravel; strongly effervescent matrix, and violently effervescent carbonate masses; moderately alkaline (pH 8.0–8.5); clear smooth boundary. Contains few to common (5–10%) masses of carbonate and some finely disseminated carbonates; some consist of 6–10 mm cylindrical carbonate concentrations, possibly formed in old insect burrows.

2Btk4—59–77 cm. Pinkish gray to light brown (7.5YR 6/3) clay loam, brown to yellowish brown (7.5–10YR 5/3 and 5/4) moist; hard, firm, sticky, plastic; many moderately thick clay films on ped faces; few very fine and fine roots; few very fine tubular pores; <1% gravel; strongly effervescent matrix, and violently effervescent carbonate masses; moderately alkaline (pH 8.0–8.5). Contains few to common moderately hard masses of carbonate.

2Btk5—77–100+ cm. Pinkish gray to light brown (7.5YR 6/3) clay loam to clay, brown (7.5YR 5/3 and 5/4) moist; weak fine prisms parting to moderate fine and medium subangular blocks; very hard, very firm, very sticky, very plastic; some possible clay coatings on peds; rare fine roots; rare fine tubular pores; strongly effervescent; moderately alkaline (pH 8.0–8.5); clear smooth boundary. Contains few to common seams and filaments of carbonate.

PROFILE DESCRIPTION 3
Terrace, Upslope of
Rock Alignment

Geomorphic setting: Backslope of fan terrace scarp, 10–11% slope.

Local setting: Terrace, 20 cm upslope of rock alignment.

A1—0–5 cm. Pinkish gray to light brown (7.5YR 6/3) very gravelly sandy loam to loam, brown (7.5YR 4.5/3) moist; weak to moderate fine and medium subangular blocks and some weak medium plates; soft, very friable, slightly sticky, slightly plastic; few to common very fine roots; few very fine tubular pores; 35% gravel, mainly on the surface; not effervescent; mildly alkaline (pH 7.5); abrupt smooth boundary. This horizon has formed in the upper terrace fill deposit, and it is covered by a patchy gravel pavement.

A2—5–16 cm. Pinkish gray to light brown (7.5YR 6/3) gravelly sandy loam to loam, brown (7.5YR 4.5/3) moist; weak fine subangular blocks and some weak medium plates at the top; slightly hard, very friable, slightly sticky, slightly plastic; common very fine and fine roots; few very fine tubular pores; 15–20% gravel; audibly effervescent; mildly alkaline (pH 7.5); clear smooth boundary. This horizon has formed in the lower terrace fill deposit.

Bk1—16–30 cm. Pinkish gray to light brown 7.5YR 6/3) gravelly sandy loam to loam, brown (7.5YR 4.5/3) moist; weak fine subangular blocks to massive; soft, very friable, slightly sticky, slightly plastic; common very fine and few fine roots; few very fine tubular pores; 25% gravel; strongly effervescent; moderately alkaline (pH 8.0–8.5); clear smooth boundary. Matrix is dominated by finely disseminated carbonates.

2Bk2—30–46 cm. Light brown (7.5YR 6/3.5) extremely gravelly sandy loam, brown (7.5YR 5/4) moist; weak fine subangular blocks to massive; soft, very friable, slightly sticky, slightly plastic; 65% gravel and some cobbles; common very fine and fine roots; strongly effervescent matrix, and violently effervescent; moderately alkaline (pH 8.0–8.5); abrupt smooth boundary. Contains both finely dis-seminated carbonates and gravel coatings on all sides.

2Bkm—46+ cm. Color of carbonate cement not described, but much lighter than above; massive, cemented; 60–70% gravel; violently effervescent; moderately alkaline (pH 8.0–8.5). This horizon has a laminar cap of carbonate above a massively cemented petrocalcic horizon.

PROFILE DESCRIPTION 4
Beneath Rock Alignment
between Two Terraces

Geomorphic setting: Backslope fan terrace scarp, 10–11% slope.

Local setting: Beneath rock alignment.

A1—0–5 cm. Pinkish gray to light brown (7.5YR 6/3) gravelly/very cobbly sandy loam to loam, brown to dark brown (7.5YR 4/3) moist; weak fine subangular blocks and some weak medium plates; soft to slightly hard, very friable, slightly sticky, slightly plastic; few fine roots; few very fine tubular pores; 15% gravel, excluding surface gravel in rock alignment; not effervescent; mildly alkaline (pH 7.5); clear smooth boundary. Upper boundary is irregular between rocks.

A2—5–18 cm. Pinkish gray to light brown (7.5YR 6/3) gravelly/very cobbly sandy loam to loam, brown (7.5YR 4.5/3) moist; weak fine subangular blocks; soft, very friable, slightly sticky, slightly plastic; few to common very fine and fine roots; few very fine tubular pores; 25% gravel; not effervescent; mildly alkaline (pH 7.5); clear smooth boundary. Surface gravel in rock alignment extends about 13 cm to 15 cm below surface.

Bk1—18–27 cm. Pinkish gray to light brown (7.5YR 6/3) gravelly/very cobbly sandy loam, brown (7.5YR 4.5/3.5) moist; weak fine subangular blocks; soft, very friable, slightly sticky, slightly plastic; few to common very fine and few fine roots; few very fine tubular pores; 30% gravel; strongly effervescent; moderately alkaline (pH 8.0–8.5); clear smooth boundary. Carbonate coatings were noted on all sides of gravel.

2Bk2—27–40 cm. Light brown (7.5YR 6/4) extremely gravelly loam to sandy loam, brown (7.5YR 4.5/4) moist; weak fine subangular blocks to massive; soft, very friable, slightly sticky, slightly plastic; 70% gravel and cobbles; few to common very fine and fine roots; strongly effervescent; moderately alkaline (pH 8.0–8.5); abrupt smooth boundary. Carbonate coatings were noted on all sides of gravel.

2Bkm—40+ cm. Color of carbonate cement not described, but much lighter than above; massive, cemented; 60–70% gravel; violently effervescent; moderately alkaline (pH 8.0–8.5). This horizon has a laminar cap of carbonate above a massively cemented petrocalcic horizon.

PROFILE DESCRIPTION 5
Terrace, Downslope of
Rock Alignment

Geomorphic setting: Backslope of fan terrace scarp, 10–11% slope.

Local setting: Terrace, 20 cm downslope of rock alignment.

A—0–3 cm. Light brown (7.5YR 6/3.5) gravelly/very cobbly sandy loam, brown to dark brown (7.5YR 4/3) moist; weak to moderate fine and medium subangular blocks to massive; loose to soft, very friable, slightly sticky, slightly plastic; few very fine roots; few very fine tubular pores; 20% gravel, mainly on the surface; effervescent; moderately alkaline (pH 8.0–8.5); abrupt smooth boundary. This horizon has formed in the upper terrace fill deposit, and it is covered by a gravel pavement.

Bk1—3–18 cm. Light brown (7.5YR 6/3.5) gravelly/very cobbly sandy loam, brown (7.5YR 4.5/4) moist; weak to moderate fine and medium subangular blocks; soft, very friable, slightly sticky, slightly plastic; few to common very fine and few fine roots; few very fine tubular pores; 20% gravel; strongly effervescent; moderately alkaline (pH 8.0–8.5); clear smooth boundary. Contains disseminated carbonates in matrix and coatings on all sides of gravel.

2Bk2—18–40 cm. Light brown (7.5YR 6/4) extremely gravelly sandy loam, brown (7.5YR 5/4) moist; weak fine subangular blocks to massive; soft, very friable, slightly sticky, slightly plastic; 70% gravel and some cobbles; few to common very fine and fine roots; few tubular pores; strongly effervescent; moderately alkaline (pH 8.0–8.5); abrupt smooth boundary. Contains few to common (5–10%) masses of carbonate and some finely disseminated carbonates; some consist of 6–10 mm cylindrical carbonate concentrations, possibly formed in old insect burrows. Contains disseminated carbonates in matrix and coatings on all sides of gravel.

2Btkm—40+ cm. Color of carbonate cement not described, but much lighter than above; illuvial clay is light brown (7.5YR 6/4), brown (7.5YR 5/4) moist; weakly cemented, massive, with some clay breaking out in blocks; many thick clay films on ped faces in clayey zones; 60–70% gravel; violently effervescent; moderately alkaline (pH 8.0–8.5). Contains few to common moderately hard masses of carbonate.

PROFILE DESCRIPTION 6
Grid Interior

Geomorphic setting: Nearly level part of alluvial fan terrace, 1–2% slope.

Local setting: Within grid interior.

A—0–3 cm. Pink to light brown (7.5YR 6.5/3.5) gravelly/very cobbly sandy loam, brown (7.5YR 4.5/3) moist; weak medium plates and weak fine subangular blocks; slightly hard, friable, slightly sticky, slightly plastic; few very fine roots; few very fine vesicular pores; 20% gravel; mildly alkaline (pH7.5); abrupt smooth boundary. This horizon has formed in the upper terrace fill deposit, and it is covered by a gravel pavement.

Bt—3–10 cm. Light brown (7.5YR 6/4) very gravelly/very cobbly sandy clay loam to loam, brown to dark brown (7.5YR 4/4) moist; weak fine to medium subangular blocks; slightly hard, friable, slightly sticky, slightly plastic; common thick clay bridges and colloidal stains on mineral grains; few to common very fine roots; few very fine tubular pores; 30% gravel and 10% cobbles; strongly effervescent; mildly alkaline (pH 7.5); clear smooth boundary.

2Bk—10–41+ cm. Light brown (7.5YR 6/4) extremely gravelly sandy loam, brown to strong brown (7.5YR 4.5/5) moist; weak fine subangular blocks; soft, very friable, slightly sticky, slightly plastic; few thin clay bridges; 40% gravel and 30% cobbles up to 12–15 cm in diameter; few to common very fine and fine roots, mainly in clusters; strongly fervescent; moderately alkaline (pH 8.0–8.5); abrupt smooth boundary. Contains disseminated carbonates in matrix, coatings on all sides of gravel, and some filaments.

Microscopic Analysis of a Tabular Knife

Marilyn Shoberg

Microwear analysis of stone tools involves the systematic recording of wear pattern attributes in order to understand the ways in which the tools were used. Current methods of analysis rely heavily on the pioneering studies of early researchers who performed extensive experiments using replica tools and then correlating types of use-wear patterns with specific tool functions. Semenov (1964) concentrated on the relationship between striations on tool edges and the kinematics (motions) of tool use. Tringham and her students (1974) correlated edge damage flake scar attributes with kinematics and relative hardness of the contact material. Keeley (1980) used a higher magnification approach (100x to 200x) to study micropolishes associated with tool use. Whether micropolishes are an additive layer of fused silica gel on the tool or an alteration of the surface by abrasion remains unresolved (Ahler 1979: 308; Kay 1996: 316). Nevertheless, the optical characteristics of polish, fine striations, and embedded abrasive particles are all important attributes in the microscopic use-wear methods used in this analysis as well as low-power observations of wear patterns on edges and surfaces of the tool.

I evaluated microscopically, at magnifications of 50x, 100x, and 200x, use-wear along the edge of one artifact from site AZ CC:1:2 (ASM). The item was tentatively labeled a "tabular knife," and I examined it with an Olympus binocular microscope equipped with polarized light Nomarski optics.

The tool examined for microwear is a thin tabular slab of rhyolite measuring 19.8 cm long, 8.35 cm wide, and 1.05 cm thick (Fig. B.1). The working edge is a slightly concave curve. Both sides of the thin

Figure B.1. Tabular knife found near Field House Structure 1, Locality 9, AZ CC:1:2 (ASM). Tool is 19.8 cm long. (Photograph by Marilyn Shoberg.)

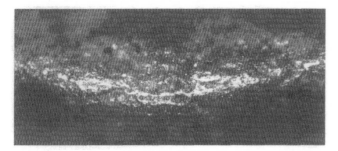

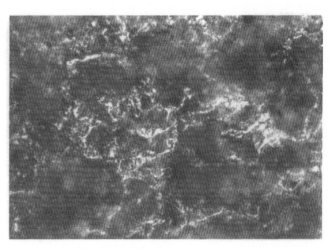

Figure B.2. Photomicrograph (50x) of a smoothed, polished point on the edge of a tabular knife. (Photograph by Marilyn Shoberg.)

Figure B.4. Photomicrgraph (200x) of weakly developed polish in a reticulate pattern on the high spots of the tool surface. (Photograph by Marilyn Shoberg.)

Figure B.3. Photomicrograph (50x) of linear strips of reticulate polish parallel to the long axis of a tabular knife. (Photograph by Marilyn Shoberg.)

working edge have been ground smooth the entire length of the tool in a strip approximately 2.5 cm to 3.0 cm wide. Side 1 has been lightly ground, smoothing off the high spots of the natural rhyolite surface. The edge of Side 1 has been ground to a steeper edge angle than that of Side 2, which has been heavily ground to a very smooth surface. The differences in the way the two sides of the working edge were ground, one much more smooth than the other, is purposeful. The less smoothly ground side curves over to meet the other edge within 0.5 cm of the edge. The sharp but relatively thick edge (0.2 cm) is stronger and less likely to fracture than if both sides had been ground equally to a very fine, thin sharp edge.

The edge is irregular due to the attrition of many flakes from both sides of the edge. Edge flaking is

unpatterned and does not appear to be the result of intentional retouch of the edge. The heavy rounding and polish on the working edge (Fig. B.2) argue for extensive use along the entire length of the tool. A number of large flakes were attrited from the edge of the tool, oblique to the edge axis; this appearance is consistent with tools that have been used in reciprocal sawing motions.

As a function of use, polish developed on the high microtopography of the broadly linear striations parallel to the long axis of the tool. These linear features are interpreted as having been produced by grinding a 2–cm to 3–cm wide strip along both sides of the proposed working edge of the tool before it was used. The polish is moderately developed in a reticulate pattern on surface high spots with large interstitial spaces of unaffected tool surface. These strips of polish extend along the entire length of the tool (Fig. B.3). There are almost no fine striations visible in this reticulate polish interior to the working edge that would indicate direction of motion during tool use (Fig. B.4).

Findings from experiments conducted at the Texas Archeological Research Laboratory (Shoberg 2001) are offered for comparison. Replica prismatic blades of Edwards chert were used in making longitudinal cuts in samples of a common reed (*Phragmites communis*). A bright, smooth-pitted, moderately well-developed polish appeared on the tool after 2,000 cutting strokes (Fig. B.5). Polish coated the edge of the blade and was incompletely linked in a reticulate pattern on the

Figure B.5. Photomicrograph (200x) of smooth, pitted polish on the surface of an experimental prismatic blade of Edwards chert. Polish is the result of 2,000 longitudinal strokes to cut a common reed. (Photograph by Marilyn Shoberg.)

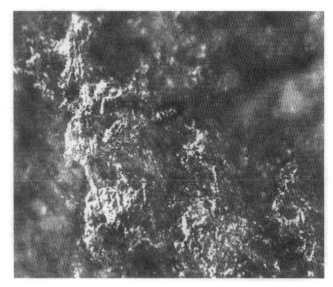

Figure B.6. Photomicrograph (200x) of fine, linear striations parallel to the long axis of the tool. (Photograph by Marilyn Shoberg.)

surface of the chert a few μm from the edge. The polish on the tool from the Safford Valley is similar in brightness, surface morphology, and pattern of development to that on the replica blade used experimentally. Therefore, it is reasonable to infer that the polish on the Safford Valley tool is also the result of contact with a vegetal material.

There are several areas of bright, well-developed, invasive polish at the edges of flake scars along the edge of the tool. Very fine striations visible in this polish are predominantly parallel to the long axis of the tool, although striations oblique to and perpendicular to the edge are also present. These fine striae indicate that the tool was used primarily in a longitudinal cutting motion parallel to the working edge (Figs. B.6, B.7).

There is extensive polish on the opposing "back" edge and high topography that would be consistent with a hand-held tool. Striations are multidirectional and unpatterned in this polish. There is no evidence that the back of the tool was ground.

FINDINGS AND MEANINGS

The bright, smooth polish on the tabular knife from the Safford Valley is composed of incomplete components developed on high topography of the tool surface, linked in a reticulate pattern around interstitial spaces of unpolished "low" spots. Polish is well

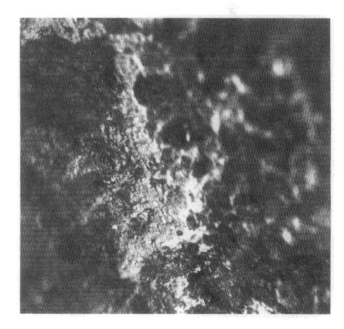

Figure B.7. Photomicrograph (200x) of the opposite face of the tool (see Fig. B.6) showing similarly fine striae oriented at a slightly oblique angle to the long axis. Also visible are abrasive particles embedded in the well-developed polish at the cutting edge of the tool. (Photograph by Marilyn Shoberg.)

developed and linked on the edges of flake scars at the edge of the tool. This bright smooth polish is similar to the polish on replica chert blades used to cut reeds experimentally. Fine striations in the polish are predominantly parallel and slightly oblique to the edge and the long axis of the tool, indicating that the tool was used in a longitudinal cutting motion. Polish may be slightly more developed on Side 2 of the tool, but the wear patterning indicates that both sides of the tool were in contact with a moderately hard vegetal material, such as agave.

References

Ahler, S. A.
1979 Functional Analysis of Nonobsidian Chipped Stone Artifacts: Terms, Variables, and Quantification. In *Lithic Use-Wear Analysis: Proceedings of the Conference on Lithic Use-Wear, Simon Fraser University, Burnaby (Vancouver), British Columbia, March 1977*, edited by B. Hayden, pp. 301–328. Academic Press, New York.

Ahlstrom, Richard V. N.
1997 Safford Valley Settlement Patterns. In "The Sanchez Copper Project, Vol. 1, Archaeological Investigations in the Safford Valley, Graham County, Arizona," edited by Gregory R. Seymour, Richard V. N. Ahlstrom, and David P. Doak. *SWCA Archaeological Report* 94–82 (Revised 1997): 9.1–9.10. SWCA Environmental Consultants, Tucson.

Ahlstrom, Richard V. N., David P. Doak,
and Gregory R. Seymour
1997 Introduction and Cultural Setting. In "The Sanchez Copper Project, Vol. I: Archaeological Investigations in the Safford Valley, Graham County, Arizona," edited by Gregory R. Seymour, Richard V. N. Ahlstrom, and David P. Doak. *SWCA Archaeological Report* 94–82 (Revised 1997): 1.1–1.16. SWCA Environmental Consultants, Tucson.

Alderfer, R. B., and F. G. Merkle
1943 The Comparative Effects of Surface Application Versus Incorporation of Various Mulching Materials on Structure, Permeability, Runoff, and Other Soil Properties. *Soil Science Society of America Proceedings* 8: 79–86.

Altschul, Jeffrey H., and Carla R. Van West
1992 Agricultural Productivity Estimates for the Tonto Basin, A.D. 740–1370. In "Proceedings of the Second Salado Conference, Globe, Arizona 1992," edited by Richard C. Lange and Stephen Germick. *Arizona Archaeological Society Occasional Papers* 19: 172–182. Phoenix.

Anderson, Kirk
1992 Lithic Raw Material Sources in Arizona. In "Making and Using Stone Artifacts in Arizona," edited by Mark Slaughter, Lee Fratt, Kirk Anderson, and Richard Ahlstrom. *SWCA Archaeological Report* 92–5: 26–36. SWCA Environmental Consultants, Tucson.

Ayres, James E.
1967 A Prehistoric Farm Site Near Cave Creek, Arizona. *The Kiva* 32(3): 106–111.

Baize, D.
1993 *Soil Science Analysis: A Guide to Current Use.* John Wiley and Sons, Chichester.

Bandelier, Adolph F.
1892 Final Report of Investigations Among the Indians of the Southwestern United States, Carried on Mainly in the Years from 1880 to 1885, Part II. *Papers of the Archaeological Institute of America, American Series* IV. University Press, Cambridge.

Barbour, M. G., G. Cunningham, W. C. Oechel,
and S. A. Bamberg
1977 Growth and Development, Form and Function. In *Creosote Bush: Biology and Chemistry of Larrea in New World Deserts*, edited by T. J. Mabry, J. H. Hunziker, and D. R. Difeo, pp. 48–91. Dowden, Hutchinson, and Ross, Stroudsburg.

Barlett, Peggy F.
1980 Cost–Benefit Analysis: A Test of Alternative Methodologies. In *Agricultural Decision Making: Anthropological Contributions to Rural Development*, edited by Peggy F. Barlett, pp. 137–160. Academic Press, New York.

Baxter, Sylvester
1882 The Father of the Pueblos. *Harpers Magazine* 65(385): 81.

Beck, W., D. J. Donahue, A. J. T. Jull, G. Burr,
W. S. Broecker, G. Bonani, I. Hajdas,
E. Malotki, and Ronald I. Dorn
1998 Ambiguities in Direct Dating of Rock Surfaces

Beck, W., D. J. Donahue, A. J. T. Jull, G. Burr,
W. S. Broecker, G. Bonani, I. Hajdas,
E. Malotki, and Ronald I. Dorn (*continued*)
    Using Radiocarbon Measurements. *Science* 280
    (5372): 2132–2139.

Benoit, G. R., and D. Kirkham
  1963 The Effect of Soil Surface Conditions on Evap-
    oration of Soil Water. *Soil Science Society of
    America Proceedings* 27: 495–498.

Berlin, G. L., J. R. Ambler, R. H. Hevly,
and G. G. Schaber
  1977 Identification of a Sinagua Agricultural Field by
    Aerial Thermography, Soil Chemistry, Pollen/
    Plant Analysis, and Archaeology. *American
    Antiquity* 42(4): 588–600.

Bierer, Susan B., and Richard V. N. Ahlstrom
  1997 Flaked Stone Analysis. In "The Sanchez Copper
    Project, Vol. 1, Archaeological Investigations
    in the Safford Valley, Graham County, Ari-
    zona," edited by Gregory R. Seymour, Richard
    V. N. Ahlstrom, and David P. Doak. *SWCA Ar-
    chaeological Report* 94-82 (Revised 1997):
    5.1–5.33. SWCA Environmental Consultants,
    Tucson.

Blake, G. R., and K. H. Hartge
  1986 Bulk Density. In "Methods of Soil Analysis.
    Physical and Mineralogical Methods" (2nd
    edition), edited by A. Klute. *Agronomy Mono-
    graph* 9(2): 363–375. American Society of
    Agronomy and Soil Science Society of America,
    Madison.

Blakemore, Michael
  1981 From Way-Finding to Map-Making: The Spa-
    tial Information Fields of Aboriginal Peoples.
    Progress in Human Geography 5: 1–24.

Bohrer, Vorsila L.
  1960 Zuni Agriculture. *El Palacio* 67(6): 181–202.
  1991 Recently Recognized Cultivated and Encour-
    aged Plants Among the Hohokam. *Kiva* 56(3):
    227–235.

Botsford, Manton, and Gay Kinkade
  1993 Cultural Resources Assessment of the BLM
    Safford District Office Project. Unpublished MS
    on file, Bureau of Land Management, Safford
    District, Arizona.

Bozarth, Steven
  1997 Pollen and Phytolith Analysis. In "Agricultural,
    Subsistence, and Environmental Studies," edited
    by Jeffrey A. Homburg and Richard Ciolek-
    Torrello, pp. 179–204. *Vanishing River: Land-
    scapes and Lives of the Lower Verde Valley: The
    Lower Verde Archaeological Project*, Vol. 2.
    CD-ROM. SRI Press, Tucson.

Brady, N. C., and R. R. Weil
  2002 *The Nature and Properties of Soils.* Prentice-
    Hall, Upper Saddle River.

Breternitz, Cory Dale, Editor
  1991 Prehistoric Irrigation in Arizona: Symposium
    1998. *Soils Systems Publications in Archaeology*
    17. Phoenix.

Butzer, Karl W.
  1982 *Archaeology as Human Ecology: Method and
    Theory for a Contextual Approach.* Cambridge
    University Press, Cambridge.

Castetter, Edward F., and Willis H. Bell
  1942 *Pima and Papago Indian Agriculture.* University
    of New Mexico Press, Albuquerque.

Castetter, Edward F., Willis H. Bell, and Alvin R. Grove
  1938 Ethnobotanical Studies of the American South-
    west VI: The Early Utilization and Distribution
    of Agave in the American Southwest. *University
    of New Mexico Bulletin* 6(4).

Chamberlin, T. C.
  1890 The Method of Multiple Working Hypotheses.
    Science (old series) 5: 92–96.

Choriki, R. T., J. C. Hide, S. L. Krall,
and B. L. Brownet
  1964 Rock and Gravel Mulch Aid in Moisture
    Storage. *Crops and Soil* 16: 24.

Ciolek-Torrello, Richard, Stephanie M. Whittlesey,
and John R. Welch
  1994 A Synthetic Model of Prehistoric Land Use. In
    "The Roosevelt Rural Sites Study, Vol. 3:
    Changing Land Use in the Tonto Basin," edited
    by Richard Ciolek-Torrello and John R. Welch.
    Technical Series 28: 437–472. Statistical Re-
    search, Tucson.

Clark, Jeffery J.
  2000 Preliminary Report on Archaeological Testing
    and Data Recovery Investigations for the U.S.
    70 Thatcher-to-Safford Project, Graham Coun-
    ty, Arizona. *Project Report* 00-117. Desert
    Archaeology, Tucson.
  2002 (Editor) The Ancient Farmers of the Safford
    Basin: Archaeology of the U.S. 70 Safford-to-
    Thatcher Project. *Center for Desert Archaeol-
    ogy Anthropological Papers* 39. Tucson.

Clark, Jeffery J., Andrew P. Dutt, and James M. Vint
  1999 U.S. 70 Safford to Thatcher Segment: Testing
    Results and a Plan for Data Recovery. *Tech-
    nical Report* 99-6. Desert Archaeology, Tucson.

Clark, S. P.
  1928 *Lessons from Southwestern Indian Agriculture.*
    University of Arizona Press, Tucson.

Colton, Harold S.
  1953 Potsherds: An Introduction to the Study of Pre-

historic Southwestern Ceramics. *Museum of Northern Arizona Bulletin* 25. Museum of Northern Arizona Society of Science and Art, Flagstaff.

Colvin, Verna R.
1997 Building Canals on the Gila River. In "Link the Past with the Present." *1997 Symposium Papers*, pp. 4–18. Graham County Historical Society, Safford.

Colwell-Chanthaphonh, Chip
2003 Signs in Place: Native American Perspectives of the Past in the San Pedro Valley of Southeastern Arizona. *Kiva* 69(1): 5-29.

Cordell, Linda S.
1984 *Prehistory of the Southwest*. Academic Press, Orlando.

Cordell, Linda S., Amy C. Earls, and Martha R. Binford
1984 Subsistence Systems in the Mountainous Settings of the Rio Grande Valley. In "Prehistoric Agricultural Strategies in the Southwest," edited by Suzanne K. Fish and Paul R. Fish. *Arizona State University Anthropological Research Papers* 33: 222–241. Department of Anthropology, Arizona State University, Tempe.

Crary, Joseph S.
1997 The Chronology and Cultures of Upper (Northern) Southeast Arizona: The Formative and Classic Periods. MS prepared for the symposium "The Archaeology of a Land Between: Regional Dynamics in the Prehistory and History of Southeast Arizona," sponsored by the Amerind Foundation, October 12–17, 1997. Dragoon.

Crary, Joseph S., Stephen Germick, and Michael Golio
1992 Las Sierras and Los Alamos: A Comparative Study of Classic Period Upland and Riverine Community Patterns in the Tonto–Globe Region of Central Arizona. In "Proceedings of the Second Salado Conference, Globe, Arizona 1992," edited by Richard C. Lange and Stephen Germick. *Arizona Archaeological Society Occasional Papers* 19: 149–160. Phoenix.

Crosswhite, Frank S.
1981 Desert Plants, Habitat, and Agriculture in Relation to the Major Patterns of Cultural Differentiation in the O'odham People of the Sonoran Desert. *Desert Plants* 3: 47–76.

Crown, Patricia L.
1984 Prehistoric Agricultural Technology in the Salt–Gila Basin. In "Hohokam Archaeology Along the Salt–Gila Aqueduct, Central Arizona Project, Vol. 7, Environment and Subsistence," edited by Lynn S. Teague and Patricia L. Crown. *Arizona State Museum Archaeological Series* 150: 207–260. University of Arizona, Tucson.
1987 Classic Period Hohokam Settlement and Land Use in the Casa Grande Ruins Area, Arizona. *Journal of Field Archaeology* 14: 147–162.

Cummings, Linda Scott, and Kathryn Puseman
1997 Pollen, Macrofloral, and Fiber Identification. In "The Sanchez Copper Project, Vol. 1, Archaeological Investigations in the Safford Valley, Graham County, Arizona," edited by Gregory R. Seymour, Richard V. N. Ahlstrom, and David P. Doak. *SWCA Archaeological Report* 94-82 (Revised 1997): 7.1-7.24. SWCA Environmental Consultants, Tucson.

Cunkle, James R., and Markus A. Jacquemain
1995 *Stone Magic of the Ancients: Petroglyphs, Shamanic Shrine Sites, Ancient Rituals*. Golden West Publishers, Phoenix.

Cushing, Frank Hamilton
1920 Zuñi Breadstuff. *Museum of the American Indian, Notes and Monographs* 8. Heye Foundation, New York.

Dart, Allen
1983 Prehistoric Agricultural and Water Control Systems Along the Salt–Gila Aqueduct. In "Hohokam Archaeology along the Salt–Gila Aqueduct, Central Arizona Project, Vol. 3, Specialized Activity Sites," edited by Lynn S. Teague and Patricia L. Crown. *Arizona State Museum Archaeological Series* 150: 345–573. University of Arizona, Tucson.
1989 Prehistoric Irrigation in Arizona: A Context for Canals and Related Cultural Resources. *Technical Report* 89-7. Center for Desert Archaeology, Tucson.

Dart, Allen, and William Deaver
1983 Appendix F: Description of Dry Farming Loci Along the Gila River in the Vicinity of the Salt–Gila Aqueduct. In "Hohokam Archaeology Along the Salt–Gila Aqueduct, Central Arizona Project, Vol. 3, Specialized Activity Sites," edited by Lynn S. Teague and Patricia L. Crown. *Arizona State Museum Archaeological Series* 150: 629–655. University of Arizona, Tucson.

Dean, Jeffery S., and John C. Ravesloot
1993 The Chronology and Cultural Interaction in the Gran Chichimeca. In "Culture and Contact: Charles C. Di Peso's Gran Chichimeca," edited by Anne I. Woosely and John C. Ravesloot. *Amerind Foundation New World Studies Series* 2: 83–103. University of New Mexico Press, Albuquerque.

Dean, Jeffrey S., and William J. Robinson
  1982   Dendrochronology of Grasshopper Pueblo. In "Multidisciplinary Research at Grasshopper Pueblo, Arizona," edited by William A. Longacre, Sally J. Holbrook, and Michael W. Graves. *Anthropological Papers of the University of Arizona* 40: 46–60. University of Arizona Press, Tucson.

Debowski, Sharon S., Anique George, Richard Goddard, and Deborah Mullon
  1976   An Archaeological Survey of the Butte Reservoir. *Arizona State Museum Archaeological Series* 93. University of Arizona, Tucson.

Dick, W. A., and M. A. Tabatabai
  1977   An Alkaline Oxidation Method for Determination of Total Phosphorus in Soils. *Soil Science Society of America Journal* 41(3): 511–514.

Dickson, Jane J., and Glen A. Izett
  1981   Fission-Track Ages of Air-Fall Tuffs in Pliocene Basin-Fill Sediments near 111 Ranch, Graham County, Arizona. *Isochron/West* 32: 13–15.

Di Peso, Charles C.
  1974   *Casas Grandes: A Fallen Trading Center of the Gran Chichimeca*. Northland Press and The Amerind Foundation, Flagstaff and Dragoon.

Doak, David P., Gregory R. Seymour,
Susan B. Bierer, and Laural Myers
  1997   Site Descriptions. In "The Sanchez Copper Project, Vol. 1, Archaeological Investigations in the Safford Valley, Graham County, Arizona," edited by Gregory R. Seymour, Richard V. N. Ahlstrom, and David P. Doak. *SWCA Archaeological Report* 94–82 (Revised 1997): 4.1–4.120. SWCA Environmental Consultants, Tucson.

Doelle, William H.
  1975   Prehistoric Resource Exploitation within the CONOCO Florence Project. *Arizona State Museum Archaeological Series* 62. University of Arizona, Tucson.

Doelle, William H., Allen Dart, and Henry D. Wallace
  1985   The Southern Tucson Basin Survey: Intensive Survey along the Santa Cruz River. *Institute for American Research Technical Report* 85–3. Institute for American Research, Tucson.

Doerge, T. A.
  1985   A Summary of Soil Test Information for Arizona's Surface Agricultural Soils: 1965–1984. MS on file, Department of Soil and Water Science, University of Arizona, Tucson.

Donkin, R. A.
  1979   Agricultural Terracing in the Aboriginal New World. *Viking Fund Publications in Anthropol-*ogy 56. University of Arizona Press for the Wenner-Gren Foundation for Anthropological Research, Tucson and New York.

Doolittle, William E.
  1980   Aboriginal Agricultural Development in the Valley of Sonora, Mexico. *Geographical Review* 70: 328–342.
  1984   Agricultural Change as an Incremental Process. *Annals of the Association of American Geographers* 74: 124–137.
  1985   The Use of Check Dams for Protecting Downstream Agricultural Land in the Prehistoric Southwest: A Contextual Analysis. *Journal of Anthropological Research* 41: 279–305.
  1988   Pre-Hispanic Occupance in the Valley of Sonora, Mexico: Archaeological Confirmation of Early Spanish Reports. *Anthropological Papers of the University of Arizona* 48. University of Arizona Press, Tucson.
  1992   Agriculture in North America on the Eve of Contact: A Reassessment. *Annals of the Association of American Geographers* 82: 386–401.
  1997   Landscapes, Locales, Fields, and Food. MS prepared for the symposium "The Archaeology of a Land Between: Regional Dynamics in the Prehistory and History of Southeast Arizona," sponsored by the Amerind Foundation, October 12–17, 1997. Dragoon.
  1998   Innovation and Diffusion of Sand- and Gravel-Mulch Agriculture in the American Southwest: A Product of the Eruption of Sunset Crater. *Quaternaire* 9: 61–69.
  2000   *Cultivated Landscapes of Native North America*. Oxford: Oxford University Press.

Doolittle, William E., James A. Neely,
and Michael D. Pool
  1993   A Method for Distinguishing Between Prehistoric and Recent Water and Soil Control Features. *Kiva* 59(1): 7–25.

Dorn, Ronald I., and M. J. DeNiro
  1984   Stable Carbon Isotope Ratios of Rock Varnish Organic Matter: A New Paleoenvironmental Indicator. *Science* 227: 1472–1474.

Dorn, Ronald I., and T. M. Oberlander
  1981   Microbial Origin of Desert Varnish. *Science* 213: 1245–1247.

Dorn, Ronald I., and David S. Whitley
  1984   Chronometric and Relative Age Determination of Petroglyphs in the Western United States. *Annals of the Association of American Geographers* 74: 308–322.

Dorn, Ronald I., D. B. Bamforth, T. A. Cahill,
J. C. Dohrenwend, B. D. Turrin, D. J. Donahue,

A. J. T. Jull, A. Long, M. E. Macko, E. B. Weil,
D. S. Whitley, and T. H. Zabel
  1986 Cation–ratio and Accelerator Radiocarbon Dating of Rock Varnish on Mojave Artifacts and Landforms. *Science* 231(4740): 830–833.

Dosh, Steve
  1988 Subsistence and Settlement along the Mogollon Rim, A.D. 1000–1150. *Museum of Northern Arizona Research Paper* 39. Museum of Northern Arizona, Flagstaff.

Doyel, David E.
  1984 Sedentary Period Hohokam Paleo–Economy in the New River Drainage, Central Arizona. In "Prehistoric Agricultural Strategies in the Southwest," edited by Suzanne K. Fish and Paul R. Fish. *Arizona State University Anthropological Research Papers* 33: 35–52. Arizona State University, Tempe.
  1993 *Prehistoric Non–Irrigated Agriculture in Arizona: A Component of the Arizona Historic Preservation Plan.* Estrella Cultural Research for the Arizona State Historic Preservation Office, Phoenix.

Dregne, H. E.
  1963 Soils of the Arid West. In *Aridity and Man: The Challenge of the Arid Lands in the United States,* by C. Hodge and P. C. Duisberg, pp. 215–238. American Association for the Advancement of Science, Washington.

Drewes, Harald, B. B. Houser, D. C. Hedlund,
D. H. Richter, C. H. Thorman, and T. L. Finnell
  1985 Geologic Map of the Silver City 1° x 2° Quadrangle, New Mexico and Arizona: *U.S. Geological Survey Miscellaneous Investigations Series* Map I–1310–C. U.S. Department of Interior, Washington.

Eastern Arizona Courier
  1998 AmeriCorps works at Hackberry Ranch. Wednesday, April 8, p. 2, sec. B.

Ebert, James I., Thomas R. Lyons,
and Dwight L. Drager
  1979 Application of Orthophoto Mapping to Archaeological Problems. *American Antiquity* 44(2): 341–344.

Ellis, Florence Hawley
  1970 Irrigation and Water Works in the Rio Grande. Paper presented at the 1970 Pecos Conference, Symposium on Prehistoric Southwestern Water Control Systems, Pecos National Monument, New Mexico. MS on file, Arizona State Museum, University of Arizona, Tucson.

Elson, Mark D.
  1996 A Revised Chronology and Phase Sequence for the Lower Tonto Basin of Central Arizona. *Kiva* 62(2): 117–147.

Elvidge, C. D.
  1982 A Reexamination of the Rate of Desert Varnish Formation Reported South of Barstow, California. *Earth Surface Processes and Landforms* 7: 345–348.

Evenari, Michael, Leslie Shanan, and Naphtali Tadmor
  1971 *The Negev: The Challenge of the Desert.* Harvard University Press, Cambridge.

Fairbourn, M. D.
  1973 Effect of Gravel Mulch on Crop Yields. *Agronomy Journal* 65: 925–928.

FAO/WHO
  1973 Energy and Protein Requirement: Report of a FAO/WHO Ad Hoc Expert Committee. *World Health Organization Technical Report Series* 522. World Health Organization, United Nations, New York.

Ferguson, T. J.
  1985 Patterns of Land Use and Environmental Change on the Zuni Indian Reservation, 1846–1985: Ethnohistorical and Archaeological Evidence. Expert testimony submitted to the United States Claims Court as evidence in the case of *Zuni Indian Tribe* v. *United States,* Docket 327–81L.

Ferguson, T. J., and E. Richard Hart
  1985 *A Zuni Atlas.* University of Oklahoma Press, Norman.

Fewkes, Jesse Walter
  1904 Two Summers' Work in Pueblo Ruins. In *Twenty-second Annual Report of the Bureau of American Ethnology to the Secretary of the Smithsonian Institution, 1900–1901,* pp. 3–195. Washington.

Fireman, M., and C. H. Wadleigh
  1951 A Statistical Study of the Relation Between pH and the Exchangeable–sodium Percentage of Western Soils. *Soil Science* 71: 273–285.

Fish, Paul R., and Suzanne K. Fish
  1984 Agricultural Maximization in the Sacred Mountain Basin. In "Prehistoric Agricultural Strategies in the Southwest," edited by Suzanne K. Fish and Paul R. Fish. *Anthropological Research Papers* 39: 147–159. Arizona State University, Tempe.

Fish, Suzanne K.
  1983 Appendix A: Pollen from Agricultural Features. In "Hohokam Archaeology Along the Salt-Gila Aqueduct, Central Arizona Project, Vol. 3, Specialized Activity Sites," edited by Lynn S. Teague

Fish, Suzanne K. (*continued*)
>   and Patricia L. Crown. *Arizona State Museum Archaeological Series* 150: 575–603. University of Arizona, Tucson.

1984   Agriculture and Subsistence: Implications of the Salt–Gila Project Pollen Analysis. In "Hohokam Archaeology along the Salt–Gila Aqueduct, Vol. 7, Environment and Subsistence," edited by Lynn S. Teague and Patricia L. Crown. *Arizona State Museum Archaeological Series* 150: 111–138. University of Arizona, Tucson.

1985   Prehistoric Disturbance Floras of the Lower Sonoran Desert and Their Implications. In "Late Quaternary Vegetation and Climates of the American Southwest," edited by B. Jacobs, P. Fall, and O. Davis. *American Association of Stratigraphic Palynologists Contribution Series* 16: 77–78.

1994   Archaeological Palynology of Gardens and Fields. In *The Archaeology of Garden and Field*, edited by Naomi Miller and Kathryn Gleason, pp. 44–69. University of Pennsylvania Press, Philadelphia.

1995   Mixed Agricultural Technologies in Southern Arizona and Their Implications. In "Soil, Water, Biology and Belief in Prehistoric and Traditional Southwestern Agriculture," edited by H. Wolcott Toll. *New Mexico Archaeological Council, Special Publication* 2: 101–116. New Mexico Archaeological Council, Albuquerque.

Fish, Suzanne K., and Paul R. Fish
2004   Unsuspected Magnitudes: Expanding the Scale of Hohokam Agriculture. In *The Archaeology of Global Change*, edited by Charles Redman, Steven James, Paul R. Fish, and J. Daniel Rogers. Smithsonian Institution Press, Washington.

Fish, Suzanne K., and Gary P. Nabhan
1991   Desert as Context: The Hohokam Environment. In *Exploring the Hohokam: Prehistoric Desert People of the American Southwest*, edited by George Gumerman, pp. 29–60. University of New Mexico Press, Albuquerque.

Fish, Suzanne K., Paul R. Fish, and John Madsen
1990   Analyzing Regional Agriculture: A Hohokam, Example. In *The Archaeology of Regions: The Case for Full-Coverage Survey*, edited by Suzanne K. Fish and S. A. Kowalewski, pp. 189–218. Smithsonian Institution Press, Washington.

1992   The Marana Community in the Hohokam World. *Anthropological Papers of the University of Arizona* 56. University of Arizona Press, Tucson.

Fish, Suzanne K., Paul R. Fish, Charles Miksicek, and John H. Madsen
1985   Prehistoric Agave Cultivation in Arizona. *Desert Plants* 7: 107–112, 100.

Flannery, Kent V.
1965   The Ecology of Early Food Production in Mesopotamia. *Science* 147: 1247–1256.

Fontana, Bernard L.
1983   Pima and Papago: Introduction. In *Handbook of North American Indians*, Vol. 10, *Southwest*, edited by Alfonso Ortiz, pp. 125–136. Smithsonian Institution, Washington.

Ford, Richard I.
1981   Gardening and Farming before A.D. 1000: Patterns of Prehistoric Cultivation North of Mexico. *Journal of Ethnobiology* 1(1): 6–27.

1985   Zuni Land Use and Damage to Trust Land. Expert testimony submitted to the United States Claims Court as evidence in the case of *Zuni Indian Tribe* v. *United States*, Docket 327–81L.

Forde, C. Darryl
1931   Hopi Agriculture and Land Ownership. *Journal of the Royal Anthropological Institute of Great Britain and Ireland* 61: 357–407.

Foth, H. D., and B. G. Ellis
1988   *Soil Fertility*. John Wiley and Sons, New York.

Fuller, Wallace H.
1975   *Soils of the Desert Southwest*. University of Arizona Press, Tucson.

Fuller, Wallace H., and H. E. Ray
1965   *Basic Concepts of Nitrogen, Phosphorus, and Potassium in Calcareous Soils*. University of Arizona, Tucson.

Gallagher, James P., and Robert F. Sasso
1987   Investigations into Oneota Ridged Field Agriculture on the Northern Margin of the Prairie Peninsula. *Plains Anthropologist* 32: 141–152.

Gallegos, R. A., and H. C. Monger
1997   Phytogenic Carbonate, Desert Shrubs, and Stable Carbon Isotopes. *1998 Annual Meeting Abstracts*. Soil Science Society of America, Baltimore.

Gee, G. W., and J. W. Bauder
1986   Particle-size Analysis. In "Methods of Soil Analysis, Part 1, Physical and Mineralogical Method," edited by A. Klute. *Agronomy Monograph* 9: 383–411. American Society of Agronomy and Soil Science Society of America, Madison.

Gelderman, F. W.
1970   *Soil Survey of the Safford Area, Arizona*. U.S. Department of Agriculture, Soil Conservation Service, Washington.

Gelles, Paul H.
1996 The Political Ecology of Irrigation in an Andean Peasant Community. In *Canals and Communities: Small-Scale Irrigation Systems,* edited by Jonathan B. Mabry, pp. 88–115. University of Arizona Press, Tucson.

Gentry, Howard S.
1972 The Agave Family in Sonora. *U.S. Department of Agriculture Handbook* 399. Washington.
1982 *Agaves of Continental North America.* University of Arizona Press, Tucson.

Germick, Stephen, and Joseph S. Crary
1992 From Shadow to Substance: An Alternative Perspective on the Roosevelt Phase. In "Proceedings of the Second Salado Conference, Globe, Arizona 1992," edited by Richard C. Lange and Stephen Germick. *Arizona Archaeological Society Occasional Papers* 19: 286–303. Phoenix.

Gile, L. H., J. W. Hawley, and R. B. Grossman
1981 *Soils and Geomorphology in the Basin and Range Area of Southern New Mexico: Guidebook to the Desert Project.* New Mexico Bureau of Mines and Mineral Resources, Soccoro.

Gile, L. H., F. F. Peterson, and R. B. Grossman
1966 Morphological and Genetic Sequences of Carbonate Accumulation in Desert Soils. *Soil Science* 101: 347–360.

Gilman, Patricia L.
1997 Wandering Villagers: Pit Structures, Mobility, and Agriculture in Southeastern Arizona. *Arizona State University Anthropological Research Papers* 49. Tempe.

Gilman, Patricia L., and Peter Sherman
1975 An Archaeological Survey of the Graham-Curtis Project: Phase II. *Arizona State Museum Archaeological Series* 65. Arizona State Museum, University of Arizona, Tucson.

Ginsburg, Karen
1987 Kitchen Gardens in the Petén Region of Guatemala: A Study of the Form, Crops, and Contributions of Gardens in Three Villages, 1978–1980. MS, Master's thesis, University of California, Davis.

Gladwin, Harold S., Emil W. Haury, E. B. Sayles, and Nora Gladwin
1937 Excavations at Snaketown, Material Culture. *Medallion Papers* 25. Gila Pueblo Foundation, Globe.

Gleason, Kathryn L.
1994 To Bound and To Cultivate: An Introduction to the Archaeology of Gardens and Fields. In *The Archaeology of Garden and Field*, edited by Naomi F. Miller and Kathryn L. Gleason, pp. 1–24. University of Pennsylvania Press, Philadelphia.

Glinski, J., and J. Lipiec
1990 *Soil Physical Conditions and Plant Roots.* CRC Press, Boca Raton.

Golub, Berl, and Herbert M. Eder
1964 Landforms Made by Man. *Landscape* 14: 4–7.

González-Jacóme, Alba
1985 Home Gardens in Central Mexico. In "Prehistoric Intensive Agriculture in the Tropics," edited by I. S. Farrington. *British Archaeological Reports, International Series* 232: 521–537.

Grant, Campbell
1965 *The Rock Paintings of the Chumash: A Study of a California Indian Culture.* University of California Press, Berkeley and Los Angeles.
1967 *Rock Art of the American Indian.* Thomas Y. Crowell and Co., New York.
1979 *Canyon de Chelley: Its People and Rock Art.* University of Arizona Press, Tucson.

Graybill, Donald D., David A. Gregory, Gary S. Funkhouser, and Fred L. Nials
1999 Long-Term Streamflow Reconstructions, River Channel Morphology, and Aboriginal Irrigation Systems along the Salt and Gila Rivers. MS to appear in *Environmental Change and Human Adaptation in the American Southwest*, edited by Jeffrey S. Dean and David E. Doyel. University of Utah Press, Salt Lake City.

Greenwood, Roberta S.
1969 The Browne Site: Early Milling Stone Horizon in Southern California. *Memoirs of the Society for American Archaeology* 23.

Hack, John T.
1942 The Changing Physical Environment of the Hopi Indians of Arizona. *Papers of the Peabody Museum of American Archaeology and Ethnology* 35(1). Harvard University, Cambridge.

Hackenberg, Robert A.
1983 Pima and Papago Ecological Adaptations. In *Handbook of North American Indians*, Vol. 10, *Southwest*, edited by Alfonso Ortiz, pp. 161–177. Smithsonian Institution, Washington.

Hard, Robert J.
1990 Agricultural Dependence in the Mountain Mogollon. In *Perspectives on Southwestern Prehistory*, edited by Paul E. Minnis and Charles L. Redman, pp. 135–149. Westview Press, Boulder.

Haury, Emil W.
1936a Some Southwestern Pottery Types: Series IV.

Haury, Emil W. (*continued*)
   Medallion Papers 19. Gila Pueblo Foundation, Globe.
1936b   The Mogollon Culture of Southwestern New Mexico. *Medallion Papers* 20. Gila Pueblo Foundation, Globe.
1945   The Excavation of Los Muertos and Neighboring Ruins in the Salt River Valley, Southern Arizona. Based on the work of the Hemenway Southwestern Archaeological Expedition of 1887–1888. *Papers of the Peabody Museum of American Archaeology and Ethnology* 24(1). Harvard University, Cambridge.
1958   Evidence at Point of Pines for a Prehistoric Migration from Northern Arizona. In "Migrations in New World Culture History," edited by Raymond H. Thompson. *University of Arizona Social Science Bulletin* 27: 1–6. University of Arizona, Tucson.
1976   *The Hohokam Desert Farmers and Craftsmen: Excavations at Snaketown, 1964–1965.* University of Arizona Press, Tucson.
Haury, Emil W., and Lisa W. Huckell, Editors
1993   A Prehistoric Cotton Cache from the Pinaleño Mountains, Arizona. *The Kiva* 59(2): 95–145.
Hausenbuiller, R. L.
1972   *Soil Science: Principles and Practices.* Wm. C. Brown Company Publishers, Dubuque.
Heidenreich, Conrad
1974   A Relict Indian Corn Field Near Creemore, Ontario. *Canadian Geographer* 18: 379–394.
Heinonen, R.
1985   *Soil Management and Crop Water Supply.* University of Agricultural Sciences, Uppsala.
Heizer, Robert F.
1958   Aboriginal California and Great Basin Cartography. *Reports of the University of California Archaeological Survey* 41: 1–9. Berkeley.
Heizer, Robert F., and Martin A. Baumhoff
1962   *Prehistoric Rock Art of Nevada and Eastern California.* University of California Press, Berkeley and Los Angeles.
Hendricks, D. M.
1985   *Arizona Soils.* College of Agriculture, University of Arizona, Tucson.
Herold, Laurance C.
1965   Trincheras and Physical Environment along the Rio Gavilan, Chihuahua, Mexico. *Publications in Geography* 65-1. Department of Geography, University of Denver.
Hester, Thomas Ray, and Robert F. Heizer
1972   Problems in the Functional Interpretation of Artifacts: Scraper Planes from Mitla and Yagul,

Oaxaca. *University of California Archaeological Facility Papers* 14: 109–110, Berkeley.
Hewes, Leslie
1981   Early Fencing on the Western Margins of the Prairie. *Annals of the Association of American Geographers* 71: 499–526.
Hewitt, Edgar L.
1906   Antiquities of the Jemez Plateau, New Mexico. *Bureau of American Ethnology Bulletin* 32. Smithsonian Institution, Washington.
Hibben, Frank C.
1937   Excavations of the Riana Ruin and Chama Valley Survey. *Anthropological Series* 2. University of New Mexico, Albuquerque.
Holmes, G. K.
1912   Aboriginal Agriculture—The American Indians. In *Cyclopedia of American Agriculture*, edited by L. H. Bailey, pp. 24–39. McMillan, New York.
Homburg, Jeffrey A.
1994   Soil Fertility in the Tonto Basin. In "Changing Land-use Practices in the Tonto Basin, Vol. 3, Field Study," edited by Richard Ciolek-Torrello and John R. Welch. *Statistical Research Technical Series* 28: 253–295. Tucson.
1997   Prehistoric Dryland Agricultural Fields of the Lower Verde. In *Vanishing River: Landscapes and Lives of the Lower Verde Valley: The Lower Verde Archaeological Project*, Vol. 2, *Agricultural, Subsistence, and Environmental Studies*, edited by Jeffrey A. Homburg and Richard Ciolek-Torrello, pp. 103–126. SRI Press, Tucson.
Homburg, Jeffrey A., and Jonathan A. Sandor
1997   An Agronomic Study of Two Classic Period Agricultural Fields in the Horseshoe Basin. In *Vanishing River: Landscapes and Lives of the Lower Verde Valley: The Lower Verde Archaeological Project*, Vol. 2, *Agricultural, Subsistence, and Environmental Studies*, edited by Jeffrey A. Homburg and Richard Ciolek-Torrello, pp. 127–148. SRI Press, Tucson.
Homburg, Jeffrey A., Jonathan A. Sandor,
and Jay B. Norton
1999   Soil Properties Associated with a Native-American Farming System: Zuni, New Mexico. Poster presented at the 91st Annual Meeting of the American Society of Agronomy, Salt Lake City.
Hough, Walter
1907   Antiquities of the Upper Gila and Salt River Valleys in Arizona and New Mexico. *Bureau of American Ethnology Bulletin* 35. Smithsonian Institution, Washington.

Houser, Brenda B.
1991 Late Cenozoic Stratigraphy and Tectonics of the Safford Basin, Southeastern Arizona. In "Geologic Excursions through the Sonoran Desert Region, Arizona and Sonora," edited by George E. Gehrels and Jon E. Spencer. *Arizona Geological Survey Special Paper* 7: 20–24.

Houser, Brenda B., D. H. Richter, and M. Shafiqullah
1985 Geologic Map of the Safford Quadrangle, Graham County, Arizona. *U.S. Geologic Survey Miscellaneous Investigations Series* I-617. U.S. Department of Interior, Washington.

Houser, Brenda B., Lisa Peters,
Richard P. Esser, and Mark E. Gettings
2004 Stratigraphy and Tectonic History of the Tucson Basin, Pima County, Arizona, based on the Exxon State (32)-1 Well. *U.S. Geological Survey Scientific Investigation Report SIR* 2004–5076.

Huckleberry, Gary A.
1995 Archaeological Implications of Late-Holocene Channel Changes on the Middle Gila River, Arizona. *Geoarchaeology* 10(3): 159–182.

Hunt, Eva
1972 Irrigation and the Socio–Political Organization of Cuicatec Cacicazgos. In "Chronology and Irrigation." *The Prehistory of the Tehuacan Valley*, Vol. 4, edited by R. S. MacNeish, pp. 162–274. University of Texas Press, Austin, for the R. S. Peabody Foundation.

Hunt, Eva, and Robert C. Hunt
1974 Irrigation, Conflict, and Politics: A Mexican Case. In "Irrigation's Impact on Society," edited by Theodore E. Downing and McGuire Gibson. *Anthropological Papers of the University of Arizona* 25: 21–42. University of Arizona Press, Tucson.

Jeffrey, D. W.
1987 *Soil-Plant Relationships: An Ecological Approach*. Timber Press, Portland.

Jenny, H.
1941 *Factors of Soil Formation*. McGraw-Hill, New York.

Jernigan, E. Wesley
1992 Hour-Glass Rock Art Figures of Southeastern Arizona. *Eastern Arizona College Museum of Anthropology Publication* 4. Thatcher.

Johnson, Alfred E., and William W. Wasley
1966 Archaeological Excavations near Bylas, Arizona. *The Kiva* 31(4): 205–253.

Johnson, Boma
1986 Earth Figures of the Lower Colorado and Gila River Deserts: A Functional Analysis. *The Arizona Archaeologist* 20.

Johnson, Gregory A.
1982 Organizational Structure and Scalar Stress. In *Theory and Explanations in Archaeology: The Southampton Conference*, edited by Colin Renfrew, Michael J. Rowlands, and Barbara A. Segraves, pp. 389–421. Academic Press, New York.

1989 Dynamics of Southwestern Prehistory: Far Outside–Looking In. In *Dynamics of Southwest Prehistory*, edited by Linda Cordell and George Gumerman, pp. 371–389. Smithsonian Press, Washington.

Kay, M.
1996 Microwear Analysis of Some Clovis and Experimental Chipped Stone Tools. In *Stone Tools: Theoretical Insights into Human Prehistory*, edited by George H. Odell, pp. 315–344. Plenum Press, New York.

Kearney, Thomas H., and Robert H. Peebles
1964 *Arizona Flora* (2nd Edition). University of California Press, Berkeley.

Keeley, Lawrence H.
1980 *Experimental Determination of Stone Tool Uses: A Microwear Analysis*. University of Chicago Press, Chicago.

Keller, Donald R., and Suzanne M. Wilson
1976 New Light on the Tolchaco Problem. *The Kiva* 41(3–4): 225–239.

Kelly, A. R.
1965 Notes on a Prehistoric Cultivated Field in Macon, Georgia. In "Proceedings of the Twenty-First Southeastern Archaeological Conference." *Southeastern Archaeological Conference Bulletin* 3: 49–51. Cambridge.

Kelly, Dorothy S.
1937 The McEuen Cave Study. Unpublished MS on file, Safford District Office, Bureau of Land Management. Safford, Arizona.

Killion, Thomas W.
1990 Cultivation Intensity and Residential Site Structure: An Ethnoarchaeological Examination of Peasant Agriculture in the Sierra de los Tuxtlas, Veracruz, Mexico. *Latin American Antiquity* 1: 191–215.

Kimber, Clarissa T.
1973 Spatial Patterning of Dooryard Gardens of Puerto Rico. *Geographical Review* 63: 6–26.

Kowta, Makoto
1969 The Sayles Complex: A Late Milling-stone Assemblage from Cajon Pass and the Ecological Significance of its Scraper Planes. *University of California Publications in Anthropology* 6. University of California, Berkeley.

Ladd, Edmund J.
1979   Zuni Economy. In *Handbook of North American Indians*, General Editor, William C. Sturtevant, Vol. 9, *Southwest*, edited by Alfonso Ortiz, pp. 492–498. Smithsonian Institution, Washington.

LeBlanc, Steven A.
1982   Temporal Change in Mogollon Ceramics. In "Southwestern Ceramics: A Comparative Review," edited by Albert H. Schroeder. *The Arizona Archaeologist* 15: 106–127. Arizona Archaeological Society, Phoenix.

Lee, Betty Graham
1975   The McEuen Cave Site Report. Unpublished MS on file, Safford District Office, Bureau of Land Management. Safford.

Lekson, Stephen H.
2002   Salado Archaeology of the Upper Gila, New Mexico. *Anthropological Papers of the University of Arizona* 67. University of Arizona Press, Tucson.

Levy, Jerold
1992   *Orayvi Revisited: Social Stratification in an "Egalitarian" Society*. School of American Research Press, Santa Fe.

Lightfoot, Dale R.
1993a   The Cultural Ecology of Puebloan Pebble-Mulch Gardens. *Human Ecology* 21: 115–143.
1993b   The Landscape Context of Anasazi Pebble-Mulch Fields in the Galisteo Basin, Northern New Mexico. *Geoarchaeology* 8: 349–370.

Lightfoot, Dale, and Frank W. Eddy
1994   The Agricultural Utility of Lithic-Mulch Gardens: Past and Present. *GeoJournal* 34.4: 425–437.
1995   The Construction and Configuration of Anasazi Pebble-Mulch Gardens in the Northern Rio Grande. *American Antiquity* 60(3): 459–470.

Lindsay, Alexander J., Jr.
1987   Anasazi Population Movements to Southeastern Arizona. *American Archeology* 6(3): 190–198.

Lindsay, Alexander J., Jr., and Calvin H. Jennings
1968   Salado Red Ware Conference Ninth Southwestern Ceramic Seminar. *Museum of Northern Arizona Ceramic Series 4*. Museum of Northern Arizona, Flagstaff.

Lyons, Thomas R., and Douglas H. Scovill
1978   Non-Destructive Archaeology and Remote Sensing: A Conceptual and Methodological Stance. In *Remote Sensing and Non-Destructive Archaeology*, edited by Thomas R. Lyons and James I. Ebert, pp. 3–19. National Park Service, Washington.

Mabry, Jonathan B.
1998a   Introduction. In "Archaeological Investigations of Early Village Sites in the Middle Santa Cruz Valley: Analyses and Synthesis," Part I, edited by Jonathan B. Mabry. *Anthropological Papers* 19: 1–29. Center for Desert Archaeology, Tucson.
1998b   (Editor) Archaeological Investigations of Early Village Sites in the Middle Santa Cruz Valley: Analyses and Synthesis," Part I. *Anthropological Papers* 19. Center for Desert Archaeology, Tucson.
2002   Diversity in Early Southwestern Farming Systems and Optimization Models of Transitions to Agriculture. In "Early Agricultural Period Environment and Subsistence," edited by Michael W. Diehl. Forthcoming in *Anthropological Papers* 34. Center for Desert Archaeology, Tucson.

Mabry, Jonathan B., Deborah L. Swartz, Helga Wocherl, Jeffery J. Clark, Gavin H. Archer, and Michael W. Lindeman
1997   Archaeological Investigations of Early Village Sites in the Middle Santa Cruz Valley: Descriptions of the Santa Cruz Bend, Square Hearth, Stone Pipe, and Canal Sites. *Anthropological Papers* 18. Center for Desert Archaeology, Tucson.

Machette, M. N.
1965   Calcic Soils of the Southwestern United States. In *Soils and Quaternary Geology of The Southwestern United States,* edited by D. L. Weide, pp. 1–22. The Geological Society of America, American Society of Agronomy, and Soil Science Society of America. Boulder and Madison.

Martin, Paul S., and W. Byers
1965   Pollen and Archaeology at Wetherill Mesa. *American Antiquity* 31(2, Part 2): 122–135.

Martin, Paul S., and J. Schoenwetter
1960   Arizona's Oldest Cornfield. *Science* 132: 33–34.

Martineau, LaVan
1973   *The Rocks Begin to Speak*. KC Publications, Las Vegas.

Masse, W. Bruce
1979   An Intensive Survey of Prehistoric Dry Farming Systems Near Tumomoc Hill in Tucson, Arizona. *The Kiva* 45(1–2): 141–186.
1981   Prehistoric Irrigation Systems in the Salt River Valley, Arizona. *Science* 214: 408–415.
1987   (Editor) Archaeological Investigations of Portions of the Las Acequias-Los Muertos Irrigation System. *Arizona State Museum Archaeological Series* 176. University of Arizona, Tucson.

1991 The Quest for Subsistence Sufficiency and Civilization in the Sonoran Desert. In *Chaco and the Hohokam: Prehistoric Regional Systems in the American Southwest*, edited by Patricia L. Crown and W. James Judge, pp. 195–233. School of American Research Press, Santa Fe.

Mauldin, Raymond
1993 The Relationship Between Ground Stone and Agricultural Intensification in Western New Mexico. *The Kiva* 58(3): 317–330.

Maxwell, Timothy D.
1995a The Use of Comparative and Engineering Analysis in the Study of Prehistoric Agriculture. In *Evolutionary Archaeology: Methodological Issues*, edited by Patrice A. Teltsev, pp. 113–128. University of Arizona Press, Tucson.

1995b A Comparative Study of Prehistoric Farming Strategies. In "Soil, Water, Biology, and Belief in Prehistoric and Traditional Southwestern Agriculture," edited by H. Wolcott Toll. *New Mexico Archaeological Council Special Publication* 2: 2–12. Albuquerque.

Maxwell, Timothy D., and Kurt F. Anschuetz
1992 The Southwestern Ethnographic Record and Prehistoric Agricultural Diversity. In *Gardens of Prehistory: The Archaeology of Settlement Agriculture in Greater Mesoamerica*, edited by Thomas W. Killion, pp. 35–68. University of Alabama Press, Tuscaloosa.

Mayerson, Philip
1961 *The Ancient Agricultural Regime of Nessana and the Central Negeb*. The British School of Archaeology in Jerusalem, London.

McLean, E. O.
1982 Soil pH and Lime Requirements. In "Methods of Soil Analysis. Chemical and Microbiological Properties," edited by A. L. Page, R. H. Miller, and D. R. Keeney. *Agronomy Monograph* 9(2): 199–222. American Society of Agronomy and Soil Science Society of America, Madison.

Mehuys, G. R., L. H. Stolzy, J. Letey, and L. V. Weeks
1975 Effect of Stones on the Hydraulic Conductivity of Relatively Dry Desert Soils. *Soil Science Society of America Proceedings* 39: 37–42.

Mills, Barbara J.
2000 Alternative Models, Alternative Strategies. In *Alternative Leadership Strategies in the Prehispanic Southwest*, edited by Barbara J. Mills, pp. 3–18. University of Arizona Press, Tucson.

Moreno, Jerryll
2003 Petroglyphs of Lake Pleasant Regional Park. *Kiva* 68(3): 185–219.

Mountjoy, Joseph B.
1982 An Interpretation of the Pictographs at La Peña Pintada, Jalisco, Mexico. *American Antiquity* 47(1): 110–126.

Munn, Nancy D.
1973 The Spatial Presentation of Cosmic Order in Walbiri Iconography. In *Primitive Art and Society*, edited by Anthony Forge, pp. 193–220. Oxford University Press and The Wenner–Gren Foundation for Anthropological Research, London and New York.

Munsell Color Company
1988 *Munsell Soil Color Charts*. Macbeth Division of Kollmorgen Instruments Corporation, Baltimore.

Muro, Mark
1998a New Finds Explode Old Views of the American Southwest. *Science* 279: 653–654.

1998b Not Just Another Roadside Attraction. *American Archaeology* 2: 10–16.

Murphy, C. H.
1984 *Handbook of Particle Sampling and Analysis Methods*. Verlag Chemie International, Dearfield Beach.

Nabhan, Gary Paul
1984 Soil Fertility Renewal and Water Harvesting in Sonoran Desert Agriculture: The Papago Example. *Arid Lands Newsletter* 20: 21–28.

National Academy of Sciences
1974 *More Water for Arid Lands: Promising Technologies and Research Opportunities*. National Academy of Sciences, Washington.

National Soil Survey Center
1996 *Soil Survey Laboratory Methods Manual*. U.S. Department of Agriculture, Natural Resources Conservation Service, Lincoln.

Neely, James A.
1974 The Prehistoric Lunt and Stove Canyon Sites, Point of Pines, Arizona. MS, Doctoral dissertation, Department of Anthropology, University of Arizona. Tucson.

1993a Prehistoric and Early Historic Agricultural Pursuits within the Bason Land Exchange. *La Cuchilla de Piedra: The Cultural Resources of the Bason Land Exchange, Los Alamos, New Mexico*, edited by John A. Peterson and Christopher B. Nightengale, pp. 231–245. Archaeological Research, Inc., El Paso.

1993b Stone Hoes from the Bason Land Exchange. *La Cuchilla de Piedra: The Cultural Resources of the Bason Land Exchange, Los Alamos, New Mexico*, edited by John A. Peterson and Christopher B. Nightengale, pp. 221–230. Archaeological Research, Inc., El Paso.

Neely James A. (*continued*)

1995a   A Progress Report on the Survey and Mapping of Six (6) Water–Management Systems in the Vicinity of Pima, Arizona. MS on file, Arizona State Museum, Tucson.

1995b   Mogollon/Western Pueblo Soil and Water Control Systems of the Reserve Phase: New Data from West–Central New Mexico. In "Soil, Water, Biology, and Belief in Southwestern Prehistoric and Traditional Agriculture," edited by H. Wolcott Toll. *New Mexico Archaeological Council Special Publication* 2: 239–262. Albuquerque.

1995c   Paleoecología, Desarrollo Cultural, y los Usos de Aguas en el Valle de Tehuacan, Puebla, México. Un reportaje al Consejo de Arqueología del Instituto Nacional de Antropología e Historia de México. Mexico.

1997a   Foothill Irrigation and Domestic Water Systems of the Safford Valley, Southeastern Arizona. Paper presented at the 62nd Annual Meeting of the Society for American Archaeology, Nashville.

1997b   A Developmental Cultural Model for the Safford Valley of Southeastern Arizona and Adjacent Areas. MS prepared for the symposium "The Archaeology of a Land Between: Regional Dynamics in the Prehistory and History of Southeast Arizona," sponsored by the Amerind Foundation, October 2–17, 1997. Dragoon.

2001a   Prehistoric Agricultural Fields and Water Management Technology of the Safford Valley, Southeastern Arizona. *Antiquity* 75: 681–682.

2001b   The Prehispanic "Fossilized" Canal Systems of the Tehuacan Valley: Their Distribution, Chronology, and Environmental Contexts. MS, Report to the National Science Foundation, Grant 9986718.

2001c   A Contextual Study of the "Fossilized" Prehispanic Canal Systems of the Tehuacan Valley, Puebla, Mexico. *Antiquity* 75: 505–506.

2002   Expedient Stone Tools as Indicators of Relic Agricultural Fields. MS, possession of author.

Neely, James A., and Joseph S. Crary

1998   The Marijilda Canyon Canal: A Complex Irrigation and Domestic Water System in the Safford Valley, Southeastern Arizona. Paper presented at the 63rd Annual Meeting of the Society for American Archaeology, Seattle.

Neely, James A., and William E. Doolittle

1996   The Goat Hill Irrigation System, Southeastern Arizona. Paper presented at the 61st Annual Meeting of the Society for American Archaeology, New Orleans.

Neely, James A., and Jennifer R. Rinker

1997   Foothill Irrigation and Domestic Water Systems of the Safford Valley, Southeastern Arizona: A Progress Report on the 2nd Field Season of Survey and Mapping of Water–Management Systems and Associated Sites in the Vicinity of Pima, Arizona. MS on file, Arizona State Museum. Tucson.

Neily, Robert B., Joseph S. Crary,

Gay M. Kinkade, and Stephen Germick

1993   The Owens–Colvin Site Revisited: A Preliminary Report of the Excavations at a Bylas Phase Settlement near Eden, Arizona. Paper presented at the 66th Anniversary of the Pecos Conference. Springerville, Arizona.

Nelson, D. W., and L. E. Sommers

1982   Total Carbon, Organic Carbon, and Organic Matter. In "Methods of Soil Analysis. Chemical and Microbiological Methods," edited by A. L. Page, R. H. Miller and D. R. Keeney. *Agronomy Monograph* 9(2): 539–579. American Society of Agronomy and Soil Science Society of America, Madison.

Nelson, Margaret C.

1991   The Study of Technological Organization. In *Archaeological Method and Theory*, edited by Michael B. Schiffer, pp. 57–100. University of Arizona Press, Tucson.

Niñez, Vera K.

1984   *Household Gardens: Theoretical Considerations on an Old Survival Strategy*. International Potato Center, Lima.

Nobel, Park S., and Robert G. McDaniel

1988   Low Temperature Tolerances, Nocturnal Acid Accumulation, and Biomass Increases for Seven Species of Agave. *Journal of Arid Environments* 15: 147–155.

Nobel, P. S., P. M. Miller,

and E. A. Graham

1992   Influence of Rocks on Soil Temperature, Soil Water Potential, and Rooting Patterns for Desert Succulents. *Oecologia* 92: 90–96.

Olsen, S. R., and L. E. Sommers

1982   Phosphorus. In "Methods of Soil Analysis. Chemical and Microbiological Methods," edited by A. L. Page, R. H. Miller, and D. R. Keeney. *Agronomy Monograph* 9(2): 403–430. American Society of Agronomy and Soil Science Society of America, Madison.

Osborne, Carolyn M.

1965   The Preparation of Yucca Fibers: An Experimental Study. In "Contributions of the Wetherill Mesa Archaeological Project," assembled by

Douglas Osborne. *Memoirs of the Society for American Archaeology* 19: 45–50.

Page, Diana
 1986 Growing Hope in Santiago's Urban Organic Gardens. *Grassroots Development* 10.2: 38–43.

Parsons, Jeffrey R., and Mary Parsons
 1990 Maguey Utilization in Highland Central Mexico: An Archaeological Ethnography. *Museum of Anthropology Anthropological Papers* 82. University of Michigan, Ann Arbor.

Patrick, Larry L.
 1985 Agave and Zea in Highland Central Mexico: The Ecology and History of the Metepantli. In "Prehistoric Intensive Agriculture in the Tropics," edited by I. Farrington, pp. 539–547. *B.A.R. International Series* 232(2).

Patterson, Alex
 1992 *A Field Guide to Rock Art Symbols Of the Southwest.* Johnson Books, Boulder.

Pool, Michael D.
 1985 The Western Apache Settlement System and Its Implications for the Prehistoric Early Mogollon Period. MS, Master's thesis, Department of Anthropology, University of Texas, Austin.

Preston, A. L., and R. A. Preston
 1985 The Discovery of Nineteen Prehistoric Calendric Petroglyph Sites in Arizona. In *Earth and Sky: The Northridge Conference on Archaeoastronomy*, edited by Arlene Benson and Tom Hoskinson, pp. 123–133. Slo'w Press, Thousand Oaks.

Prewitt, Elton R., and Robert K. Holz
 1976 Application of Orthophoto Mapping to Archaeological Problems. *American Antiquity* 41(4): 493–496.

Rafter, John
 1985 Archaeoastronomy of Counsel Rocks, A Ring of Pictured Stones. In *Earth and Sky: The Northridge Conference on Archaeoastronomy,* edited by Arlene Benson and Tom Hoskinson, pp. 109–122. Slo'w Press, Thousand Oaks.

Ramenofsky, Elizabeth L.
 1984 *From Charcoal to Banking: The I. E. Solomons of Arizona.* Westernlore Press, Tucson.

Rankin, Adrianne G., and Keith Katzer
 1989 Agricultural Systems in the ACS Waddell Project Area. In "Settlement, Subsistence, and Specialization in the Northern Periphery: The Waddell Project," edited by Margerie Green. *Cultural Resources Report* 65: 981–1020. Archaeological Consulting Services, Tempe.

Raynor, G. S., J. V. Hayes, and E. C. Ogden
 1970 *Experimental Data on Dispersion and Deposition of Timothy and Corn Pollen from Known Sources.* Brookhaven National Laboratory 957 (T–398).

Raynor, G. S., E. C. Ogden, and J. V. Hayes
 1972 Dispersion and Deposition of Corn Pollen from Experimental Sources. *Agronomy Journal* 64: 420–427.

Richter, D. H., B. B. Houser, and P. E. Damon
 1983 Geologic Map of the Guthrie Quadrangle, Graham and Greenlee Counties, Arizona. *U.S. Geological Survey Miscellaneous Investigations Series*, Map I-1455. U.S. Department of Interior, Washington.

Rinker, Jennifer Rebecca
 1998 The Bryce-Smith Project: Irrigated Agriculture and Habitation from A.D. 1000 to 1450, Lefthand Canyon, Safford Valley, Arizona. MS, Master's thesis, Department of Anthropology, University of Texas, Austin.

Rinker, Jennifer R., and James A. Neely
 1998 Habitation Sites and Upland Canal Irrigation in Lefthand Canyon, Safford Valley, Southeastern Arizona. Paper presented at the 63rd Annual Meeting of the Society for American Archaeology, Seattle.

Rogers, Malcolm J.
 1939 Early Lithic Industries of the Lower Basin of the Colorado River and Adjacent Desert Areas. *San Diego Museum Paper* 3.

Rose, Martin R.
 1994 Long Term Drought Reconstructions for the Lake Roosevelt Region. In "The Roosevelt Rural Sites Study, Vol. 3, Changing Land Use in the Tonto Basin," edited by Richard Ciolek-Torello and John R. Welch. *Technical Series* 28: 311–359. Statistical Research, Inc., Tucson.

Ross, Winifred
 1944 The Present Day Dietary Habits of the Papago Indians. MS, Master's thesis, Department of Home Economics, University of Arizona, Tucson.

Rucks, Meredith
 1984 *Safford District Rock Art: Cultural Resources Management Plan.* U.S. Department of Interior, Bureau of Land Management, Safford.

Rule, Pam
 1993 The Owens-Colvin Site of the Safford Valley. *Eastern Arizona College Museum of Anthropology Publication* 3. Thatcher.

Russell, Frank
 1908 The Pima Indians. *Twenty-sixth Annual Report of the Bureau of American Ethnology to the Secretary of the Smithsonian Institution, 1904–1905*, pp. 3–289. Washington.

Sahlins, Marshall D.
1972   *Stone Age Economics*. Aldine de Gruyter, New York.

Saini, G. R., and A. A. MacLean
1967   The Effect of Stones on Potato Yield, Soil Temperature, and Moisture. *American Potato Journal* 44: 209–213.

Salls, Roy
1985   The Scraper Plane: A Functional Interpretation. *Journal of Field Archaeology* 12: 99–106.

Sandor, Jonathan A.
1995   Searching for Clues about Southwest Prehistoric Agriculture. In "Soil, Water, Biology, and Belief in Prehistoric and Traditional Southwestern Agriculture," edited by H. Wolcott Toll. *New Mexico Archaeological Council Special Publication* 2: 119–137. Albuquerque.

Sandor, Jonathan A., and Jeffrey A. Homburg
1997   Soils and Prehistoric Agricultural Sites on Piedmont Slopes Near Paquime, Chihuahua, Mexico. MS, draft report for National Geographic project, submitted to Paul Minnis, Department of Anthropology, University of Oklahoma, Norman.

Sandor, Jonathan A., P. L. Gersper, and J. W. Hawley
1986   Soils and Prehistoric Agricultural Terracing Sites in New Mexico. I, Site Placement, Soil Morphology, and Classification. II, Organic Matter and Bulk Density Changes. III, Phosphorus, Selected Micronutrients, and pH. *Soil Science Society of America Journal* 50: 160–180.
1990   Prehistoric Agricultural Terraces and Soils in the Mimbres Area, New Mexico. *World Archaeology* 22: 70–86.

Sauer, Carl, and Donald D. Brand
1930   Pueblo Sites in Southeastern Arizona. *University of California Publications in Geography* 3: 415–458. University of California Press, Berkeley.

Sayles, E. B.
1945   The San Simon Branch: Excavations at Cave Creek and in the San Simon Valley, Vol. 1, Material Culture. *Medallion Papers* 34. Gila Pueblo Foundation, Globe.

Schaafsma, Polly
1975a   Rock Art in the Cochiti Reservoir District. *Museum of New Mexico Papers in Anthropology* 16.
1975b   *Rock Art in New Mexico*. University of New Mexico Press, Albuquerque.
1980   *Indian Rock Art of the Southwest*. School of American Research and University of New Mexico Press, Santa Fe and Albuquerque.

Schiffer, Michael B., Alan P. Sullivan, and Timothy C. Klinger
1978   The Design of Archaeological Surveys. *World Archaeology* 10: 1–28.

Schlegel, Alice
1992   African Political Models in the American Southwest: Hopi as an Internal Frontier Society. *American Anthropologist* 94: 376–397.

Schmidt, Robert H., Jr., and Rex E. Gerald
1988   The Distribution of Conservation–Type Water-Control Systems in the Northern Sierra Madre Occidental. *The Kiva* 53(2): 165–179.

Schroeder, Albert H.
1952   *A Brief Survey of the Lower Colorado River from Davis Dam to the International Border*. The Bureau of Reclamation, Boulder.

Sellers, William D., Richard H. Hill, and Margaret Sanderson-Rae, Editors
1985   *Arizona Climate: The First 100 Years*. University of Arizona Press, Tucson.

Semenov, S. A.
1964   *Prehistoric Technology*. Adams and Dart, Bath.

Seymour, Gregory R.
1997   Ceramics. In "The Sanchez Copper Project, Vol. 1, Archaeological Investigations in the Safford Valley, Graham County, Arizona," edited by Gregory R. Seymour, Richard V. N. Ahlstrom, and David P. Doak, *SWCA Archaeological Report* 94–82 (Revised 1997): 6.4–6.6. SWCA Environmental Consultants, Tucson.
1998   The Civilian Conservation Corps in Arizona: A Context for Erosion-Control Features. *Kiva* 63(4): 359–377.

Seymour, Gregory R., Richard V.N. Ahlstrom, and David P. Doak
1997a   Prehistoric Exploitation of the Sanchez Project Area. In "The Sanchez Copper Project, Vol. 1, Archaeological Investigations in the Safford Valley, Graham County, Arizona," edited by Gregory R. Seymour, Richard V. N. Ahlstrom, and David P. Doak. *SWCA Archaeological Report* 94–82 (Revised 1997): 10.1–10.6. SWCA Environmental Consultants, Tucson.
1997b   (Editors) The Sanchez Copper Project, Vol. 1, Archaeological Investigations in the Safford Valley, Graham County, Arizona. *SWCA Archaeological Report* 94–82 (Revised 1997). SWCA Environmental Consultants, Tucson.

Seymour, Gregory R., David P. Doak, and Richard V. N. Ahlstrom
1997   Prehistoric Farming and Resource Use. In "The Sanchez Copper Project, Vol. 1, Archaeological Investigations in the Safford Valley, Graham

County, Arizona," edited by Gregory R. Seymour, Richard V. N. Ahlstrom, and David P. Doak. *SWCA Archaeological Report* 94–82 (Revised 1997): 8.1–8.14. SWCA Environmental Consultants, Tucson.

Shackley, M. Steven
2000 Late Prehistoric Farmers/Foragers at the Foot of the Mogollon Rim: The McEuen Cave Archaeological Project. MS, proposal submitted to the National Science Foundation, on file, Hearst Museum of Anthropology, University of California, Berkeley.

Shoberg, Marilyn B.
2001 Untitled and unpublished manuscript on file at the Texas Archeological Research Laboratory, University of Texas, Austin.

Sofaer, Anna, Volker Zinser, and Rolf M. Sinclair
1979 A Unique Solar Marking Construct: A Unique Archaeoastronomical Site in New Mexico Marks Solstices and Equinoxes. *Science* 206: 283–291.

Soil Science Society of America
1987 *Glossary of Soil Science Terms*. Soil Science Society of America, Madison.

Soil Survey Staff
1993 *Soil Survey Manual*. U.S. Department of Agriculture, Washington.
1998 *Keys to Soil Taxonomy*. U.S. Department of Agriculture, Natural Resources Conservation Service, Washington.
1999 *Soil Taxonomy, A Basic System of Soil Classification for Making and Interpreting Soil Surveys*. U.S. Department of Agriculture, Washington.

Solbrig, O. T.
1977 The Adaptive Strategies of *Larrea. Creosote Bush: Biology and Chemistry of* Larrea *in New World Deserts*, edited by T. Jonathan Mabry, J. H. Hunziker, and D. R. Difeo, pp. 1–9. Dowden, Hutchinson, and Ross, Stroudsburgh, Pennsylvania.

Spencer, Joseph E.
1966 *Shifting Cultivation in Southeast Asia*. University of California Press, Berkeley.
1973 *Oriental Asia: Themes Toward a Geography*. Prentice-Hall, Englewood Cliffs.

Spencer, Joseph E., and Gary A. Hale
1961 The Origin, Nature, and Distribution of Agricultural Terracing. *Pacific Viewpoint* 2: 1–40.

Stanbury, Pamela C.
1996 The Utility of Tradition in Sri Lankan Bureaucratic Irrigation: The Case of the Kirindi Oya Project. In *Canals and Communities: Small-Scale Irrigation Systems*, edited by Jonathan B. Mabry, pp. 210–226. University of Arizona Press, Tucson.

Stevenson, Matilda Coxe
1904 The Zuñi Indians: Their Mythology, Esoteric Fraternities, and Ceremonies. *Twenty-third Annual Report of the Bureau of American Ethnology to the Secretary of the Smithsonian Institution, 1901–1902*, pp. 73–634. Washington.

Stewart, Guy R.
1939 Conservation Practices in Primitive Agriculture of the Southwest. *Soil Conservation* 5: 112–115, 131.
1940a Conservation in Pueblo Agriculture: I. Primitive Practices. *The Scientific Monthly* 51: 201–220.
1940b Conservation in Pueblo Agriculture: II. Present-Day Flood Water Irrigation, *The Scientific Monthly* 51: 329–340.

Stewart, John H.
1998 Regional Characteristics, Tilt Domains, and Extensional History of the Late Cenozoic Basin and Range Province, Western North America. In "Accommodation Zones and Transfer Zones: The Regional Segmentation of the Basin and Range Province," edited by J. E. Faulds and J. H. Stewart. *Geological Society of America Special Paper* 323: 47–74.

Streuver, Stewart
1968 Woodland Subsistence-Settlement Systems in the Lower Illinois Valley. In *New Perspectives in Archaeology*, edited by Lewis R. Binford and Sally R. Binford, pp. 285–312. Aldine, Chicago.

Suttles, Wayne
1951 The Early Diffusion of the Potato Among the Coast Salish. *Southwestern Journal of Anthropology* 7: 281–288.

Tello-Balderas, J. Jesus, and Edmundo García-Moya
1985 The Mescal Industry in the Altiplano Potosino-Zacatecano of North-central Mexico. *Desert Plants* 7: 81–87.

Tisdale, S., W. L. Nelson, and J. D. Beaton
1985 *Soil Fertility and Fertilizers*. Macmillan, New York.

Towner, Ronald H.
1994 Lithic Artifacts. In "The Roosevelt Rural Sites Study, Vol. 2(2), Prehistoric Rural Settlements in the Tonto Basin," edited by Richard Ciolek-Torrello, Steven D. Shelley, and Su Benaron. *Statistical Research Technical Series* 28: 469–533. Statistical Research, Inc., Tucson.

Tringham, Ruth, Glenn Cooper, George Odell, Barbara Voytek, and Anne Whitman
1974 Experimentation in the Formation of Edge Damage: A New Approach to Lithic Analysis. *Journal of Field Archaeology* 1: 171–196.

Tuohy, Donald R.
1960   Archaeological Survey and Excavation in the Gila River Channel Between Earven Dam Site and Buttes Reservoir Site, Arizona. MS, report to the National Park Service, on file, Arizona State Museum Library, Tucson.

Turner II, B. L.
1992   Comments. In *Gardens of Prehistory: The Archaeology of Settlement Agriculture in Greater Mesoamerica*, edited by Thomas W. Killion, pp. 263–273. University of Alabama Press, Tuscaloosa.

Turney, Omar A.
1929   *Prehistoric Irrigation*. Arizona State Historian, Phoenix.

Valenzuela-Zapata, A. G.
1985   The Tequila Industry in Jalisco, Mexico. *Desert Plants* 7: 65–70.

Van Buren, Mary, James M. Skibo, and Alan P. Sullivan III
1992   The Archaeology of an Agave Roasting Location. In "The Marana Community in the Hohokam World," edited by Suzanne K. Fish, Paul R. Fish, and James H. Madsen. *Anthropological Papers of the University of Arizona* 56: 88–96. University of Arizona Press, Tucson.

Vanderpot, Rein
1992   Rockpile Areas and Other Specialized Activity Sites on the Gila River Terrace: An Appraisal of Hohokam Auxiliary Agricultural Strategies near Florence, Arizona. *Statistical Research Technical Series* 32. Statistical Research, Inc., Tucson.

Van West, Carla, and Jeffrey H. Altschul
1994   Agricultural Productivity and Carrying Capacity in the Tonto Basin. In "The Roosevelt Rural Sites Study, Vol. 3, Changing Land Use in the Tonto Basin," edited by Richard Ciolek-Torrello and John R. Welch. *Statistical Research Technical Series* 28: 361–435. Statistical Research, Inc., Tucson.

Vivian, R. Gwinn
1974   Conservation and Diversion: Water-Control Systems in the Anasazi Southwest. In "Irrigation's Impact on Society," edited by Theodore E. Downing and McGuire Gibson. *Anthropological Papers of the University of Arizona* 25: 95–112. University of Arizona Press, Tucson.

Wallace, Henry D.
1997   (Organizer) The Archaeology of a Land Between: Regional Dynamics in the Prehistory and History of Southeast Arizona. Symposium sponsored by the Amerind Foundation, October 12–17, 1997. Dragoon.

2000   Origins of the Hohokam Cultural Tradition. *Glyphs* 50(11): 8–11. The Monthly Newsletter of the Arizona Archaeological and Historical Society, Tucson.

Wallace, Henry D., James M. Heidke, and William H. Doelle
1995   Hohokam Origins. *Kiva* 60(4): 575–618.

Ward, Albert E., Editor
1978   Limited Activity and Occupation Sites. *Contributions to Anthropological Studies* 1. Center for Anthropological Studies, Albuquerque.

Waters, Michael R., and John C. Ravesloot
2000   Late Quaternary Geology of the Middle Gila River, Gila River Indian Reservation, Arizona. *Quaternary Research* 54(1): 49–57.

Welch, John R.
1994   Ethnographic Models for Tonto Basin Land Use. In "The Roosevelt Rural Sites Study, Vol. 3, Changing Land Use in the Tonto Basin," edited by Richard Ciolek-Torrello and John R. Welch. *Statistical Research Technical Series* 28: 79–120. Statistical Research, Inc., Tucson.

White, Carleton S., David R. Dreesen, and Samuel R. Loftin
1998   Water Conservation Through an Anasazi Gardening Technique. *New Mexico Journal of Science* 38: 251–278.

Wilcox, David R.
1978   The Theoretical Significance of Fieldhouses. In "Limited Activity and Occupation Sites: A Collection of Conference Papers," edited by Albert E. Ward. *Contributions to Anthropological Studies* 1: 25–32. Center for Anthropological Studies, Albuquerque.

Wild, A.
1993   *Soils and Environment: An Introduction*. Cambridge University Press, Cambridge.

Wilken, Gene C.
1987   *Good Farmers: Traditional Agricultural Resource Management in Mexico and Central America*. University of California Press, Berkeley and Los Angeles.

Williams, Oran A.
1937   Settlement and Growth of the Gila Valley in Graham County as a Mormon Colony 1879–1900. MS, Master's thesis, Department of History, University of Arizona, Tucson.

Wilson, D. R.
1982   *Air Photo Interpretation for Archaeologists*. St. Martin's Press, New York.

Winter, Joseph
1978   Anasazi Agriculture at Hovenweep I: Field Systems. In "Limited Activity and Occupation

Sites: A Collection of Conference Papers," edited by Albert E. Ward. *Contributions to Anthropological Studies* 1: 83–98. Center for Anthropological Studies, Albuquerque.

Woodbury, Richard B.
1961   Prehistoric Agriculture at Point of Pines, Arizona. *Memoirs of the Society for American Archaeology* 17.

Woodson, Michael Kyle
1995   The Goat Hill Site: A Western Anasazi Pueblo in the Safford Valley of Southeastern Arizona. MS, Master's thesis, Department of Anthropology, University of Texas, Austin.
1999   Migration in Late Anasazi Prehistory: The Evidence from the Goat Hill Site. *Kiva* 65(1): 63–84.

Woosley, Anne I.
1980   Agricultural Diversity in the Prehistoric Southwest. *The Kiva* 45(4): 317–335.

Wright, Thomas E.
1993   *Keeping the Boys Busy: Archaeological and Documentary Investigations of AR–03–12–06–1391, A Civilian Conservation Corps Erosion Control Site in the Tonto Basin, Gila County, Arizona, with a Brief Account of CCC Activities on Tonto National Forest Lands and a Suggested Historic Context and Research Issues for CCC Erosion Control Sites on the Tonto National Forest*. Archaeological Research Services, Inc., Tempe.

Wrucke, Chester T., Calvin S. Bromfield, Frank S. Simons, Robert C. Greene, Brenda B. Houser, Robert J. Miller, and Floyd Gray
2004   Geologic Map of the San Carlos Indian Reservation, Arizona. Map I–2780, Scale 1:100,000. *U.S. Geological Survey Miscellaneous Investigations Series*.

Yaalon, D. H.
1957   Problems of Soil Testing on Calcareous Soils. *Plant and Soil* 8: 275–288.

Young, H. M., Jr.
1982   *No-Tillage Farming*. No-Till Farmer, Brookfield.

Zeilnik, Michael
1985   The Fajada Butte Solar Marker: A Reevaluation. *Science* 228: 1311–1313.

Index

Abstract

For more than a century, archaeologists have wondered about an expanse of rock alignments oriented more or less parallel and perpendicular to each other on the Pleistocene terraces overlooking the Gila River in the Safford Valley of southeastern Arizona. The rock alignments form a network of grids of various sizes and shapes, most averaging about 4 meters to 5 meters square. The largest set of these grids covers more than 80 hectares and involves nearly 90 kilometers of alignments. Although long thought to be prehistoric and agricultural, these features remained enigmatic. Archaeologists speculated on their purpose and function, but no one systematically investigated them, their related features (rock piles, roasting pits, field houses, and rock art), or their associated artifacts (ceramics and lithic tools). This volume reports the findings of a project sponsored by the National Geographic Society to explain when and why the grids were built.

The multidisciplinary research team included experts outstanding in their respective fields of geology, soil science, remote sensing, geographical information sciences (GISc), hydrology, botany, palynology, and archaeology. The cumulative findings of these independent, but intertwined, investigations are that the grids were constructed between A.D. 750 and 1385. The grids captured direct rainfall and kept it from running off the slightly sloping terrace surfaces. Water retained by the grids percolated into the soils and accumulated under the rock alignments that acted as mulch and reduced evaporation. The prehistoric inhabitants of the area planted agave among the rocks forming the grid borders, but apparently did not farm the grid interiors. Agave provided a dietary supplement to maize, beans, and probably other crops that were cultivated with the help of canal irrigation on the bottomlands nearby. As a perennial rather than an annual crop, agave could be relied on when staple crops like corn failed because of drought or heavy floods. Agave may also have been used as a trade commodity in times when yields were high.

Resumen

Por más de un siglo, los arqueólogos han debatido la naturaleza de ciertos alineamientos de rocas orientados más o menos paralela y perpendicularmente, que se localizan en las terrazas pleistocénicas a lo largo del Río Gila en el valle de Safford, Arizona central. Los alineamientos de rocas forman redes con retículos de varios tamaños y formas, la mayoría midiendo entre 4 y 5 metros cuadrados. La más grande de estas redes cubre más de 80 hectáreas y contiene casi 90 kilometros de alineamientos. A pesar de haber sido considerados rasgos agrícolas prehistóricos, estos alineamientos continúan siendo enigmáticos. Los arqueólogos han especulado sobre su propósito y función, pero nadie ha investigado sistematicamente los alineamientos u otros rasgos (pilas de rocas, hoyos asaderos, casas de campo y arte rupestre) y artefactos (cerámica y lítica) asociados a ellos. Este volumen reporta los hallazgos de un projecto financiado por National Geographic Society para explicar cuándo y por qué se construyeron estas redes.

Un equipo de investigación multidisciplinario incluyó expertos en geología, suelos, teledetección, sistemas de información geográfica (GIS), hidrología, botánica, palinología, y arqueología. Los hallazgos cumulativos de estas investigaciones demuestran que las redes fueron construídas entre A.D. 750 y 1385. Estas redes capturaron precipitación directa y por lo tanto impidieron la pérdida de agua en la superficie inclinada de las terrazas. El agua retenida en las redes percoló los suelos y se acumuló debajo de los alineamientos de rocas, reduciendo así la evaporación. Los habitantes prehistóricos de esta área plantaron agave entre las rocas al borde de los retículos, pero aparentemente no utilizaron el interior de las redes. El agave suplementó la dieta de maíz, frijoles, y probablemente otros productos que fueron cultivados en áreas vecinas irrigadas por canales. Como el agave es perenne en lugar de estacional, esta planta proveyó alimento cuando otras cosechas fallaron debido a la sequía o inundaciones. El agave también pudo ser utilizado para intercambio en tiempo de buena cosecha.

ANTHROPOLOGICAL PAPERS OF THE UNIVERSITY OF ARIZONA

Anthropological Papers listed as O.P., D are available as Docutech reproductions (high
quality xerox) printed on demand. They are tape or spiral bound and nonreturnable.